Journey Across Tibet

A Young Woman's Trek Across the Rooftop of the World

Sorrel Wilby
Foreword by the Dalai Lama

Seal Press

Cover design by Clare Conrad
Cover photograph by Sorrel Wilby
All insert photographs by Sorrel Wilby

"Where Is Love?" words and music by Lionel Bart, © 1960 and 1968
Lakeview Music Co. Ltd., London England. All publication rights for
the U.S.A. and Canada controlled by TRO-Hollis Music, Inc., New
York.

Library of Congress Cataloging-in-Publication Data
Wilby, Sorrel.
Journey across Tibet : a young woman's trek across the rooftop of the
world / Sorrel Wilby ; foreword by the Dalai Lama.
p. cm.
Originally published: Chicago : Contemporary Books, 1988.
ISBN: 1-58005-053-0 (alk. paper)
1. Tibet (China)—Description and travel. 2. Wilby, Sorrel—Journeys—
China—Tibet. I. Title.
DS786 .W47 2001
915.1'50458—dc21   2001049004

Printed in Canada

First Seal Press edition, December 2001

10   9   8   7   6   5   4   3   2   1

Distributed to the trade by Publishers Group West
In Canada: Publishers Group West Canada, Toronto, Ontario

Journey Across Tibet

For Jigme, Patricia, and, of course, my mother

CONTENTS

F O R E W O R D
by His Holiness,
the Dalai Lama

Since Tibet's borders have been opened to foreign visitors, many people have published their impressions of my country and my people. Unfortunately, the majority of them have stuck to the few big towns like Lhasa, Gyantse, Shigatse and other places which have comparatively easy access.

Sorrel Wilby, however, has taken the more difficult path in traversing the regions inhabited by the nomads. She has managed to reveal the enduring Tibetan-ness of my people despite the long years of stresses and strains they have endured.

I have called foreigners who visit Tibet witnesses to what the country once was and what it is becoming now. This book is a lucid testimony to these facts.

The attitudes of the Tibetans whom the writer met on her journey show that no matter what situation they may be in, their determination lives on.

Tenzin Gyatso
McLeod Ganj
Himachal Pradesh
1987

An Acknowledgment

"Lone Aussie on Top of the World." "Solo Across Cloudland Tibet." The press had a field day creating "one-woman-against-the-world" clichés for my adventure in Tibet. Let's set the record straight once and for all. There is no such person as "Solo Sorrel." She had and still has a huge support army.

To all my friends and family who honored me with their confidence and good wishes, those whose tattered photographs I carried on my journey, thank you for being there near my heart every step of the way. (Thanks too to those whose ridicule merely strengthened my resolve!)

Equally important to my adventure were those who helped in a more practical way. My thanks to Dick Smith and Howard Whelan at *Australian Geographic*, for their backing; Downia Feather Mills, the makers of my life-saving sleeping bag; Bill Johnston whose supply of Eve-ready batteries and torches kept my need for night-vision to a minimum; and Ian Day of Best Foods for the generous supply of Uncle Toby's Muesli Bars.

The friendship, encouragement, last-minute material, and emotional support given by Shubu Sengupta and Hyo Bergman will never be forgotten.

Last, but not least, I thank the land of Tibet and its remarkable people. From the great Dalai Lama to the humblest pilgrim and poorest nomad, I have learned how to survive, how to laugh, how to love. Life is a gift—a precious parcel to be held and unwrapped layer by layer. Mine passed from the hands of one Tibetan to another, so gently I did not notice them peeling away veneers of ego and vanity, and discarding paper-thin dreams of "fame and fortune." Tibetans nourished and enriched me with passion and warmth. This, in gratitude, I share now with those who choose to listen.

Sorrel Wilby
1988

INTRODUCTION

Many enthusiasts fired with grandiose plans come through the doors of *Australian Geographic*. Of those who dream, few have the ability and drive to achieve their ideals.

When I first met Sorrel Wilby she was working eighteen hours a day to save enough money to cycle around Asia. She was determined to pursue her plan, come what may, and this determination, together with her unique combination of talents in writing and photography, impressed all who met her. It was a delight to be able to help her.

Sorrel embodies the spirit of Australian adventure. In her Tibetan journey, she has shown that the far horizon is within the reach of all who have the courage to try.

Dick Smith, Publisher
Australian Geographic

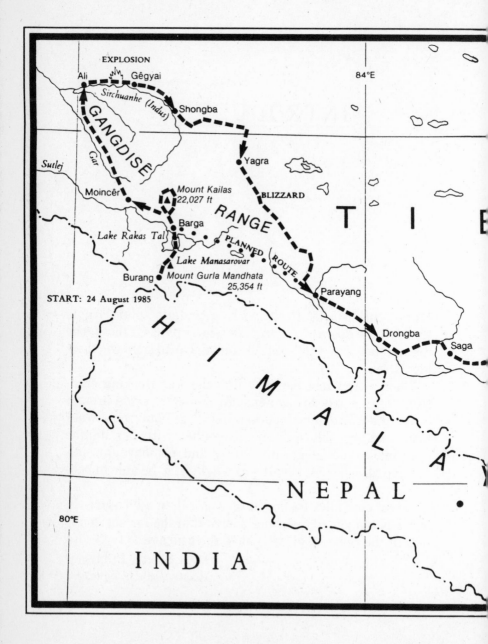

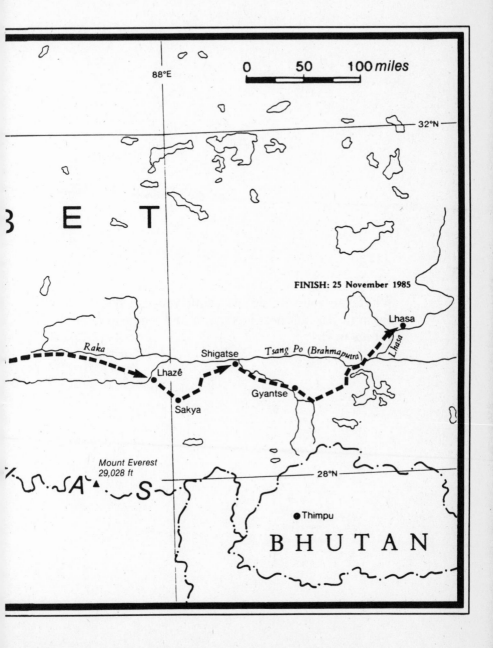

88°E

0   50   100 *miles*

32°N

B E T

FINISH: 25 November 1985

Raka

Shigatse   *Tsang Po (Brahmaputra)*

Lhasa

Lhazê

Sakya

Gyantse

Mount Everest
29,028 ft

28°N

A · S

●Thimpu

B H U T A N

Whatever you can do, or think you can do—
begin it. For boldness has power and magic and
genius in it.

Goethe

CHAPTER 1
Realizing Dreams and Facing Fears

Hyo turned his face from mine. I followed his line of vision to a distant mountain ridge, now black and half-buried beneath layers of monsoon cloud. A violent storm thrashed across the sky. All tempest sounds dimmed, as my mind swept away with the wind and submerged in the blue ocean of his thoughts. I seemed to be floating, small and insignificant, toward a nameless horizon. The inspiration of Hemingway and Conrad infused my consciousness, I reached for Hyo's hand, and sighed.

The monumental challenge of my undertaking overwhelmed me. Tomorrow, Hyo would be gone. Shubu would be gone. Their little green dome-shaped tents would vanish, and I would be alone. Reality would turn those blue, white-crested waves of my dreamtime into a daunting tableau of snow-capped peaks. The gentle beaches would become deserts. The land of Tibet lay before me, as unpredictable and challenging as Everest itself.

Two years ago, almost to the day, I had sat with friends

1

and a cask of wine beneath the sweet-smelling acacias and eucalyptus in their Australian garden, watching the stars and speculating on my future. For three years, I had pursued a disastrous relationship and now, finally, it was all over. At twenty-two, I was disillusioned, prematurely old and cynical. Part of me just wanted to curl up in a listless ball of melancholy and die. The other parts wanted to pull together and live—really live. It was time to change the focus of my life from romance to career—to stop feeling sorry for myself. I needed a new vocation! But what? What could I, the classic "Jill-of-all-trades," do now? All my life, I had followed a patchwork-quilt career with no clear pattern or definable path.

After dropping out of art college in 1980, I had tried my hand at numerous pursuits: everything from geriatric nursing to working as an usherette for a circus troupe. Initially, I had abandoned my studies as a protest against rigid educational curricula, which attempted to mold my attitude and to direct my creativity. I had wanted to make it as an artist on my own; not to reproduce the artistic tastes of my professors, but rather to create for art's sake—not for As and Bs and credit points. Away from the institution, however, I quickly discovered a marked lack of self-discipline. I failed to fit into the struggling artist guise and, tired of filling out social security forms, I sublet my studio space to a more passionate, would-be-if-he-could-be sculptor, and decided to try my luck on the professional music circuit instead. I sang and played my guitar in wine-bars and clubs around Sydney for a while, but achieving fame and fortune through song demanded more dedication than I possessed. I packed up my microphone and fled to the more anonymous realm of CBS Records where I assumed a more down-to-earth role—packing mail-order records off to discerning listeners.

I waited on tables in a Mexican restaurant, picked fruit in outback NSW, and eventually saved enough money to share in buying an old Toyota Land Cruiser. Then I set out with my partner, the other half of that ill-fated relationship, on my first travels through the eastern half of the Australian continent. By the time I reached Ayers Rock—the dead center—I was flat broke, and thankfully accepted employment running the dining room of a field-mouse-infested two-star hotel. I made beds and cleaned toilets from 8 A.M. until 5 P.M. and then served badly cooked meals to sometimes-tolerant tourists from 6 P.M. until midnight. I was paid the princely sum of $30 a day, and had Sundays off.

It was on those precious Sundays off, escaping from both the hotel regime and the declining state of communication between my companion and me, that I started taking photographs. Steadily, my interest in this art form was reawakened. At the age of twelve, when little girls are supposed to dream glamorous destinies for themselves as models in *Vogue*, I had sworn allegiance to a quite different magazine. I wanted to work for *The National Geographic*. I dreamt of a life of high adventure—discovering lost tribes, rafting rivers, and scaling mountains. With body and soul, I wanted to be an intrepid photojournalist. But with the onset of puberty, my ambitions succumbed to conformity, to more conventional career objectives like nursing and teaching. The challenge of mountains and rivers was not completely forgotten though, just cleverly transferred to the hobby department, where it would attract no social ridicule and appear to be a passive interest—something to pursue on weekends and between boyfriends.

Now, bitter experience was trying to tell me something else. Perhaps boyfriends were something the truly sane woman pursued between mountains? Now, after my return from Central Australia, the Riesling-and-gum-tree evenings of discussion took effect. I felt I was ready to follow my star—to be that intrepid and adventurous camerawoman. I swore to my friends, to the sweet-smelling acacias, and to the now empty cask of cheap wine, that I

would indeed try my hand at professional photojournal-
ism. And for the first time in my life, I would stick it out
until I succeeded.

Still intimidated by the bonds of formal training, I began my writing and picture-taking career in a typically
unorthodox fashion. I resurrected all my transparencies
from Ayers Rock (and beyond) and spent a few months
typing up the diaries I had kept on that journey into a
manuscript form. I scoured the Sydney phone directory
and plucked out the names of several dozen publishing
houses. After many phone calls, I actually got to meet two
publishers, but without success. All unknowing, I had
strayed into one of the most competitive fields of human
endeavor—and I had armed myself with the poorest of
portfolios.

Sensing my naiveté, one sympathetic editor put his personal—albeit condescending—criticisms in writing, and
ventured to suggest that I channel my energies into something more exciting. He intimated my Australian material lacked originality. I really hadn't done anything
worth writing about. In his opinion, there were already
too many picture books about Australia on the market. In
short (and no doubt to prevent any further correspon-
dence), he suggested I canoe down the Amazon or attempt
some equally dangerous and exciting feat. If I survived, I
was welcome to call him again. So, to guard against receiving any more demeaning rejection notices, I shelved
my fledgling manuscript and photographs, wiped the
tears of self-pity out of my eyes, and decided to take the
editor's sardonic advice.

I had nothing to lose; the words *dangerous* and *exciting*
held no fears—they spelled adventure. I had no commit-
ments, no children, no house nor car repayments to meet
every month, no cares in the world. I was totally free.

But the Amazon? No. I wasn't inspired. India? Yeah,
that's getting close. Eventually, I pieced together an elaborate plan—a journey across Asia: alone, and by bicycle.

I had never ridden a bicycle farther than the local shops

before, but that hardly seemed relevant. What I most
needed in order to embark on my dream journey was
money. Obviously I wasn't going to make a fortune out of
my writing and photography just yet, so it was back to
nursing homes, restaurants, and, quite literally, the drawing board. My art school training came into its own and I
actually sold a few sketches.

I worked eighteen hours a day on six, sometimes seven
days a week for six solid months. I bought an 18-speed
Shogun touring bicycle for what seemed an exorbitant
$600 and gradually outfitted it with front and rear pan-
niers, headlights, spare parts, and a very special padded
Italian seat—specially designed for women cyclists—what
a breakthrough!

When I had paid off the bicycle, I pedaled it out of the
store and all the way to the railway station. It was a
beautiful, maroon-and-chrome machine—by far the best
looking 'baby' in the shop. I made a beeline for home.
Embarrassed by my lack of cycling prowess, I waited
until the dead of night to try riding my piece of hi-tech
wizardry for the first time. I was completely unfamiliar
with the gears and had never ridden a bike with toe-clips
on the pedals.

After a few days of pedaling and walking my bicycle,
friends nicknamed my superb steed "Pushy"* and made
jokes about the length of time it would take to traverse
Asia that way. But a week of night practices later, I had
mastered the twentieth-century pedal-power routine and
felt confident enough to make my first daytime expedition: an inaugural ride to my parents' Carlingford home—
no less than 42 miles from my own in Springwood, Sydney.

I arrived elated and hid the blisters and the shooting
pains in my wind-chilled neck. I smiled and told my
mother I was ready for the real thing—the All-Asia ride.

Hours and hours of reading books and poring over maps
eventually led me to decide on a starting point for my first

---

*In Australia, a bicycle without a motor is a "pushbike."

two-wheeled adventure: southern Japan. If I survived
that, I could go on to conquer South Korea, northern Japan, Taiwan, China, Thailand, Malaysia, Indonesia, and—
saving the best for last—India. I estimated the journey
would take me two years to complete and I planned to
cycle an average of 60 miles a day. I sought sponsorship
for my journey and tried to interest travel-oriented magazines in on-the-road tales of my (mis)adventures. Rejection
slips failed to daunt my enthusiasm. I was going to cycle
around Asia, with or without outside financial and material support. I worked an extra two shifts every week at
the restaurant and bought my own tent, camera, and fuel
stove with the proceeds.

Come Christmas 1983, the dream had become rock-hard
reality. Even my family (who believed all along that the
trip was just another of my all-talk-and-no-action
schemes) had come to accept the strength of my conviction. My parents, brothers, sisters, and relatives all
chipped in to buy me extra travelers checks, bringing the
total value of my purse to $4000 Australian—more than
enough for two years once I started selling photographs
and stories. On December 29, 1983, Pushy and I finally
flew to Tokyo, and the months and miles rolled by and by.

To wake up in a new place each day—whether it was
among the lonely craggy peaks of a South Korean mountain range, or beneath a traffic-jammed bridge somewhere in Japan's jumble of cities—was an absolute joy to
me. For the first time in years, I felt totally alive, free as a
bird, my head ever in the clouds and depression over my
failed romance long forgotten. I remembered reading
somewhere that in our lives we choose our own reality—
and for the first time in mine, I felt I had chosen not just
wisely, but perfectly. And what of love? No greater affair
had I ever experienced than that with the mystical orient.
I was like a little boat in an enormous unknown ocean—
tossed, turned, caressed, directed, and at times overawed
by unpredictable storms of emotion and waves of experi-

ence. Asia, and the challenge to cycle through her wide expanses alone, were molding me, shaping me into something I vaguely liked and respected. I was growing, adapting, learning so much—about myself, the world, and most importantly, about the beauty of its cultural and physical diversity. People, languages, attitudes, lifestyles, religions—I was taking more than a passive glimpse of the East, I was in it, eating, breathing, feeling it through every fiber of my being; talking and laughing as I never had before.

I was captivated with Asia, and for some bizarre reason, Asia became a little captivated with me. Just enough, in fact, to titillate my photojournalistic ambitions. Apparently it was not a normal sight, a woman on her own on a bicycle, or in a tent a night; a woman on her own fixing flat tires by the side of the road or scaling some little-known mountain. After cycling around Japan and Korea, I returned to Tokyo and attracted an unprecedented amount of attention and world-wide publicity. I climbed the sacred Mount Fuji—all 12,388 feet of it—on my bike, and unwittingly created history by becoming the first woman in the world to do so. I actually rode Pushy halfway, then strapped her across my back for the four-hour climb to the summit. It was really a lot of fuss about nothing, but this little adventure put my journey on the map. After this publicity, my tales and pictures started selling—even back in Australia, land of skeptics!

Everywhere I ventured after that exploit, the media was curious as to what the crazy lady (nicknamed "Wombat" to save my parents undue embarrassment) would do next. In Taiwan I was given permission to climb 13,000 feet to the top of Yu-Shan Mountain, and in China I was allowed to ride Pushy down a section of the Great Wall near Beijing.

While pedaling around various parts of that vast, over-populated chunk of the Asian continent, I occasionally bumped into other tourists from the West. Since I was not permitted to pitch my tent in any of China's mainland cities, I usually spent the night in a cheap dormitory room of some antiquated city tourist hotel.

It was now November 1984, and everywhere I went in China I heard travelers singing the praises of a city called Lhasa, only re-opened to the individual visitor in September—although group tours had been permitted there earlier. Lhasa lay in the vast mountainous country of Tibet. Once it was claimed to be the most exotic destination in the world—a land shrouded in almost medieval mystery. Until 1980, it had been visited by a mere handful of intrepid European explorers. I knew nothing about the country really, only that it could now be reached by domestic aircraft from Chengdu, the capital of China's Sichuan Province. Stories of smiling faces (something lacking in most of China-proper), snow-capped mountains, and mystic monasteries and temples whetted my appetite. I wanted to see Lhasa—more out of simple curiosity than soul-searing desire. I wanted to see the place that had fired so many imaginations, awakened so many adventurous spirits that it became the ultimate destination on the "Do-Asia" checklist. So as step one toward Tibet, Pushy and I caught a train to Chengdu—it was too far to ride.

I stayed a week in Chengdu and talked to a lot of people about Tibet, reading everything I could lay my hands on. The country had a fascinating history and culture, more than any other I had heard about. From what I could gather, Tibet's recorded history began in the seventh century. The country was ruled by a succession of kings with impossible-to-pronounce names, who had warred endlessly with their neighbors—bloody battles to gain and occupy land in an effort to expand the kingdom. The country eventually broke up into independent feuding principalities. Fighting continued, only this time it was internal. Lots of revolutions. As the authority of the nobility dwindled, the power of the Buddhist clergy—a presence in Tibet since the third century—increased. Tibetans formed their own unique variation of Buddhism. Gradually the religion and politics of Tibet entwined, and a single leader emerged under the title of "Dalai Lama," "Ocean of Wisdom"—the God-King of Tibet.

I tried to imagine what a Dalai Lama would look like. I had always believed a lama to be a two-headed animal from the wonderful world of Doctor Doolittle. The ignorance produced by a state school education is unique.

According to the Tibetan religion the spirit of the Dalai Lama had been reincarnated fourteen times. On its most recent return to earth, it entered the body of one Tenzin Gyatso. That was in July 1935 when the bizarre, fascinating culture of Tibet—writing, literature, medicine, arts and architecture, and above all, monastic studies—was flourishing.

In 1950, three months after the creation of the new People's Republic of China, Radio Peking announced that the People's Liberation Army would, among other things, liberate Tibet. The Chinese moved into the mountain kingdom with troops and tanks, claiming that the country had always been a part of China and never independent. In 1959, they officially annexed Tibet. The Dalai Lama fled to India. The infamous Red Guards began wreaking havoc across the nation. Monasteries were destroyed, some said in the thousands. The ancient feudal and monastic systems fell under new, Communist rule.

I couldn't find out anything about the following decades, for China had sealed Tibet off completely from the outside world. Travelers' theories conflicted with the propaganda of leaflets and books available in Chengdu. If my education was to be furthered, I myself simply had to get to Lhasa, the capital.

The thought of going by plane was uninspiring. I met a couple of people who had successfully made the trip back to China from Tibet by road. It was illegal, and a highly dangerous thing to do at that time. But if they could get out by that route, then surely I could get in.

Bold as brass, I presented myself at the Sichuan Province Security Police office and asked for a permit to visit Lhasa.

"My name is Sorrel Wilby and I'm a journalist and photographer from Australia. I have been traveling throughout Asia collecting material for a book. I'm very interested in including Tibet in my record. I would like to travel to Lhasa overland. I get airsick, you see. And I have a bicycle with me. It's in the courtyard. Would you like a ride?"

Very cagey. I had never let anyone so much as touch my precious bike before. If I couldn't charm the young security officials with my smile, then good old Pushy would, with her shining chrome and alloy rims. To Western eyes, my bicycle was nothing out of the ordinary, but to the Chinese, it was an object of wonder. It was indisputably foreign. Like television sets, tape decks, and disco music cassettes, it was the cause of much envy among modern-minded Maoists.

As it happened, Pushy and I had appeared in several Chinese newspapers after our ride down the Great Wall at Badaling, east of Beijing, and the security police in Chengdu had read those fabulously complimentary articles.

My plea went before the Sichuan Province directors and won approval. I would indeed be permitted to reach Lhasa by road, but not by bicycle. Pushy would have to travel on the roof of the bus—for which I was issued a permit to obtain a ticket.

I was overcome with shock and delight. How easy it all seemed. Easy, until I tried to find the office and actually buy the bus ticket! Finally, four days later I was organized. On a cool and misty mid-November morning, I secured Pushy to the roof rack of a dilapidated government bus and climbed aboard, fully prepared for the two-week journey to Lhasa, 1,500 miles away. I had a big bag full of mandarin oranges and garlic to ward off infection, lots of warm clothes, and plenty of film.

When the bus finally left the depot four hours later, I

was riding high on a wave of excitement. I saw the journey ahead and the permission I had obtained to make it as the most prodigious miracle. I felt untouchable. I had no idea then, that this pilgrimage through eastern Tibet was merely a catalyst: the first in a series of miracles which would ultimately lead me, seven months later, back to Tibet for the greatest and most demanding adventure of my life.

On the second evening of the trip, I very nearly lost my hitherto-unshakeable cool. I had met a couple of young Swiss travelers in Chengdu—Thomas and Ingrid—who had their "Lhasa-by-bus" request flatly rejected by the security police. They had decided to risk making the journey by road illegally, and I was determined to help them. So that they could purchase tickets and to lessen their chances of being caught *en route* later and sent back to Chengdu, I added their names to my own permit and changed the figure "1" in the ticket allocation box to a "3." At 10 P.M. on this evening, five local security police burst into our room in the guest house in Kangding Village and challenged our "authority" to be there. Shaking like a leaf, the lank blond Thomas surrendered our papers. Ingrid and I stopped breathing. The police lit cigarettes and invited themselves to sit down on our beds. I offered them coffee, trying to conceal my fear with a smile. One of the police officials left with our permits and passports and another started asking impertinent personal questions in English.

We joked with them and gradually a few of the stony-faced officials broke their silence with laughter. Two hours later, when we were exhausted from our labored conversation, the permit was returned and the uniformed contingent left. Their parting words were, "Have a nice trip!" We delayed our shouts of joy until they were well and truly out of earshot.

Early the next morning, the blue-and-white single-decker bus began to climb upwards—snaking slowly

through the western Sichuan Province. It got colder and
colder. Thawing ice and snow moistened the sheer rock
cliffs from which the road had been etched. We climbed
through the clouds, then above them. At the top of one
13,000-foot pass, the vehicle labored to a standstill. The
driver and the other thirty-odd Han Chinese traveling on
the bus quickly scrambled out into the thin, crisp air and
began to throw cups of water from a nearby stream
through the wire grill at the front of the bus in an attempt
to cool the overheated radiator. From that moment on,
until we reached the Tibetan border on the Yangtse River,
the bus broke down frequently, so we had early-morning
starts and late-night ends to our days in order to reach the
city of Qamdo on schedule. Qamdo was 180 miles over the
border into Tibet, and despite the discomforts of all-day
travel, Thomas, Ingrid, and I were elated to reach the
city—our halfway post to Lhasa. Gradually, tiny groups of
very un-Chinese houses—squat, whitewashed, mud-brick
compounds—had appeared on the vast vistas of bare
mountains around us. A three-day stopover in Qamdo
meant we could at last explore and meet our first
Tibetans.

The city, the third largest in Tibet, was crowded with
brown-faced, almond-eyed Tibetans, trying to cadge lifts
to the holy city. They were handsome people—always
smiling, poking their tongues out at me, and showing me
their palms (which I didn't understand), laughing when I
responded by mimicking their odd gestures. The tall,
proud men wore their hair bound in a halo of red tassels.
Jeweled hair-rings circled their thick, unkempt plaits and
huge, turquoise-studded loops pierced their left ears. The
women's hair was either braided into dozens of thin plaits
or twisted with colored, cotton threads and looped like a
crown atop their heads.

The men wore long swords attached to their wide woven
waist-sashes. Their cloaks, or "chubas" as they called
them, were made from several thick sheepskins, sewn
together with handspun wool. The exterior hides were

grubby to say the least and the sleeves of this traditional costume drooped almost to the ground. The women generally wore more tailored garments—long wraparound dresses in black felt or cotton, over which hung a tightly woven, colorful striped apron.

The most fascinating building in the Tibetan city wa situated at the end of a foot track which wound from the bridge spanning the upper reaches of the mighty Mekong River. Prominently positioned on the top of a small bare hill lay the magnificent Qamdo monastery complex, built of mud bricks.

My first visit here was filled with wonder. As I gazed at the three-story whitewashed temple, it seemed deserted. A pile of appliquéd felt boots lay outside. Suddenly, as I stood savoring the almost ghostly silence, a crowd of at least one hundred barefooted monks poured from the temple doors like blood from a severed vein. They surged past me, burgundy-red robes flapping in the icy breeze. Their laughter carried them to the edge of the hill where, to my absolute bewilderment, they squatted as one, and quickly relieved themselves. As quickly as they had emptied from the huge building, they returned. This time, beckoned by one of the older monks, I followed.

Inside the temple, all fell silent. The atmosphere was electric until (very softly at first) a low, foghorn-like note was blown from a conch shell, and then the throb of a small drum signaled to the monks that they could commence their meditative chanting.

They were seated in parallel rows inside the huge, poorly lit hall—physically and mentally cut off from the rest of the world. Nothing save a few rays of sunlight filtered in from outside. I too felt similarly moved, enveloped in the shadows of the leather-curtained doorway. My scattered thoughts had centered on the scene before me. Time stood so absolutely still; the world beyond the Qamdo temple room remained in suspended animation. This was the only reality.

The shafts of light coming through the small vents in

the ceiling fell upon the Buddhist holy scriptures, propped on low benches between each row of monks. These men, ranging in age from very young to very old, sat cross-legged, and leaned forward from their cushions to read and chant words from the printed pages. Every twenty minutes or so, they punctuated their ramblings with a sip of soupy-looking tea—served to the monks from a large copper and brass pot by a small, robed boy. My eyes wandered from one mysterious object to another within the temple room—the brass cups holding burning candles, the red wooden columns covered in carvings and reaching toward the smoke-blackened ceiling they supported, the wall frescoes, altars, and the huge cobweb-covered tapestries hanging from the rafters. Then I followed the teaboy out of the temple and into an adjoining kitchen.

Two older monks were preparing a meal—cutting up sheep carcasses and placing each joint into a large pot of boiling water, hanging over a deep, open fire pit. I was taken aback—Buddhists, as far as my experience had led me to believe, were vegetarians. Then I remembered how barren Tibet had seemed so far—the lack of vegetation, save for the occasional poplar tree, and the rocky, freezing landscape—and I put the Tibetan meat-eating habit down to necessity. Apart from vegetables and fruit occasionally delivered to Tibet by truck from China, I guessed there was little else for the monks to eat—at least in this region.

I spent most of the next two days at the monastery, for it seemed the hub of activity in Qamdo. People came and went all day, walking around and around the temple extremities; many seemed in an almost trancelike state of religious contemplation. Apart from this building, and several small commune-style dwellings strung out along the river banks or dotting the landscape far away into the distance, Qamdo boasted only Chinese building-block architecture. I had seen enough of that elsewhere in my travels—cold, unyielding concrete-slab structures, often surrounded by steel picket fences and always enclosing the most depressing, spartan interiors. Variety came only in the color of the spear-tipped fence rods—green, blue, and in some cities, yellow. Here and in my later journey through Tibet, I noticed a great deal of new buildings under construction. Schools, hospitals, shopping complexes. I thought it was all part of the surge of growth after the Cultural Revolution, but also due to the Chinese wish to make Tibet part of her empire. Certainly, the Chinese military presence was obvious. But . . . the Chinese seemed to be the worst town planners in the world. It was sad they had turned Qamdo into such an eyesore.

I tried to imagine what the city must have looked like before Chinese domination—tried to duplicate in my imagination the few Tibetan-style structures. Made of mud, these single-story houses complemented their surrounding environment. In fact, they seemed to grow out of the very landscape. Windows were adorned with brightly painted flower designs or carved timbers and beams. They had a Swiss-chalet look about them, the larger-scale temples were like the medieval castles from my dimly remembered childhood fairy tales.

I couldn't wait to reach Lhasa now, for Qamdo Monastery was surely just a taste of what lay in store at the capital.

We were to ride in a different bus for the second leg of the journey, and Thomas and Ingrid secured themselves a seat on the left-hand side, about halfway down the aisle. By the time I reached the depot, the vehicle was full to the roof with Tibetans and their simple but bulky belongings and I had to fashion myself a seat from some old wooden boxes which I wedged between the engine casing and the front windscreen.

Day after day we traversed the desolate, majestic landscape leading into Lhasa. My position next to the driver forced me to share the thrills of his daredevil driving on roads more precarious than any other I'd been on in my life—even through the Australian Outback. They were gouged by streams, littered with landslides, and so narrow it seemed a mere gust of wind would send the sluggish vehicle careening down the sheer mountainsides.

We crossed a series of dry, windswept plains and hurtled past glaciers and half-frozen rivers. We were still many miles from Lhasa itself, when I saw the strangest vision ahead: three men rose out of the dust on the side of the road. They seemed to stand to attention, hands clasped together above their heads, then threw themselves forward on the ground. For just a moment they stayed spread-eagled on the road with their hands outstretched, then rose to attention again. Each time they repeated the sequence, they took a long step forward to the point where their hands had previously reached—as if using their bodies to measure the entire length of the road. The Han Chinese driver pointed at the three ragged and dusty men as we passed, and smirked. He uttered the words *Lhasa* and *Buddha* and clicked his tongue in sheer disbelief. I shrugged my shoulders, not comprehending. Surely the threesome were not going to measure the dirt highway with their bodies all the way to Lhasa? But who could tell, in a land as strange as Tibet?

Five days after leaving Qamdo, we rattled into the fog-covered outer limits of Lhasa itself. Mile after mile of dismal, gray, semi-industrial squalor set the scene for a classic anticlimax. "Lhasa? This is Lhasa?" I cried in disbelief to Thomas and Ingrid. Then, right on cue, the mighty Potala—the colossal mud-brick winter palace of Tibet's succession of Dalai Lama leaders—came into view and lifted us from disillusionment to wonder. It appeared through the mist, all thirteen tiered, whitewashed floors— soaring toward the sky from a single hill, linking earth to heavens and rising from the Chinese ghettos like a victorious, battle-scarred star. Shining, literally beaming with Tibetan-ness. I had made it to Lhasa. Lhasa at last!

CHAPTER 2
Lhasa at Last!

I was eager to explore but before I could view the great Potala itself at close range, I had to find a place to stay. After returning the bus to the company depot, our driver kindly led Thomas, Ingrid, and me to a cold, concrete building that someone—in a moment of misplaced inspiration—had labeled with a glossy bronze plaque "Lhasa's Number One Hotel."

My passport and cardboard "Aliens Permit to Enter Lhasa" were scanned at the reception office and shoved into a tatty cardboard box half full of similar papers. At a quick glance I guessed another fifteen or so foreigners had also found lodgings within the bowels of Number One. Judging by the level of fluid in the stairwell spittoons I noticed on the way to my assigned dormitory bed, thousands of Chinese visitors must also have registered before us. Thomas and Ingrid checked into a private room and I later lost touch with them in the hectic weeks that followed. I made my way to a dormitory on the third floor. It was a canary yellow room with nine beds, no bath, and was

cold as a tomb. I flung my cycle packs onto the only unoc-
cupied mattress.

It was 11 A.M., but curiously, five of my eight roommates were still in the throes of their morning ablutions,
sponging themselves with hot water poured from an array
of large, gaudily painted thermos flasks into shallow
enamel basins. Breakfast—tinned peaches, yogurt, and
sweet, warm, powdered milk with a rationed sprinkle of
instant coffee—was prepared for collective consumption
by a shivering English girl called Chris. I introduced
myself to the group, tuning in to their amusing and impatient "this-is-not-the-paradise-we-hoped-it-would-be" ob-
servations. Jen, from New Zealand, had lost her luggage
at the airport. Her boyfriend, Vass, had altitude sickness
and looked pale as death. Lhasa sits at an altitude of
11,352 feet above sea level and many visitors of all ages
experience difficulties in adjusting to the city's rarified
air. Two French travelers were debating the best way to
smuggle out a knife stolen from the sky burial site near
Sera Monastery, two miles northeast of the city center.
Presumably the other three occupants were still asleep
beneath the mounds of cotton eiderdowns and sleeping
bags heaped on the sagging wire frame beds. I was
warned that early risers were not welcome in Room Seven
... unless of course you were taking in the sunrise—that is,
the sunrise funeral rites.

The account given by the two French girls of watching
the traditional burial rites horrified me. They explained
how bodies were dismembered on an exposed slab of stone
near Sera. Skin and flesh were removed from the bones,
which were pulverized, mixed with flour, then offered
together with the flesh to the ever-waiting flock of hungry
vultures circling the skies above. One of the French
women told me a holy man presides over the rites, chanting scriptures to the steady beat of his small, hand-held
drum, which is itself fashioned from two human skulls,
joined crown to crown. A leather bead on a string swings
as the instrument is twirled, and this beats out a rhythm

on the skin-covered hollow surface of the skulls. When I
asked them why Tibetans disposed of cadavers by feeding
them to the vultures, they simply could not answer. And
why had they taken photographs, apparently against the
will of the undertakers? They just laughed.

I had never heard of sky burial before, but from what I
had seen of the Tibetan landscape perhaps the technique
was a very practical one. The ground would be too hard to
dig graves and the lack of vegetation made cremation a
limited possibility for the disposal of the dead. After some
thought, I was more disgusted with the lack of respect on
the part of the French travelers than the bizarre local
ceremony itself.

I spent the rest of the day with Chris, exploring the
Barkhor, the market streets surrounding the Jokhang
Temple, the central cathedral of Buddhism in this part of
Tibet. We ventured down several streets lined with the
usual uniform, concrete-cube buildings characteristic of
most Chinese cities, before reaching the true Tibetan center of Lhasa. Once there, it was easy to forget the Chinese
presence. We were swept up into the surging crowd of
Tibetan pilgrims and shoppers and swirled around the
Barkhor three times before I realized we'd actually circled the temple itself. The people—their costumes, their
jewelry, their wares, and their easy acceptance of foreigners like us in their clockwise parade—made it plain to see
what had charmed all who had beheld the city.

Several roads splayed out from the main Barkhor complex. Two-story earth-and-stone buildings, whitewashed
like the Potala itself and supported by wooden beams
painted red, orange, blue, and black, made the center of
town look like a huge, handcrafted merry-go-round. Alleys shot off every corner, turning the whole street ar-
rangement into a veritable maze.

One of the major arteries leading from the Barkhor
boasted Lhasa's open meat market. On either side of the
thoroughfare, a row of ragged canvas canopies shaded
huge trestle tables and stalls. These displayed partly

butchered carcasses of yaks, sheep, and goats. Blood clotted in the dusty gutters of the roughly cobbled road. Some vendors sold chunks of what looked like rancid butter, wrapped in pieces of animal hide.

Vegetables—cabbage, turnips, potatoes, and the odd bunch of carrots—were sold from a central, more permanent-looking market set out on a concrete slab beneath corrugated iron roofing. The rest of the Barkhor circuit resembled a massive, hectic white elephant stall: a jumble sale of ready-made incense sticks, fragrant juniper bushes, cutlery and crockery, clothing and printed materials, plastic trinkets and glassware, Chinese tinned food and Nepalese glucose biscuits, curious beads, turquoise and coral stones, jeweled daggers, antique ornaments and flint boxes, herbal medicines, and potions—in fact everything the fashionable Tibetan could want. I even spotted a glass baby's bottle shaped like a breast—complete with rubber nipple!

Many Tibetans carried strange copper cylinders on sticks which they turned as they walked. They seemed to be talking to themselves, continuously mumbling as they fumbled one-handedly through the displayed goods. Between produce and goods stalls, dentists and optometrists had set up small, open-air clinics. Han Chinese teeth "specialists" pedaled foot-operated drills and filled or capped Tibetan teeth in full view of the public, while self-styled eye doctors sold secondhand prescription spectacles to not-too-discerning customers.

I noticed several men, women, and children throwing themselves onto the ground after every step they took among the spectacular stream of Barkhor shoppers. I remembered the three men I had seen from the bus in the middle of nowhere. In the courtyard of the Jokhang Temple (not apparent at first, because new construction rubble and scaffolding had hidden the entrance), I came across hundreds of people repeatedly performing the same strenuous exercise. If this was a measure of religious devotion, I would think more than twice before becoming a convert.

Massive versions of the inscribed copper cylinders carried by so many Tibetans spun slowly in an external passageway surrounding the huge inner sanctum of the temple. I followed the procession of wide-eyed Tibetans filing past the six-and-one-half-foot-high tubes, then squeezed slowly into the interior building.

The rank smell of burning butter candles made me nauseous, yet the solemn atmosphere seduced me to stay with the crowd. When my eyes adjusted to the gloomy light, they focused on gigantic frescoes of gods and monsters writhing in agony throughout at least a dozen hellish scenes.

Still moving clockwise, the crowd ebbed in and out of blackened anterooms, gazing in awe and lightly touching the gold and jewel-encrusted sculptured deities housed in each. At one point Chris tapped me on the shoulder—and I jumped. She pointed out that I was unconsciously mumbling, like the Tibetans around us!

The Jokhang was mysterious, yet compelling; mesmeric with the pungent odor of incense and in the incomprehensible orgy of sculptures and paintings which bedecked its walls. Maroon-robed monks moved in and out of the shadows and mingled with the crowd. I reached the entrance to the inner temple again, and followed the throng back out into daylight. I had been going around in circles for hours and now my thoughts were doing the same. I vowed to return to the temple again and hoped with each visit I would come to understand more of its many mysteries.

On my second morning in Lhasa, I cycled out to Drepung Monastery. I had been told that it was once a great center of Buddhist learning. My hands were freezing, even inside the ski gloves my mother had sent me from Australia. I envied all the other foreigners, still snug and warm inside their beds back in the dormitory. How wise they were, not to surface before 10 A.M.! On the way I passed a group of pilgrims, walking into Lhasa from goodness-knows-where. They were worn out, slowly limping on beneath the weight of their bamboo backpacks. What an extraordinary journey they must have had to the holy capital. They were filthy, their faces lined and calloused by wind and sun. They were chanting, spinning the same strange copper cylinders on sticks as they walked.

I roamed around the exterior of the huge monastery and climbed the hill behind restored buildings to some old, weather-beaten ruins. Huge paintings of Buddhist deities colored the rocks. The mist hanging in the valley below slowly lifted, and the sun rose to strike its first rays on the painted gods. They came alive. The sunshine was intense, but still my hands and toes were numb. I sat down on a rock, shoved my hands into the pockets of my down jacket, and looked out over the valley leading into the city of Lhasa. Incredible. Everything around me—behind, below, beneath, and above—was so different, so fascinating and mysterious. My mind grew heavy with questions. Why this? And why that? I had absorbed everything I had seen, but not understood it at all. I wanted to know everything about Tibet. I wanted to be able to look at paintings and know what gods they represented. I wanted to hear the lamas chant and know what their prayer meant. I wanted to look at the architectural splendors of Lhasa and know how and why each mud brick and wooden pillar had been laid. I sat for ten minutes on that rock, aware this thirst for understanding could become an obsession. There was magic in the mountains around me; Tibet was a sorcerer and I was ensnared in its spell.

In an internal courtyard in the monastic complex, a group of monks were having a heated and animated argument beneath the trees. Sunlight dappled their thick maroon robing and ruddy, flushed cheeks. I watched them for a few minutes, amazed at the intensity of their debate, wondering when the first punch would be thrown. Their behavior struck me as being completely out of character. Did priests and archbishops fight such wars with words back home? I couldn't understand it, and as with everything else I had seen, I wanted to know why.

I walked away from the monastery, its interior unexplored, jumped on my bike and pedaled back to Lhasa, anxious to see my Western friends whose conversations, thoughts, philosophies, and antics made complete sense. There is something very comforting about being in familiar surroundings, listening·to familiar sounds, and smelling familiar smells. For my mind had suddenly short-circuited, slipped into sensory overload. I felt I needed to get back to familiar territory. Enough of this Tibet stuff for one day, Sorrel.

In a way I admired my roommates' nonchalant acceptance of all things Tibetan. This was this and that was that and it was completely unnecessary for them to get to the bottom of it all and ask why. When their time came to leave Lhasa, most of them would say, "Been there, done that—didn't buy a T-shirt, because there weren't any." Then they would simply wander off to different lands. It was a curious attitude which made sense for them, I suppose, for it never stressed the heart or mind into perplexing states of confusion. It was like looking at the page of a book, mechanically registering all the letters spaced into words, sentences, and paragraphs, then turning to the next page without having read and made sense of the first. When I read a book, I read every word, then go one step further. I want to know what lurks in the author's mind, how many cups of coffee and cigarettes, sleepless nights, and hung over mornings it took to produce the first and final chapters.

I parked my bike and ran up the stairs to the dormitory.

"Hi Chris. Hi Jen. How's Vass?"

"Well, he's breathing again."

Vass smiled, and poked his fingers out of his sleeping bag and waved. Because I had traveled gradually from near sea level into Tibet, I did not suffer from Lhasa's rarified air. My acclimatization had been gradual, unlike my roommates who had flown up to Lhasa in under two hours. Vass had taken it harder than most and lay in his sleeping cocoon with a long tube sticking out of his nose, carrying oxygen from a green canvas air bag.

I went to plonk myself down on the end of Chris's bed, ready to beg another filtered English cigarette from her. She coughed.

"Ah, Sorrel, you've got visitors."

I turned around then and noticed five people were sitting on my bed.

"Oh. Hi. Ah . . . what can I do for you?"

I wandered over.

Jigme Surkhang introduced himself and comrades—an assortment of personalities from Radio Lhasa, the local newspaper, the dreaded security police, and the Tibetan Women's League. Jigme, representing the Tibetan Sports Service Company (formally the Tibetan Sports Federation), flashed a cheeky smile across his dark, smallpox-scarred face, and welcomed me to Lhasa. His long black hair and faded blue jeans belied both his age (he was in his late forties) and position of authority.

Jigme had learned of my arrival in Lhasa through the security police. The people from his sporting organization habitually scoured Chinese newspapers and cut out any interesting articles related to sport. He held two about me in his hand. He smiled and told me I looked fatter in real life. Stronger too. I told him it was probably because the photographs accompanying the articles had been taken after riding down the steepest section of the Great Wall, and had captured me pale and drawn—scared to death in fact. And now, here in Lhasa, I puffed out with joy. He laughed. Jigme could understand *everything* I said, concrete or abstract. The occasional Aussie colloquialism had him stumped, but never for long. He was young at heart and we got on tremendously well.

As I answered each question he posed about my cycling journey through Asia, he translated all I said into Chinese and Tibetan, for the benefit of his companions. Pens were plied across pages, smiles stretched across faces. Every now and then, someone would blush, grimace, or bellow with raucous laughter.

And then it was my turn to ask a question, and I rephrased my query that had gone unanswered from the beginning.

"So, Jigme. Why are you here? What is this all about?" There was a hint of hesitancy in his voice.

"Oh. Ahh, I just wanted to find out who you are. And congratulate you for managing to get here by road *with* permission—you are the first to succeed, you know. And I wanted to congratulate you on your achievements so far, for they are remarkable—especially being the first woman to climb Mount Fuji with your bicycle."

At this point I was blushing, embarrassed by his flattery. But there was more.

"We here,"—he passed his hand through the air, gesturing toward his companions—"wish to welcome you to Lhasa and if there is anything you need or want, just say so."

Jigme saved the best for last.

"Sorrel, if there is anything special you would like to do in Tibet, I may be able to help you get the necessary permission. I want to help. Your spirit of adventure is an admirable quality. I like it. So . . . what would you like to do?"

My jaw dropped.

"What do you mean, what do I want to do? Something special? What could be more special than the privilege already extended to me?"

"Well, maybe—I thought maybe you may like to ride your bicycle to Shigatse. It's about two hundred miles from here and no one has ever ridden there before, even *without* permission. You'd indisputably be the first."

My mind raced. Ride my bicycle in Tibet? It's never been done before. Ride my bicycle in Tibet? Think of the flat tires! The mountain passes! A fuse blew somewhere in my brain again. A voice spoke, but I could scarcely believe it was my own.

"No, Jigme. I want to walk across Tibet."

The words were out before I had had a chance to think about their implication. Where had such a preposterous idea come from? The words had tumbled out automatically. Up until that moment, the thought of crossing Tibet on foot had never entered my conscious mind, yet suddenly I knew it was exactly what I wanted to do, what I was meant to do. I knew right then and there that I would get permission, I would walk, and I hoped would succeed. But that didn't stop bucket loads of doubt and fear from attempting to drown my inspiration. Those bucket loads fell then, in the following days and months, and on just about every single day of the epic journey itself.

Jigme and his companions left the dormitory a little confused by my response to their offer but determined to make my desire a reality. I turned to face my own, equally stunned friends. I walked over to the large wardrobe in our room and banged my head against its door. I hadn't been dreaming. I was awake, and now my head hurt.

That evening a man called Claus arrived at the dormitory. He was from Holland, and had studied Tibetan Buddhism. He was trapped beneath my avalanche of questions for the next few hours, stunned by my complete ignorance, yet happy to be able to share his knowledge of Tibetan culture and history. All the missing information from those decades of Chinese occupation jigsawed into place.

After the Dalai Lama fled from Tibet, thousands of his followers did likewise. They formed refugee camps in various parts of India. Eventually a Tibetan government-in-exile, headed by the "Ocean of Wisdom" himself, established its roots near the old British hill station of Dharamsala, at a place called McLeod Ganj. The Tibetan communities were plagued by many problems, notably poverty, disease, and above all, the devastating psychological effect of statelessness. They had lost their country. Overnight, aristocrats became paupers. The journey from Tibet into India cost many lives, split up many families. It took a lot of courage for those people to pull the threads of what remained together and start anew. They found that courage and succeeded, many taking their skills and theological philosophies beyond India to places like America and the European continent.

Back in Tibet, the Chinese were ardently repressing the religious beliefs and practices of the people, indoctrinating them with Communist Party dogmas. The Cultural Revolution was in full swing throughout China, but in Tibet it reached proportions of genocide. Religious persecution, and famine due to interference with old, established agricultural systems, killed many thousands of Tibetans.

Following the end of the Cultural Revolution, China opened her doors to foreign trade and tourism. In 1980, she opened those of Tibet also—but only to a small number of wealthy people. They were led by the hand around Lhasa, allowed to see the famous Potala Palace and the Jokhang Temple. Tourism flourished throughout China and more and more people were able to fly in and out of Lhasa at slowly diminishing expense. Finally, we young travelers on a shoestring were allowed into Tibet with little more than an Alien's Travel Permit, issued at the paltry cost of one yuan (about 40 cents).

While all this was going on, the Chinese started pouring money into the restoration of a few of the many temples and monasteries they had earlier destroyed. They were trying to compensate for their dreadful mistakes, as well as to encourage tourist dollars. In 1982 they even lifted the ban restricting the religious practices of the Tibetans.

Claus started to expound his views on Tibetan socioeconomics and politics, but as this was (at that time) outside my realm of interest, I steered the conversation onto the extraordinary Tibetan idiosyncracies and paraphernalia that had aroused my curiosity to date. First, there was that copper cylinder on a stick. It was called a prayer wheel. Inside the squat copper tube was a roll of paper, like the tape in a cash register, with the words "Om Mani Padme Hum" written over and over again on it. This "mantra," or prayer, when translated into English, means "Bless the jewel in the lotus." Hmmm—exotic, but a bit too esoteric for me to yet comprehend. The prayer wheel was a timesaving device. Spinning the words of the mantra around and around was the same as uttering them. One could do the shopping, talk to friends, *and* pray all at the same time. Worship, it seemed, was not confined to churches and Sundays. It was an integral part of everyday life. If the wheel was spinning, you were praying. Simple. Even logical.

I asked Claus about the presence of the sometimes colorful, but more often weather-bleached and tatty rags flying on houses and hillsides everywhere throughout eastern Tibet and Lhasa. They were prayer flags. Like the prayer wheel papers, the little banners were printed with "Om Mani Padme Hum," he told me, and other significant mantras. As they flapped about in the breeze, those printed prayers flew up to the Heavens. The flags were printed in five colors—white, yellow, red, green, and blue and reflected the Buddhist states of mind: form, feeling, recognition, karmic formation, and consciousness. At a higher level, the colors stood for the five Buddhist wisdoms: the abilities to reflect what the mind sees, to compare, to differentiate, to accomplish, and finally the perception of truth—Buddha-hood.

And what was the purpose of lying on the ground, or prostrating—that odd practice I had first come across on the road to Lhasa? The simple answer is that as Christians choose to kneel or cross themselves, Tibetans prostrate themselves in supplication to their god.

Finally, I asked Claus about the times Tibetan people had poked their tongues out at me in the streets of Qamdo and Lhasa. Why? Well, it is a very ancient greeting—and an extremely courteous one. According to a superstitious belief, a person who would poison another has a black tongue. Displaying a pink tongue indisputably reveals one's harmlessness. The open palm gesture which accompanies this strengthens the claim: look, no weapons either.

And so the lesson in Tibetan customs came to an end. Claus had not only enthralled me, but my roommates too.

They really cared after all. Such is the charm of Tibet. I told Claus of my plan to walk across the country. He was astounded.

"Sorrel, if they really let you do it, you must try and get to Kang Rinpoche—Mount Kailas. It's somewhere in the western corner of Tibet—one of the holiest places and a center for pilgrims. Oh, Sorrel, you must go there."

And with that I climbed inside my sleeping bag and stretched out on the narrow bed, my head buzzing with ideas.

Jigme came by in the morning and whisked me off to meet some other officials from his sporting organization. The Tibetan Sports Service Company took charge of all mountaineering expeditions within Tibet. The communal office was adorned with pictures of Mount Everest and a huge map of Tibet—I was amazed at its size, equal to that of western Europe. Jigme laughed. "Why don't you climb Mount Everest? That's easy—well, easy for us to organize. We've had a lot of foreign mountaineering clubs here to do that. There was an Australian team here a few months back, but I didn't meet them because I was in America." He pulled out a stack of papers from a file. "Look at this! Look how much we charge these climbing parties. Peak fees, portage fees—it's $140 American a day for each member just to be in this country!"

My heart sank. I suddenly felt sick. "Jigme, I—ah, I don't have any money . . ." He cut me short. He had no intention of charging me a cent for my proposed expedition. He genuinely wanted to foster my spirit of adventure, not throw me into debt for the rest of my life. He planned to convince his more money-hungry overlords of the virtues of goodwill. What a man! This was a bigger miracle than I had ever imagined.

The next week was spent meeting more Tibetan government delegations by day and disco dancing in the newly opened discotheque with Jigme and his friends at night. It came as quite a shock to find the large, prestressed concrete hall, festooned with gaudy streamers and garlands beneath the majestic 300-year-old Potala Palace. Dancing, an activity banned during the Cultural Revolution, had only been revived as a legal activity in the last few months. I was amazed to see a place as geographically isolated as Lhasa already locked into the current modern trend. We jived away the hours to the beat of Michael Jackson and Boney M. Jigme had learned how to dance in America. I had learned to dance in Australia. Together, with the help of Chris, Jen, and Vass (when he had recovered) we were shamelessly responsible for exerting a new wave influence on the youth of Lhasa. Their recently mastered foxtrots and waltz steps flew right out of the proverbial window. Lhasa had already moved—irreversibly—into the twentieth century; we just made it jump up and down a bit. It had to happen sooner or later.

Come Tuesday December 18, there was more than sufficient reason to dance. I received my permission to walk around Tibet. On paper, no less! The next day Jigme asked me to his home to meet his family. He had prepared a special celebratory feast of lamb stew, knowing the tender meat to be a great favorite of all Australians. He had spent the day searching the marketplace for a whole carcass, and returned with just a leg and apologies. But there was plenty to go round.

Jigme's wife was a teacher at the College of Lhasa, soon to be declared a university. She could speak a little English, and took great pleasure in practicing it on me. We laughed a lot, talked a lot, and munched our way through Jigme's stew, then watched Chinese dramas on the television Jigme had brought from America.

Winter was really starting to set in. The days were fast getting shorter and colder in Lhasa. It was insane to even consider starting my trek across Tibet right then and there. I was totally unprepared for such a venture. I had all the wrong equipment, lacked high-altitude experience, and did not consider I knew enough about the country and its people to make such a journey yet. Climatically, Tibet was supposed to be at its best from May until mid-Septem-

ber, when the brief, high-altitude summer ended, and obviously that was when I should be out trekking. Despite near-constant sunshine, Lhasa by day was seldom warmer than 45°F in the daytime now, and with the temperature dropping almost to zero at night, the prospect of venturing to even higher altitudes within the country was a grim one indeed.

On the other side of the world, sweltering beneath the rays of the southern hemisphere summer sun, Aussie friends were diving into backyard pools and sparkling oceans. It was nearly Christmas . . . dare I venture to make it my very first white one? The thought of yak meat and cabbage was far from appealing. My first true white Christmas would be nothing without all the traditional trappings. Roast turkey and cranberry sauce, chocolates and plum pudding, fresh nuts and mangoes—my stomach called! I wasn't ready for home just yet, but the prospect of eating festive fare in nearby Hong Kong was too good to resist.

So Chris and I plotted to leave wintry Tibet by plane. Since Lhasa airport lies a good sixty miles from the city, it was first necessary to arrange tickets for a bus. Surprisingly, these were issued along with the plane tokens— reducing the usual Eastern ticketing procedure to just a single day-and-a-half ordeal! Normally, as we had both experienced elsewhere in China, it takes the independent (often referred to by the authorities as "unorganized") traveler at least four days to battle bureaucracy and arrange transport. Four days to wait in queues, and be directed to numerous other offices or ticket depots, then be redirected back to the first, confront security police— either to have your intended destination stamped on your Alien's Permit, or apologize (in writing) for the civil unrest you "ashamedly" created out of frustration back at the first ticket office . . . and so it goes on.

Once on the airport-bound bus, however, the apparent organization quickly deteriorated. The bus came to a complete standstill just eight miles out of town. No one explained why, or what was happening. In fact, no one moved, not even the driver. Chris and I just giggled nervously and stared at all the Mao-jacketed Han Chinese passengers surrounding us. There were no Tibetans on the bus at all—presumably they would have no reason to fly to mainland China, nor any money to do so. About an hour later, a blast shook the bus violently. Billowing clouds of dust raced down the valley and enveloped not only our vehicle, but the several dozen now hissing behind us like a long, impatient snake. A traffic jam in Tibet! We realized that road gangs were literally building the road before us. Massive landslides alternated with crater-like obstacles along its intended course.

I couldn't believe the travel authorities had not been informed of the afternoon road closure. We missed our designated plane and did not arrive at the airport until the following morning. Chris and I, together with all the other passengers, had been left at a cold concrete compound in the dead of night, and told simply: "Tomorrow, okay tomorrow." Lack of sufficient bedding forced us to snuggle up together in a single room occupied by no less than twelve people.

The following day, through eyes blurry from lack of sleep, I gazed down at Tibet, steadily unfolding beneath me as the aircraft gained altitude. It was magnificent. Desolate. So arid, so vast, so imposing. Mountain after mountain, on and on, as far as I dared imagine. I strained to see a sign of life, even a single village, amid the endless dry-blown landscape. Was this the land I had vowed to traverse—on foot? For the first time, I realized the extent of my challenge. How far was I going to walk? How long would it take? Soon I had to make some pretty important decisions. But it was obvious that the projected "walk across Tibet" would take shape in much the same way as my "ride around Asia": slowly, piecemeal, and its success would owe as much to chance as any careful planning.

My mind was brought back to the present by a sudden

tilting motion of the plane. For no apparent reason, all the Chinese passengers had decided simultaneously to unbuckle their seat belts and rush to the right hand side, although the view was no different from the left. Watching them move to and fro for collective viewing made me laugh so hard that I quickly snapped out of my apprehensive state. We reached Chengdu, a little shaken, and transferred to a Canton-bound flight. Then we traveled all night on a luxurious ship from the mainland port and arrived in Hong Kong on December 24th. Christmas in civilization, by the skin of our teeth!

Lhasa, the Potala, the Jokhang, the Hobbit's ring of magic mountains, was suddenly a vague memory—a distant dream. Colored lights adorned Nathan Street, Christmas trees filled hotel foyers, everywhere the angels sang and bells jingled, and kings brought gifts from far-off lands. There was mail awaiting me in Hong Kong. I tore open dozens of letters and greeting cards from friends with the enthusiasm of a five-year-old and devoured them word by word; each one as tantalizing as the bubbles in French champagne. I was quickly drunk on the thoughts and glad tidings of far-off friends.

We danced and we sang and we partied till dawn. Christmas became new year, and I polished my bicycle and flew to Bangkok. Chris departed on her own travels.

My plan was to explore the East further and return to Tibet in the spring month, June. I had received an invitation to take part in an Indian all-women's mountaineering training course in Manāli, in northern India. It was scheduled to take place in late May and June and would give me the experience in high-altitude trekking, rock, snow, and ice-climbing I so desperately needed. The invitation was another godsend, the timing was perfect.

I rode up to the northern hills of Thailand, singing all the way. Every bit of my body and mind was filled with the goodness of life. Oh, how beautiful the trees were, the rice fields, the warm tropical air! A thousand pieces of a

giant puzzle had fallen from heaven, and slotted into place
for me with miraculous ease. Everything, absolutely everything was perfect.

Then disaster struck. I had been commissioned to write
an article about cycling around Thailand for a Bangkok-
based adventure magazine. They wanted a really special
photograph of me and Pushy for the front cover, and in a
moment of inspired madness, I cooked up a brilliant idea.

In Japan I'd put wheels on Mount Fuji. In China, I had
cycled on the Great Wall. Following tradition, I decided to
put myself and Pushy atop the symbol of Siam. And unfortunately for me the symbol of Thailand is an elephant.

In the jungles near Chiang Mai, I composed my fateful
photograph. One elephant, one bicycle, one ladder, one
camera, one assistant, and—ho-hum—one ghastly accident. Three seconds after the photograph was taken, the
elephant reared her ugly head. I tumbled from my precarious perch and plummeted to the ground. It was a long
way down. Assuming I was winded, Tanome, the elephant
trainer, scooped me up and began bouncing me up and
down on the ground, holding me around the waist with the
strength of a cobra. Put me down, put me down . . . I tried
to say. I collapsed in his arms, blacked out and came to
again in a matter of seconds. I lay motionless on the
ground. I couldn't move. Something had happened. I
looked up at Tanome's blurred, frightened face. In broken
Thai, I managed to say, "Did you get the photograph?" He
nodded. "Great! How's the elephant?" A nervous little
smile creased his face and he told me to lie very still while
he went to get help. Lie very still. That was easy. What did
he think I was going to do? Jump up and cartwheel all the
way back to Australia? I remember thinking I couldn't
have broken my back, for I'd have been as dead as a
doornail after Tanome's violent shaking. I watched the
clouds sail overhead and finally heard footsteps running
toward me. Six normally rowdy Thai boys stood above me,
their faces expressing horror. I smiled up at them, and
managed to giggle. Two boys bent down and secured a

grip around my ankles. Two slid their hands beneath the small of my back and the others lifted me up by the shoulders. I screamed. Searing pain rushed through the lower part of my body. Oh God, what's happened? I thought. The boys, like pallbearers shouldering a coffin, carried me out of the jungle and over a gushing river to the roadside. I was biting hard on a stick of bamboo, trying not to scream. I kept blacking out from the pain. In my head I kept repeating: I'm okay. I'm okay. But I really wasn't at all.

Hours later a car came, and rushed me off to the Lanna Hospital in Chiang Mai. X-rays revealed a small fracture in my pelvis. It was so small, it almost didn't show up on film. But I had torn all the muscles in my thigh and lower back, and that, according to my doctors, was the source of my excruciating agony. I stayed in the hospital for several weeks. Physiotherapy was unbelievably painful, but I wanted to walk—I didn't have time to lie around and heal. I shed oceans of tears, dragging myself on crutches and walking frames up and down the sterile-smelling ward.

The hospital rang the Australian Embassy in Bangkok, they in turn rang my mother, and she rang me. It was wonderful to hear her voice; so full of love and assurance. "Why don't you come home, darling? You can always go back again." I suddenly felt defeated. An imaginary chorus of "I-told-you-so's" rattled around in my mind. Oh, how they would mock me.

My mother hung suspended in my silence, intuitively interpreting its meaning. I hadn't uttered one word, yet she simply said, "No they won't, Sorrel. You have made it. We are all proud of what you have achieved. Especially your father. Come home and get the strength you need to go on." And on—and on and on. I loved my mother more than anything in the whole world, and ached to see her. And my father—proud of me. I flew home.

While recuperating, I labored over the great Tibetan plan. Jigme wrote to me, saying he had permission for me to make a documentary film of the adventure, if I so

desired. I was very keen on the idea. But my "Hail, Hollywood" hallucinations were short-lived. The logistics of getting financial backing, a cameraman, and an assistant
were horrendous. It was impossible, and, with some regret, I refocused on my original plan. To trek across Tibet,
alone.

Plans for my proposed journey found their way into the
hands of Dick Smith, a successful Australian business-
man. He invited me to his office at Terry Hills and filled
me in on his own adventurous undertakings. He was working with infectious enthusiasm on the production of a
journal of discovery and adventure for the Australian
market—a quarterly magazine with a positive outlook,
about Australia and Australians. He offered to pay my air
fare to the East and back, to support my expedition, and
hoped I would write about it for what he envisaged would
become the most prestigious and widely read magazine
ever to take root in Australian soil. I accepted.

So *Australian Geographic* magazine became my major
sponsor for the Tibetan trek and who knows? Maybe even
a dozen more adventures still unplanned.

I simply used my own common sense and experience to
work out exactly what equipment I needed for this journey (which still had no specific route, no specific mileage,
and no specific time limit!). My old down-lined waterproof
jacket and an ultra-thick down sleeping bag (donated by a
Sydney-based manufacturer) would keep me warm at
night—even in subzero temperatures. I planned to pick up
a secondhand heavy-duty high-altitude tent on my way
through Nepal, since the price of a new one in Sydney
stores was exorbitant.

I intended to use a yak, the Tibetan all-purpose beast of
burden, to carry all my goods and chattels across Tibet,
and as I knew a yak could easily carry between 125 and
200 pounds, I amassed about 75 pounds of food, additional
warm clothing, books, ropes, solid fuel blocks, a tiny aluminum burner with its pot, a plastic ground sheet, plus a
bulky, tube-shaped bean-sprouting kit to fill my need for

fresh vegetables! I also took an assortment of bandages, antiseptics, basic medicines, and an array of vitamin supplements. I purchased foodstuffs which I hoped would complement those I would buy locally, such as meat and flour. So I took with me mostly the dehydrated or dried varieties of soups, fruits, muesli, peas and beans, milk, coffee, tea, rice. I had $800 Australian in my wallet—more than enough to pay for the mountaineering course, travel by truck to Lhasa, and buy a yak.

Attempting to ease the burden of worry on friends and family, I assured everyone that Jigme had arranged a guide to accompany me on the expedition—white lies were made for occasions such as this. Finally I crammed all my gear into two cheap backpacks, donned my hiking boots, and boarded the jet for India.

Delhi was sweltering, even before sunrise. Sacred cows and Sadhus, ragged beggars and diseased dogs lined the filthy gutters of New Delhi Road. Dawn cast its golden rays through the haze of humidity and billowing clouds of dust created by the gutter traffic, as it shuffled in silence toward the railway station. The dogs and cows scrounged for food from the garbage bins, the Sadhus and beggars scrounged coins from Sikhs and businessmen. An ancient woman in a faded, stained sari struggled to turn her roadside bedding into a street stall, slinging her sheets between two leaning poles to form a canopy over her broken-boxed brassware. She had a bucket of wilting flowers for sale as well. I bought a bunch and passed them around the lost souls outside the railway station. I took a deep breath, and all that putrid, Eastern air came rushing into my lungs. Ahh. Asia. It was so good to be back!

I found my way to the bus station and secured a ticket on the "video bus" bound for Manāli. Since the journey would take fourteen hours, I opted for this form of transport in place of the ordinary bus, presuming that the more expensive ride would include a measure of luxury. Air conditioning and the latest feature-length movies were the ad-

vertised benefits. Since the temperature had already
reached 95°F, I happily handed over the extra dollars to
the ticket seller. The realities of the situation were soon
apparent.

Air conditioning came in the form of a fan, six inches in
diameter, nailed to the cracked black vinyl roof trim
above the driver's head. The casing was covered in fly dirt
and the blades whirred to a standstill after the first few
miles. My legs stuck to the seat with sweat and the oppres-
sive heat made me drowsy. An hour later, the caterwaul-
ing of India's musical movie stars jolted me awake. Enter
the Indian video—the entertainment favorite of the eight-
ies. Sitars and tabla drums, distorted by the full-blast
positioning of volume and tone knobs on the video player,
twanged and thumped out inharmonious rhythms. The
actresses and actors pranced around on rolling green hills
and picnicked in fields of wildflowers, screeching love
songs like bestial banshees. Enter a headache.

The bus reached Manāli at midnight and a dozen touts
for hotels and lodges milled around the depot soliciting
clientele. I haggled for a cheap room and followed one
swarthy barker to his father's guest house. It was in the
Tibetan quarter of town. Gone were the smells and humidity of Delhi. This was mountain country, the air was sweet
with the fragrance of pine and deodar cedars and cooled
by a northwesterly breeze. The hotel manager saw me to a
room, then brought a mug of hot, spiced tea. I remembered him putting it down near my bedhead, and
mumbled "Danyavad" in thanks, but the next eight hours
were a complete blackout. No dreams, nothing. I slept so
well, stretched out on a bed for the first time in forty-eight
hours.

When I awoke in the morning, it was to find myself in
paradise. Never had I seen such a beautiful place. Manāli
lay at the foot of the Western Himalayan Ranges high in
the valley of the Beas River. The Beas roared down from
the snow-capped mountains and sliced the township of
Manāli in two, then gurgled all the way through the Kulu

valley and out to meet the Sutlej River, over two hundred miles away. Coniferous forests covered the steep, rocky foothills. Here, the valley was just wide enough to accommodate the river and the ramshackle houses of Manāli, but splayed out to lush, green fields farther downstream. After throwing buckets of cold water all over myself in an attempt to free the last, clinging cobwebs of jet and video bus lag, I wandered off to find the mountaineering school.

It was situated on the left bank of the Beas, a few miles down the valley, an assortment of dingy administration buildings and dormitories set in gorgeous, almost manicured gardens. I introduced myself to the superintendent of the complex, filled out some enrollment forms, then returned to the guest house to retrieve my belongings. Since the course was not due to commence for another four days, I decided to do a little exploring. With Tom, an Einstein look-alike from Canada, whom I had met on the bus from Delhi, I walked down the Kulu valley to Nagar and on to Buntar.

We walked and talked together through two sun-filled days, absorbing the exquisite beauty of the vale and the many tiny villages which clung to its sides. My pelvic fracture had healed beautifully and I felt confident it would withstand the rigorous training program in the weeks ahead.

I was wrong. Walking down a solid dirt track to Buntar was one thing; but dragging myself up cliff faces and trudging through deep, powder snow was something else entirely. I ached in silence day after day, hiding tears of pain and fighting off fears of being physically unable to endure the long Tibetan trek before me.

The training course was exhausting, but I learned an incredible amount—how to tie knots, tie myself in knots, and then eventually undo myself with the grace of Houdini. Once I had mastered the art of half hitch and bowline-tying, I learned the technique of climbing rock faces on my finger tips and boot toes, learned how to fall—and how to curse in Hindi dialect. The fifteen women enduring

all this with me were from various parts of the country—
all keen to equal one day the achievement of the first
Indian woman to reach the summit of Mount Everest. Two
of them in fact had young children, whom they had left in
the care of their husbands. I was delighted to learn a sense
of independence had emerged in Indian women and together we joyfully progressed from climbing to abseiling—I leaped like a lemming from the top of Vashist Rock,
a 150-foot cliff, over and over again, until the ropes grew
threadbare. We moved from the Manāli institution up into
the mountains and I learned how to climb ice walls and
snow slopes. I learned all about avalanches and caused a
few through clumsiness. I deliberately fell down crevasses
and subsequently learned mountain rescue procedures.

All this may sound frightfully easy and carefree, but
believe me, it wasn't. I lived with fear most of the time,
and every inch of every rock face, snow slope, and ice wall
I found utterly daunting. I learned a lot about different
mountaineering skills, although I failed to really master
most of them. I learned more about myself though, and
perfected the power of determination. I was by no means
ready to take on the Empire State Building dressed in a
Spiderman costume, nor challenge the Pentecost Island-
ers in their ritual leaps into nothingness. But I was, I
believed, ready for Tibet.

While I was in Manāli, the most bizarre coincidence
occurred. His Holiness, the Dalai Lama sailed into town
with his entourage, in a fleet of yellow limousines. He had
left his home-in-exile at McLeod Ganj in Himachal Pradesh, to holiday for two weeks in this picturesque village.
The mountaineering school directors, aware of my intention to trek across Tibet, gave me time off from my studies
to arrange a meeting with the holy man.

First I met Tempa, the Dalai Lama's private secretary,
and talked my way into his heart. His Holiness hadn't
planned to give private audiences during his vacation, but
Tempa would see what he could do for me. Three days
later, he phoned the school. A date and a time had been

set. I would indeed get to meet the God-King of Tibet. I was ecstatic.

On the morning of the meeting, I could hardly concentrate on the knot-tying tasks of the day. My mind was about as far removed from bowlines and half hitches as Manāli was from Melbourne. What would he look like? What would he say? More to the point, what was I going to say? I leapt off good old Vashist Rock a dozen times, oblivious to its dizzying height.

At 3 P.M. with abseiling ropes and rock pitons still in hand, I marched off to meet the incarnate, living Buddha. A smiling guard searched me at the gate and removed the rock pitons and a pocket knife from my person, then he led me over to Tempa's office. Tempa tried for half an hour to calm my excitement and nervousness. Eventually he gave up and led me to the veranda of a quaint little cottage on the other side of the garden of the small resort. A heavy curtain separated Tempa and myself from His Holiness. My heart pounded erratically.

I turned to Tempa. "What do I say. What do I do? Do I kiss his ring or prostrate myself a dozen times in front of him?"

Tempa laughed, "Oh you don't have to be formal."

So I wasn't. The curtains parted like the Red Sea, and there on a cushion sat the Ocean of Wisdom, the Dalai Lama, bending over a neat pile of written Buddhist scriptures.

"G'day! You must be the great Dalai Lama!" I reached down to shake his hand. "How are you?"

I heard Tempa choke on a giggle and felt instantly embarrassed by my nervous impertinent introduction. I tried to make amends.

I had read somewhere that it was the Tibetan practice to give a white scarf or "khata" on auspicious occasions and had bought one from the local Tibetan curio shop in the main street. The shop proprietor had shown me how to fold it properly for presentation, and that morning while my climbing colleagues had fumbled with ropes and harnesses, I had fumbled with my scarf, trying to fold it perfectly. Succeeding at last, I had shoved it in the pocket of my tracksuit pants and promptly forgotten all about it until now.

I reached into my pocket but only caught one mysteriously loose end of the cloth. I pulled and pulled, and out it came, bit by bit, all crinkled and undone, like an endless, knotted string of magician's handkerchiefs. I blushed and handed the six-foot length of fake silk to the smiling Dalai Lama.

After my initial blundering, I found it surprisingly easy to relax in the presence of His Holiness. He was so warm and human and spoke fluent English. We talked for an hour about a hundred things. He told me all about the plight of his people and the temperament of yaks. I told him all I knew about the Australian Aborigines and the character of kangaroos. While yaks and kangaroos are hardly comparable, I could see parallels between the indigenous Tibetan and Aboriginal races, strong similarities in their past situations and present circumstances. We talked and talked and talked some more.

As I was leaving, the Dalai Lama rose to his feet and shook my hand again. Then, in a gesture of love and fatherly concern, he put his arm around me and pinched me hard on the cheek. He laughed—how he laughed! A Dalai Lama chuckle starts at the toes and works its way up beneath the maroon and yellow robes, sending little rivulets of mirth across the fabric. It reaches the shoulders and sets them shaking, then explodes across the face, crinkling the nose and causing the eyes to vanish behind suddenly rosy, puffed cheeks. That laugh had been reincarnated fourteen times, burst forth from fourteen different beings. No wonder it was perfect. Then he pinched my cheek a second time and gave me a pile of books, a white khata, and a thin red string, explaining that the latter was a protection cord to wear around my neck. He had blessed it dozens of times and it would guarantee me a safe journey across Tibet.

Tempa invited me to visit McLeod Ganj when I finished the mountaineering course. He wanted me to see the settlement, and to use their library resources to learn more about Tibet in days of old. He told me they had some maps I would be welcome to use, and he himself offered to help me plan my trekking route across the country.

We finished our course with a climb almost to the summit of Friendship Peak, using our newly acquired skills on the mountain as a practical examination. It was June 19th, my birthday. The day after, I waved goodbye to my climbing colleagues and caught a bus to McLeod Ganj.

Now the difference between an ordinary bus and a video bus may seem quite obvious, but apart from the former vehicle missing a TV and player, it also lacked padding on the seats, a licensed driver, several windows, and half the engine. The windscreen was decorated with pictures of Shiva and eight rows of the last decade's Christmas tinsel. The dashboard was decorated with dusty plastic floral arrangements, a plaster replica of Buddha's nativity scene, a buxom "Parvati" carved from a tree stump, and a line of burning incense sticks shoved into blobs of dirt-gray clay. The driver had a square foot of unadorned glass to see through, but even that was filthy with grime and dust. His driving got worse. The "holy roller" careened along precariously narrow roads at the speed of a Grand Prix challenger. How the bus managed to reach McLeod Ganj in one piece, with all its passengers and cargo relatively intact, I will never know. The Indian travelers had taken the whole horrendous journey in stride. Even when a scrawny villager hopped on board with a leaking plastic container full of petrol, they didn't panic. They just lit cigarettes and flicked their still-burning matches toward the potential bomb. On recollection, I think surviving that bus ride may have been a miracle.

I stayed for three days in McLeod Ganj and on the second, attended a local wedding with Tempa. The daughter of New Delhi's liaison officer to the Dalai Lama was getting married and the family wanted some photographs

taken of the Hindu ceremony. I had offered with enthusiasm to do the job.

It was a long affair, but all the vow-making and religious rituals were fascinating. I photographed everything. The wedding took place on the veranda of a stately
old home—once the residence of some affluent British Raj
dignitary. Tibetan women had prepared a sumptuous
banquet for the reception party on the spacious lawn before the house. I was asked to put down my camera and
join in the afternoon's feast. The bride's sister painted my
hands with henna, which didn't wash off for several
weeks—a curious traditional custom.

During those three days His Holiness was busy doing
some special meditation or religious ceremony, and
Tempa allowed me to sit inside the temple with the monks
and listen to the holy man for half an hour. It was all very
mysterious, and the Dalai Lama's low eerie chant scared
the daylights out of me. Was this the same man who had
tweaked my cheek and chuckled with such innocent joy?

That afternoon, I returned to my lodgings to find an
Indian film crew had taken over the restaurant attached
to it, and turned it into a stage setting resembling a busi-
nessman's office. They were producing a documentary-
style film on business management, and I was offered a
starring role in a short scene. My wildest fantasy was
fulfilled! Hollywood! Well, not quite, but at least my face
would grace the screens on India's infamous video buses
for a few seconds. I played the part of a business tycoon's
foreign secretary and penned shorthand for my actor-
boss. Oh, I did look the part—all dressed up in my grubby
tracksuit pants and maroon cheesecloth shirt. I had to say
inane things like, "Oh, very good, Sir." and "Is this correct,
Sir?" and bat my eyelids a lot. Bette Davis couldn't have
done it better. Because the session ran late, I missed my
bus down to lower Dharamsala, so the film producer offered to drive me there to meet my connecting bus to
Delhi.

From Delhi, I caught a plane to Kathmandu. When

Himalayan trekking became a popular pastime for Westerners in the early 1970s, Kathmandu quickly established
itself as a major center for the industry. Businesses flourished, catering to the whims and appetites of the influx of
visitors, and now, fifteen years later, the city is a melting
pot of cultures. It is widely touted as the best place to get a
"real" (that is, Western) meal in Asia. It was no wonder the
number of similar-looking foreigners on my flight
doubled that of returning Nepalese. Over 200,000 Westerners a year visit Nepal these days to trek the mountain
vistas, but I was Kathmandu-bound for essentially a very
different reason. I planned to travel by road from the city,
across the border between Nepal and Tibet and into
Lhasa. The border had opened only three months previously, and from all accounts, the tourist industry in
Lhasa was booming.

It was the beginning of July and the monsoon clouds
were filling the Kathmandu valley. The fields were iridescent green, the roads a sticky red quagmire. Rickety rick-
shaws bogged in the mud, taxis crawled along behind
endless processions of massive gray bullocks, people ran
through the puddles dodging carts, buses, and bicycles—
their cotton bloomers clinging like wet tissue paper to
their thin, tanned legs. Huge black umbrellas formed a
dark canopy over everyone and everything in the marketplace. Black dye leaked from the wet umbrellas and
stained saris and dhotis. Flower petals and bidi (cigarette)
butts floated by in the monsoon streams. The wares from
fruit and fabric shops overflowed onto the crowded
streets. The roads became narrow lanes lined with the
Newari gingerbread houses. It was easy to get lost in the
network of back streets and alleys, and pure joy to do so.
Eventually I found my way to Thamel, the budget travelers' section of town, and collapsed in a dripping muddle
inside Le Bistro restaurant. Ahhh, yak cheesecake and
instant Nescafé. Paradise!

The restaurant was part owned by Kerry, a woman I
had been introduced to in Sydney, and she appeared

shortly afterwards with her boyfriend, Garry. We laughed
and talked for hours with Pandey, their Nepalese partner.
Pandey never stopped smiling. He was the most aptly
named person I had ever met, for he reminded me of the
cuddly pandas I had seen in the zoo at Beijing.

Ten days rolled by in Kathmandu. I was anxious to get
into Tibet, but the Chinese ambassador was creating problems—he refused to issue me an independent visa for his
country, claiming I could not enter by road unless I was on
a group tour. I argued with the embassy officials day after
day, but they remained obnoxiously adamant.

One company in town was operating tours to Tibet,
charging exorbitant prices—in U.S. dollars, no less. But it
was the only way to get to Tibet from Nepal, so I had to
pay. And I can't deny that it hurt.

While I waited for the departure date, I filled in the
many hours with Kerry, Garry, Pandey, and a continuous,
changing stream of other travelers floating through their
restaurant, talking about Tibet and my great plan to trek
across it. I would buy a yak to carry my equipment, and
we mused at length about its name and appearance. Ever
the patriot, I planned to fly a rather battered Australian
flag from its left horn and, just so Pushy would be with me
in more than spirit, I intended putting her bicycle bell on
the other horny handlebar.

There were many new friends who scoffed at my plan;
many who no doubt thought I was little more than an over-
inflated bag of wind. There were those who shared in my
excitement and those who laughed at it. But the ones who
laughed and mocked were then the greatest help of all, for
they strengthened my resolve, my power of determination
to see the plan through to its fruition. Later I would draw
strength from those who half-believed in me.

Beneath all the scheming and laughter, there was ap-
prehension. When I was finally ready to leave Kathmandu, Pandey hosted a fabulous party in my honor. We
drank and danced, and when it was time to say goodbye, I
was the recipient of hugs and kisses which were so acutely
final that they scared me. They were the hugs of brothers

and sisters, standing on wet shipping docks, farewelling a
soldier bound for battle.

Apart from the hugs and kisses, I received two other
gifts. The first was a pair of brand, spanking-new ski
overalls from Conel Ongdi, a Bhutanese trekking company director who had also kindly lent me a high-altitude
tent for the journey, thus solving that problem. The second
was a dysentery-inducing amoeba, from a thoughtlessly
consumed glass of unfiltered Nepalese water. There were
no drug stores open when the minute amoeba latched
itself onto my intestine, so I had to leave Kathmandu with
the little bug intact. The tour company was anxious to
leave the city before dawn to begin the journey to the
Tibetan border before the road became heavy with traffic.

It was a horrible trip. I was suffering from acute diarrhea and nausea and had to beg the driver of the jeep to
stop every half hour so I could get out. There were three
jeeps in our entourage, all carrying paying customers who
were no doubt not impressed by the frequent delays. We
crossed the border on foot, for the road bridge had yet to
be constructed, and reached the ugly town of Khasa in the
early evening. Tibet. I had returned at last. And I felt at
death's door.

The expensive tour only went as far as Khasa; if you
wanted to go through to Lhasa, you had to pay a few
thousand dollars more, or find your own way there. I
neither knew nor cared what the rest of the group planned
to do but in the morning, I paid thirty yuan (about twelve
dollars) to a truck driver, pulled myself up into the open
tray of his ancient vehicle, curled up inside a big spare
tire, covered myself up with my yellow plastic raincape,
and began my second journey to Lhasa.

It took three days to reach the holy city and I was so ill
when I arrived I could scarcely walk. I had phoned Jigme
from Shigatse to let him know I would be arriving, and so
he met me at the truck depot.

"Gee, you're thin. And weaker too. What's happened to
you?"

I explained all the intimate details to my old friend. It

was so good to see my Tibetan "father" again, after all those hectic months. There are people you know will be lifelong friends the first time you meet them, and Jigme was one. He took me to the guest house at the Tibetan Sports Service Company, got me all comfortable and tucked up beneath a pile of heavy quilts, and went to find a medicine to cure my ills. He returned an hour later with two rabbit-dropping-sized black balls, guaranteeing they would bring instant relief.

But they didn't work. This form of dysentery can only be flushed from the system with one of two drugs—Tiniba or Flagyl. I telegramed my parents to send a supply of either antibiotic by express post, and sat back to await its arrival.

I'm not very good at sitting, even when I'm ill. I coerced Jigme into letting me out of my sick room so I could re-explore the city of Lhasa. I could not believe how different it looked from my first visit in December, only seven months before. A new plaza had been built in front of the Jokhang Temple. On either side of it, three-story apartment blocks had been constructed in the old tiered, Tibetan style. Gardens in the plaza held neat rows of newly planted shrubbery; all the plants were carefully protected from the elements by transparent plastic bags. The streets around the Jokhang had been paved with roughly hewn cobblestones and the market stalls were flooded with more Chinese and Western goods than ever before. There were considerably more tourists, too, clicking Nikons at this and that, buying turquoise and trinkets from vendors and vagabonds on the busy streets. It didn't matter much that Lhasa's surface was changing. In its heart, in my heart, it would always be the same—always enchanting.

I wandered inside the temple and reacquainted my senses with the rank smell of burning yak butter and the squeaking sound of huge un-oiled prayer wheels turning in the hallway, around the central cathedral. The Jokhang was the hub of a wheel—the spiritual heart of Tibet itself—which turned and throbbed with the rhythm and meaning of life.

I was getting impatient about my trek across Tibet. Jigme had lost his light-hearted air, and a deep worry line now furrowed his brow. He started to create little danger-packed scenarios for me; our conversations were full of "What if this happens?" questions, and "You have no idea what you are in for!" statements. July threatened to become August.

He tried to talk me out of starting the trip, and when he failed, he took me to meet lots of other people who, he hoped, would succeed. But, as Jigme had really expected all along, nothing, absolutely nothing, anyone could say would change my mind. I was going to walk across Tibet, and not even the little Nepalese amoeba would stop me. I was as stubborn as an ox, even when I was as sick as a dog.

While Jigme lacked the power to change my mind, he did have the influence to alter my plan. Ever the romantic, I had anticipated buying a yak and simply wandering off into the sunset. I had a vague sort of route to follow; from Lhasa, I wanted to head north to Amdo, then due west to Sirchuan He or Ali, then loop back to Lhasa. I had a compass in case my usually reliable sense of direction played out during the many months I would be on the road. Those mad whims were now rightfully suppressed by my mentor, who pointed out the distance I had set myself amounted to something like 3,600 miles. Since that would take five or six months, given the late start I seemed doomed to make, I would have to endure the full extent of a Tibetan winter on the road.

Jigme and I labored for hours over maps, and finally we reached an anticlimactic agreement. I would begin my journey in the far southwest corner of Tibet, in a town called Burang, and follow the southern road all the way through to Lhasa. If I survived that, I could continue along the roadway to Qamdo in the east. I hated the idea of walking along the road, imagining a paved, four lane

highway. What a bore. But Jigme's reasoning was sound.
My highway was no more than a rough dirt track, occasionally frequented by trucks taking supplies to distant
villages, and jeeps carrying Chinese military personnel to
far-off outposts. If I ran into any major catastrophe, I
probably wouldn't have to wait more than three days for a
passing vehicle to scoop me out of trouble and whisk me
and my shattered pride back to Lhasa. There would,
Jigme said, be no problems in finding water either, for the
thousand-mile road followed the Tsang Po River for most
of its length.

My travel permits were prepared in readiness for my
departure. Jigme assured me I would find a donkey
"somewhere out West." The only thing I needed now, before I could start, was Flagyl, that amoeba-slaying drug
from Australia. I was growing thinner and weaker by the
minute and had long grown tired of spending half my days
squatting over a toilet that invariably wouldn't flush.

Flagyl finally came, but not through the post. A team of
twelve New Zealand and two Australian climbers arrived
in Lhasa for an expedition to Mount Everest, bringing
with them a mountain of equipment and a medical kit
which rivaled the supplies of most of the major hospitals
on the Asian Continent. The team's doctor reckoned they
were prepared for any accident or disaster. They could
remove a splinter, perform tracheotomies and appendec-
tomies, or deliver a baby if they had to—not that that was
likely, for there were no women on their team, let alone
pregnant ones. There was nothing they couldn't handle.
And yes, that included the minor disaster of my stomach
trouble. Doctor Dick prescribed a seven-day course of
Flagyl, and after popping the first of the twenty-one tablets, I felt better instantly.

Jigme was delighted, but still wanted me to regain some
of my former strength before I began my trek across
Tibet. He suggested I go out to the Everest base camp with
the New Zealand climbing contingent, and walk around in
the high altitude for a few days. See how I felt. Then I

could come back to Lhasa in the empty supply truck. My
return would coincide with the departure of a western-
bound European four-wheel-drive tour on a filming expedition. Jigme intended asking them to transport me and
my enormous pile of equipment and supplies out to a
location near Burang, a place called Mount Kailas. Hmm,
that mysterious mountain again—the one I had been told
to visit by Claus when we first talked of the trek months
before.

Everest. I had always wanted to see it. Jigme's face
grew lined with worry again. He made me promise I
wouldn't get carried away and climb the thing. But even I
knew that was completely out of my sphere of abilities,
both physical and mental.

And so I went to Everest base camp and I walked
around a bit. I felt fine. In fact, I really didn't want to
leave. It was so much fun being with a bunch of old moun-
tain-rascals, listening to their well-calculated plans to conquer Everest. "Look, all we've got to do is run up this
section here, chuck in an ice screw or two, whack on a few
ropes, run along that ridge there and we're on the top! No
worries! We'll piss-bolt it in!" What a delightful piece of
New Zealand slang, "piss-bolt." It sounded like something
one of Jigme's famed yaks would do. Piss—then bolt!

I returned to Lhasa fighting-fit and raring to go. Ten
days had passed since the German film crew had arrived.
Jigme introduced me to Shubu, the Tibetan leader of the
four-wheel-drive expedition. Apart from the crew, there
was an assortment of European tourists, who had actually
paid to make this, the first-of-its-kind expedition. Shubu
decided that I would travel in the back of their supply
truck to Shigatse, then take a more comfortable seat for
the last lap in one of the five Land Cruisers they had for
their journey.

In the morning, Jigme came to say goodbye. He hugged
me and said, "I'll probably never see you again. You are
mad. Take care, please." He had a gift for me—a beautiful
piece of flawless turquoise set in a silver ring. He showed

it to me, looked into my eyes, then changed his mind. "No, I'll save it for when you return. When I know you've survived." At least that was more positive than his first remark. I jumped in the hold of the truck bound for Shigatse. Yahoo! I'm finally going to get my show on the road!

It took me seven days to cross to western Tibet, traveling over roads more atrocious than any others I had been on, anywhere—even those which zigzagged the mountains of eastern Tibet. The west was daunting—vast, hauntingly beautiful. So different from the east, from Lhasa and its surrounding valleys. Day by day as the barren landscape unfolded, the harsh realities of what I had undertaken began to sink in. I tried to block the numerous, growing fears from my mind. I tried to listen to the little voice inside me that kept insisting I could make it.

I camped out with the members of the Kailas-bound expedition, and spent many of the evening hours talking to Shubu and Hyo. Hyo Bergman was the man responsible for producing the film about Tibet and about the inaugural tourist journey across it. It was the first time a group had been given permission to travel through the western reaches of the mysterious land; and a West German television station had sponsored Hyo and his three colleagues, Gerry, Yaro, and Peter, in making the hour-long documentary. When I first saw Hyo—tall, tanned, blond, and Wiesbaden-born—I had ruthlessly repressed the instantaneous flutterings of my heart. How dare I be so girlish, so immature. This was no time to go weak at the knees. This was no time to go and fall in love. But Hyo was not only exceptionally good-looking. He proved to be exceptionally intelligent, exceptionally witty, and exceptionally talented.

For every Adam, there is an apple. For every Eve, well, need I say more? The miles rolled by and by; the days wore on and on, and all too soon we reached that detestable location: that barren, desolate plain before Mount Kailas.

So, now I sat with Hyo, holding his hand, staring toward the stormy horizon. Tomorrow, we would go our separate ways. Tomorrow, I would go by truck alone to Burang, buy my donkey, and begin my long, long trek across Tibet. Alone. Had I really gone mad? Did I really believe I could make it? Handle all those days of loneliness, all those mountains, all those deserts?

Second thoughts? Yes, and third thoughts, too. Fear and doubt had suddenly spread throughout my mind, grabbed my stomach, and knotted it into a hundred bowlines and half hitches. But it was too late, too late to turn back now.

CHAPTER 3
Clashes Before Kailas

Over the past months, a lot of people had questioned my motives for trekking across Tibet. It had been hard to find an excuse which would satisfy all those who asked, for how could I expect them to accept that the whole plan, the whole journey was simply something I *knew* I had to do? Hyo was the only one who had never asked, "Why?" In the morning, as he prepared to leave for Mount Kailas, he questioned only the strength of my conviction. "Do you still want to do this, Sorrel?" I looked into his eyes. I had been thinking about this trip for so long there was only one answer, it was preprogrammed in my brain.

"Yes Hyo, I do. I must."

Smart little independent inner voice. I felt like strangling it, drowning it, and saying with my own, "No! Take me back to Germany! Marry me! Anything! I'll sweep your floors, wash your dishes—anything! Anything but this."

The expedition team motored away to Mount Kailas. Shubu took me to a nearby settlement called Barga and helped me arrange my midafternoon passage to Burang.

He hugged me tight. "Oh, my little sister, take care. Be brave. You can do it. I know." He hugged me again, and I didn't want him to let go. "Goodbye, my little sister. You will find what you are looking for. I know that too."

I climbed aboard the open tray of a military truck and jostled for space between the cargo of petrol drums and Han Chinese soldiers. Destination Burang: the trilateral border town in the far southwest corner of Tibet, a hundred miles away. I was lost in my thoughts, oblivious to the landscape.

Shortly after dusk, the truck thundered down the last pass into Burang. A pink shaft of light soared upward from behind a silhouette of ancient fortress ruins. Like glowworms on the walls of darkened caves, low-watt globes and flickering candles dotted the valley sides. I leapt off the back of the military vehicle, sneezed out one last noseful of road dust, and listened.

A river somewhere below me roared through the night. The clank of hand-beaten tin bells and the clip-clop of hooves vibrated on the breeze. Cart wheels grated, laboring through mud and gravel. The subtlety and gentleness of the setting dissolved under the fiery sky of my own anticipation. Donkey, where are you? I'm ready. Optimism replaced the tears and fears of yesterday. The inner voice was winning.

The town lay in a sheltered basin surrounded by mountains, and I started my donkey-hunt the next morning in the Indian marketplace in the southern corner. Rows of calico-covered stalls selling bales of wool and leather saddlebags similar to the wares of Kathmandu sprawled out from a shopping center consisting of three rows of head-high, claustrophobic mud-brick rooms bulging with incense, brassware, sari cloth, brocades, plastic trinkets, and jewelry. Nepalese and Indian traders moved freely across the border, carrying daunting loads on their backs to stock these shops. There were donkeys pulling carts and carrying firewood; donkeys practicing obstinacy and ignoring the hoarse commands of their masters; donkeys in the nearby fields, but there were no likely looking, unemployed donkeys for sale in the marketplace of Burang.

The Chinese part of town boasted the usual bleak, concrete array of red-starred institutions and government amenities—not a hee-haw to be heard above the noise of construction workers nor amid the rustle of papers shuffled by Chinese bureaucrats. The only redeeming feature of this eastern quarter was its jasmine-tea-and-noodle restaurant.

The western cliffs directly behind the river were dotted with cave-like dwellings tunneled into the mountainside. To the north, along both sides of the river, both Tibetans and pilgrims sheltered in tents and small mud-brick houses. A colorful market extended from the east bank settlement over the bridge, and open stalls sold turquoise stones and prayer flags. Traders from faraway Kashgar offered bruised apples and dried apricots grown in their province. No one, alas, sold donkeys.

Another two days passed before I had any luck. The Chinese officials who were responsible—on paper—for my stay in Burang and for my safe departure, hired two Tibetans as donkey-detectives, to seek out the most capable ass from the agricultural region south of the township. They demanded a daily payment of twenty yuan (about seven dollars) each; 75 percent of which would inevitably end up greasing the palms of the officials. To save money, I was sleeping in the construction rubble of a new concrete building and resented having to redistribute my wealth in this manner. Finally, at five o'clock on August 23rd, my super sleuths returned from their long day's search, smiling. They'd found it! They'd found the sacred donkey of nonbiblical Burang. In fact, they had found three of them.

After dinner, the owners of the asses came to the construction site with their charges. I felt like the contender on a TV game show. Contestant number one had a limp. On a trek across Tibet, he'd have about as much chance as Jimmy Connors trying to win at Wimbledon with tennis elbow. Number two appeared to be on the verge of collapse: a well-loved teddy bear with moth-eaten ears and unstitched seams, the product of childhood torture, fed evil concoctions of snail bait and mud, buried alive just once too often in sandpits. He was ready for the compost heap, not a two-thousand-mile trek across Tibet. The third donkey in the show terrified me. Black, defiant, rooted to the ground like a Moreton Bay fig tree.

This would never have happened in Bethlehem. What a choice! Two couldn't move, and one wouldn't. Since a personality flaw seemed easier to rectify than gross physical inadequacy, number three won the holiday. Two hundred and eighty yuan (about one hundred dollars) changed hands. It was easy to see who was getting the better end of the bargain. The Nepalese pilgrim, his wallet now bulging with my money, tweaked a small clump of hair from his donkey's head and rolled it into a ball. He popped it down his ballooning calico pants, and vanished. I paid off my two detectives. The donkey was mine, and I christened it "Budget." A tank full of gas and the first fifty miles free. I couldn't believe it. I was actually ready to start walking. I was so excited, I could barely sleep.

I was up before dawn, packed and ready. The Kashgari apple traders were the only people to see me leave town. The oldest merchant gave a long, incredulous stare, tugged thoughtfully on his wispy white beard, and called for me to stop. He ran up the slope from his riverside stall, arms laden with the small, bruised fruits of his labor. He crammed his gift into Budget's backpacks and quickly eyed the little beast's burden. Tying ropes was definitely his forte; he corrected my poor attempt and altered the weight distribution of my luggage. Budget groaned and passed wind. Poor little beggar. He really looked depressed. He had eaten so much the night before, he now had a severe case of indigestion. I grabbed his lead rope and laughed at the irony of it all. Apart from the obvious definition, I knew the word *ass* meant a stupid, obstinate, or perverse person. Hand in hoof, two asses would traverse

Tibet. Budget backfired again and we were off.

When the sun rose from behind the snow-capped peaks circling Burang, we caught up to a couple of horsemen and their yaks. They helped Budget and me to cross the river and we flew up the first pass behind them. Then Budget turned to face the slowly diminishing township of Burang. The nylon lead rope I held loosely in my hand yanked tight. His little black body filled with fear and homesickness and he pulled me off balance in a last-minute bid to return to Burang.

"Forget it, kid." I said. "You're coming with me."

I pulled on the lead rope to correct the donkey's direction and cursed. Even *I* could handle a donkey. Ha! I would have been better off trying to tame an elephant. But on second thought, no. My track record with those beasts wasn't very good either. I thanked God for not making me a zookeeper.

The horsemen left me at the next pass and pushed their herd down into a spring green valley. Budget and I floundered on. The heat of the day was upon me, burning a Tibetan glow into my cheeks and forearms. Budget began stopping for small feasts of Scotch thistle flowers. I hoped they would ease his chronic flatulence. The pace of our trek had slowed considerably. Then Budget stopped, his legs rooted to the ground. He wouldn't budge. For two hours I whipped and swore till I was blue in the face and hoarse. I sat down, back against a boulder, and cried until my tear glands were as dry as the desert around me. Mountains, detestable mountains. Nothing but rocks and sand, and more stupid barren mountains.

"Why me? Why me?" I screamed to the heavens. Why on earth am I doing this? Two hours of pushing and pulling a stubborn old ass no more than one hundred feet was not the way I had planned to discover Tibet, to discover myself. I felt so alone. So pathetic. Budget just stood there, glaring balefully at me.

With the bone-handled knife Hyo had given me as a

parting gift, I cut my beast a handful of thistle flowers from a nearby bush. With all the charm I could muster, I managed to coax him a further ten paces.

I picked a dozen more bouquets and presented them to my little man. Sorry, love. Sorry for burning the toast this morning. Sorry I forgot to pay the electricity bill. Sorry for burning a hole in your favorite shirt. Sorry, sorry, sorry. Reluctantly, old Budget wobbled slowly onward. My first lesson in donkey management was thus learned. The way to a man's heart was indisputably through his stomach. Mummy was right—again.

The sky above filled with charcoal clouds. A storm swept across the horizon. An Indian monsoon had crept over the Himalayan Ranges and into Tibet. An unprecedented amount of rain had fallen in recent weeks and filled the rivers everywhere—even in this vast desert of gibber and sand, waterways overflowed. We negotiated a deep stream and tumbled downhill to a beautiful, lush, riverside camping spot. I staked Budget near a row of his beloved thistles and bathed my aching feet in the icy river water. I reached into my pack and pulled out a bar of Toblerone chocolate Shubu had given me. My spirits soared. Day one was over. It had been a pretty tough old day, but now that it was drawing to a close, I felt great. No day would ever be as difficult as the first. Such were the words of inspired wisdom from every explorer and adventurer that had ever lived. I pulled out my maps and studied the route I would take back to Barga. There was plenty of water, two huge lakes, in fact—Lake Rakas Tal and Lake Manasarovar, the latter being the holiest lake in the world. Mount Kailas is the home of gods, to both Hindu and Buddhist. According to legend, Manasarovar was formed when two sages, absorbed in mortification and prayer for twelve years at Mount Kailas, finally asked their gods for water to drink and bathe in. Manasarovar appeared, and the sages went on praying. The lake became as holy as the mountain, and all who venture on pilgrimage to Kailas bathe in its waters. I planned to spend the next night at one or other of the lakes and cleanse not only my soul, but my filthy, sweaty body too.

By morning, the storm clouds had passed. I loaded Budget and paused to watch the landscape around me stir from slumber. What a glorious day! I turned the key to Budget's ignition and pushed him over the hills, into another winding, barren vale.

Despite all the refueling, the old black ass never got beyond first gear and reverse. He'd overdone the thistle-eating and was backfiring with the explosive regularity of a Lewis machine gun. His homesickness had worsened. At every short pass, every hilltop, every twist in the track, I would gaze toward the future and Budget would turn to face the past. Burang was long out of sight but Budget's body quivered each time he stopped and turned around. His sad, hollow eyes searched mine, pleading to be returned to his former master. "Sorry, buddy," I said. "You're mine now, and I need you. You ain't going anywhere but ahead. Ahead, through Tibet. With me."

At last Lake Rakas Tal came into view, a massive body of sapphire-blue water, ebbing toward a vast yellow plain. Beyond, the sacred, pyramid-shaped peak of Mount Kailas stood alone. Over thousands of years, Indian and Nepalese pilgrims had crossed the Himalayas and stood where I now stood, taking in their first glimpse of the holy mountain. A deep gully cut through the horizontal rock strata of the mountain's southern face, forming a natural swastika—the Buddhist talisman of immutability and strength. Even at this great distance, the symbol was discernible. Despite being neither Hindu nor Buddhist, I was completely overawed by this vision of Kailas. So great was its aura, it even managed to win Budget's gaze. For a moment, just for a moment, he stopped scanning the bare earth for edible plant matter. Incredible!

A wind raced across the lake's surface and a hundred small white horses galloped toward the shore. Still mesmerized by the mountain, I let the tiny waves lure me to the water and another perfect resting place. I pitched my

tent, kicked off my shoes, and led Budget to the lakeside.
He balked at the gentle tide. He hadn't had a drop of water
all day and refused, even now, to quench his thirst. Stubborn little beast. A green carpet of creeper weed softened
the sharp rubble of the crescent-shaped beach. I tied
Budget's rope to a large rock and left him, contentedly
gnawing away at the pile. Then I stripped off and plunged
into the crystal-clear waters of Rakas Tal. My sunburned
skin smarted and my heart skipped a few beats. It was
freezing. Budget had found himself an old pilgrims' fireplace and was busy rolling in the gray ashes, sending up
smoke signals and wheezing as they penetrated his nostrils. I was getting clean, he was getting filthier by the
minute. Our personality differences seemed infinite.

Eventually, we ambled back to the tent together and
watched a descending sun turn the snow-covered massif of
Gurla Mandhata mountain into a shimmering vision of
pink and crimson. I let go of Budget's lead rope and dived
inside the tent, grabbing my camera, anxious to record
this sunset beauty. I clicked off a few frames. Wonderful!
Budget appeared in the viewfinder. His dusty back grew
wings and he flew like a jet-propelled Pegasus toward
freedom. Oh no! He was running away! The nylon umbili-
cal cord linking him to my demanding world had been
thoughtlessly severed and he was free! I dropped my camera and bolted after him.

I hate running at the best of times and at an altitude of
over 12,000 feet, in pursuit of a hairy male I didn't even
like, I hated it even more. The tiny, sharp stones of the
Tibetan desert floor pitted my bare feet. Tears filled my
eyes. "If I catch that cantankerous little ass, I'm going to
turn him into the fattest Hungarian salami this planet has
ever seen. . . ." Budget, that scrawny little ratbag who had
to be pushed and pulled along all day, had cunningly saved
his strength for this one moment. He was literally charging head first into one of the most spectacular sunsets I'd
ever witnessed. Alternate pink and blue shafts of light

were radiating across the sky from a single point on the horizon.

"I'll kill you, Budget!" I screamed.

He stopped to catch his breath and took off again when I was within arms reach of his haggard little throat. He ran and ran, all the way back into the stone valley of the afternoon, visible only by the small cloud of dust he left in his wake, and the dancing end of his long, dangling rope. Mile after mile, on and on. Then nothing. Budget had dissolved completely into the darkness. I kept on running, gulping air—coughing, heaving, and retching, nothing but tears and fear. But it was hopeless. Budget was gone, no doubt all the way back to Burang.

Somewhere among the rocks and thistles I collapsed and let sleep free me from the pain of exhaustion. My body became a great white sail and the breeze of the evening pushed me away on a gentle wave, far away from the shores of reality. The calm, rhythmic ebb of my dream slowed my thumping pulse and soothed my aching limbs.

Hours later I awoke to find the moon intensely bright on the landscape. I was shivering. My clothes were wet with sweat and a strong wind now worked its way between the clammy layers. I hugged my arms around my chest and began the long walk back to camp. I felt completely devastated. Assless. Jigme's words rang in my ears. "Even you could handle a donkey, Sorrel." Jigme had obviously never met Budget and grossly overrated my abilities.

I looked down at my feet, swollen and blood-splattered, stumbling through the moonlit dust. The cold had numbed all pain and I could feel only a light, burning sensation as I took each drunken step. A few toenails were missing. One big toe was badly stubbed and both soles were a mass of bleeding cuts and bruises.

Finally, I caught sight of the lake for the second time that day. Moonlight had turned its surface into a sequinned robe, floating magically between the jet-black hills. The snow-capped peak of Mount Kailas was illumi-

nated by an eerie ring of light. I consciously retraced my
steps toward camp. Too tired to care about anything, I let
the wind push me through the arched doorway of my tent
and fell flat onto my half-opened sleeping bag. I couldn't
lift either arm, nor bend at the knees in order to climb
inside it. There wasn't an ounce of energy left within me.
No day could ever be as difficult as the second.

In the morning, I tried to accept my fate without fears. I
concluded that the loss of Budget was not due to misman-
agement on my part; rather it was heaven's sweet way of
letting me know I had misinterpreted "the plan," attempted to alter my destiny. I sat by the lake for an hour,
waiting. Waiting for a yak to fall down from the sky.

It was all right for Jesus to use a donkey and all right for
Harrer to use a yak, but me—well, gradually it became
obvious I was meant to go on alone. I took stock of the
situation and my enormous pile of supplies.

Methodically I set about dismantling the two backpacks
I had sewn together to fit over Budget. I had hacked off
various straps and now it was clearly apparent that
neither remained suitable for human use. The shoulder
loops were half-severed and the waist belts were probably
still in the construction site rubble at Burang. I crammed
everything I could safely label nonessential into the
smaller of the two packs: my bean-sprouting kit and spare
clothes, my wooden Nepalese flute, half my food supplies,
camera tripod and chocolate bars, medical supplies—bar
a few band-aids and aspirins. Two pairs of shoes seemed
unnecessary. I bandaged up my toes and plastered the
worst cuts on my soles, threw away my sneakers, and
donned my heavy, snow-climbing boots, deciding it would
be far better to wear rather than carry them. It was high
time they were broken in anyway.

At a rough guess, the weight of what remained was
around seventy-five to eighty-five pounds. My tent, sleeping bag, down jacket, cooking equipment and solid fuel,
five-gallon water containers, writing material, packets of
dry soup mix, muesli, milk powder, a small tin of coffee,

dried fruit-and-nut bars . . . it felt like a load of bricks once I had hitched it onto my back and fastened it in place with a thin nylon rope from my tent fly. I slung my equally cumbersome camera bag over one shoulder and limped away from the shores of Rakas Tal over the roadway.

Every 200 paces, I stopped and bent forward, resting the weight of my load on the center of my spine in order to give my shoulders a moment's relief. Each time a desperate whimper forced its way from between my wind-cracked lips. I had never felt so utterly pathetic in all my life. Blisters had formed on my heels and were adding to my misery. I had to keep going. I couldn't stop and rest; I knew I would never get up again if I did. I had struggled a mere five miles from the lakeside. There were thousands more ahead of me. Two hundred paces. Stop, bend, and bleat like a frightened sheep. Two hundred paces. Stop, bend and bleat again. The thin plastic rope was slicing me in two. I couldn't take shortcuts. I had to stay on the two-wheel tracks. I prayed I would run into Shubu and Hyo and the four-wheel-drive expedition. They had to be in the area somewhere. They just had to be. And I had to run into them. It was my only chance. I had to beg, borrow, or steal a better backpack, or abandon my dream. I could never make it to Lhasa beneath such an ill-fitting load as mine.

And then it appeared. Out of the corner of my eye, I spied a little red backpack on legs disappearing around the rocky cliff to my left. Yippee! Bless you Buddha, and all the Jewels in your Lotus! It had to be a member of the four-wheel-drive film expedition! Who else would have such a modern piece of mountaineering equipment in these remote parts? A red backpack. And friends! I jumped up and ran, oblivious to the pain in my flayed feet.

Beau, an unassuming French geologist, who was a member of the expedition, was picking away at a rock face with his tiny tools of trade. He had been fascinated by the mineral composition of Tibet. I sneaked up from behind and hugged him tight, laughing and crying and blurting out my saga of misadventures. The expedition camp was

only an hour or two away. I was lucky, for they had decided to stay another day in the Kailas region. According
to their schedule, they should have been heading north to
Kashgar. Beau pointed out the long ridge I had to climb in
order to sight the camp, and returned to picking at his
beloved rocks.

I fought against the weight of my pack, and all the pain
the long day's march had etched into my body. One foot in
front of the other, I walked slowly on toward my friends.
And their backpacks. The little voice inside me was singing with confidence. I knew I would be okay.

The tent city seemed deceptively close from the top of
the ridge. Every inch of the way down was a struggle. I
tried to look positive. In control. I didn't want to cry. I
didn't want anyone down there thinking I wasn't strong
enough to make it. The closer I came to the camp, the
farther it seemed I had to go.

Yaro, one of the professional photographers on the expedition, came out of his tent and stood facing Manasarovar.
My parched throat found moisture enough to whistle and
Yaro turned and ran toward me. Good old Yaro, he still
had his baseball cap on. It's nice how people never change,
even their clothes.

"Sorrel! Whoa! Where's the donkey?"

I had shared a lot of jokes with them all—with Yaro,
with Horst, the other "stills" man, and with Gerry and
Peter, the cameramen, during the brief time—was it
seven or ten days?—I had previously spent in their company. They were the nearest thing I had to longtime
friends out there in the wastes of western Tibet. Emotions
exaggerated by fatigue and partial realization of my fragility surged to the surface, and I greeted Yaro as if he
were a long-lost, much loved kindred spirit. I collapsed on
the ground in tears. The others wandered over.

There were lots of laughs as I told my tale. The flight of
dear Budget had everyone in fits and their encouragement
gave me so much renewed energy I even found strength to
sit up. Hyo was above me then, his long, tanned legs

stretching toward the sky. He felt the weight of my backpack and bent to caress the dark, peeling skin of my right
forearm. He muttered something in German to the others.
It felt so wonderful to see all those familiar faces again.
Slowly they drifted away, and I was alone with Hyo.

We talked of courage, of Mount Kailas, and of the film he
had ventured here to produce. We talked about the various
people in the expedition; their lives and ambitions. We
talked long into the warm, evening hours. I was so tired,
but who could sleep on a night such as this? The wind had
dropped and the midnight sky was completely cloudless.
Oh, to have the power to stop time.

The next morning, beads of silver laced the orange hue
of dawn. A few water birds landed noisily on the surface of
Manasarovar and I turned to shake Hyo awake. An hour
later, everyone had gone. Sadly, I watched the last Land
Cruiser disappear over the arid hills. I was alone again,
but this time for good.

Shubu had left me his brand new backpack and Horst
and Yaro had left a small pile of tinned luncheon pork,
dried fish, and sweet biscuits in the doorway of my tent.
The team's doctor had left a bottle of antiseptic and fresh
bandages for my feet. Hyo had left me a small piece of his
heart.

I had planned to rest the whole day by the lake to give
my broken blisters a chance to dry out in the sun and my
shoulder muscles a moment to recuperate from yesterday's burden. But the now-deserted lakeside swamped me
with an unsettling emptiness. I could better escape from
my somber thoughts if I kept moving. The task of walking,
even the physical pain itself, would be better than an
afternoon on emotional skid row. Better a masochist than
a depressive.

I set out for Barga. A huge mushroom-shaped cloud
billowed above the waters of Manasarovar, filling the entire eastern sky. It looked like the aftermath of a nuclear
holocaust. What would happen in the big wide world
beyond Tibet during the months ahead? No newspapers—

no news. Political leaders would topple and fall. Planes
would be hijacked. Doubtless, someone would invent a
new religion. Earthquakes would reduce whole cities to
rubble. People would die and others would be born to take
their place in the never-ending circle of life. But all the
real, everyday stuff seemed already some sort of weird
fantasy from another time. My world, for today, tomorrow, and the next, was one of mountains and deserts. A
small world indeed.

I argued the concept through in my head, imagining the
repercussions of all the possible dilemmas I faced within
my own undertaking. My crises would be so small in rela-
tion to those in Libya or Lebanon. The decisions I would
make would affect only me—not whole nations of trusting,
desperate people. If I had to suffer, there was only myself
to blame for it. No one had given me a tin hat or gun, or
sent me away to this war.

My thoughts were marching out across the illusory bat-
tlefield with such strength and determination. If only I
could hold on to these qualities and not let my poor physical state, or unexpected adversity undermine my conviction. In the past few days, I had made this land my enemy.
If I kept believing this notion, I would be waving a white
surrender flag at the mountains within a week.

Tibet could not be my enemy. If she were, it implied I
had to fight against her to conquer her. I was no fame-
seeking mountaineer, no imperialist general. I had no
desire to conquer peaks or climb them simply "because
they were there." My motives were simple. I wanted to eat,
breathe, and feel Tibet—to experience the country and its
people as deeply as I could. In doing so, I knew I would be
challenging myself, not the mountains—extending the
boundary of my own limitations and learning something
new. I pressed on.

By the time I reached Barga and the low, mud rest
house at the western crossroads of Tibet, my feet were not
fit to stand on. I spent the next day propped up by a wall in
the sunshine, trying to dry out my blisters and rest my

shoulders. Shubu's pack was comfortable, but my load weighed far too much and my shoulders still ached in consequence. I halved my food supply and gave the manager of the guest house my spare flashlight and batteries.

A little crowd of Tibetans had gathered around me. The women stared at my poor, bloodied feet and clucked their tongues in sympathy. The men stared at me and shook their heads in disbelief. Children poked their curious little fingers into everything I owned, including the softer bits of my body. They giggled and squealed with delight as they prodded. One pigtailed little urchin went running back to find her mother, screaming, "Ama, ama,"—which I knew meant "mother." Much curving gesticulation revealed her surprise that I was not a man after all! A few men shuffled forward and tried on my fashionable rucksack, and gave it the thumbs-up sign of approval. They studied its design intently, discussing the positioning of each pocket and strap at length.

My travels in countries where English is rarely spoken meant I had become an expert in interpreting body language. After all, deaf-and-dumb people can communicate without words, but I always enjoyed learning as much as possible of the local dialects and languages and so I seized this opportunity to extend my knowledge of Tibetan beyond my ten-word Jigme-inspired vocabulary. I pulled out my little Tibetan phrase book purchased in Kathmandu. Very quickly it became apparent the author had never ventured into the remoter regions of western Tibet. Every phrase listed was so utterly useless! "Chu tsha-bo du gay?" *Is there any hot water?* Not bloody likely. "Ngay kang miy-giy di-mi kaba to?" *Where is the key to my room?* My "room" didn't even have a door on it. "Dra-gang ka ba to?" No, no post office here, no post office for hundreds of miles. "San-ju ka ba to?" Someone pointed to the plains behind me and laughed. The whole world is a toilet. Go anywhere your heart desires. The crowd swelled and the air was thick with laughter as I struggled to pronounce dozens of stupid phrases. *Can I have eggs on toast for breakfast? I want to go to a movie; will you take me?*

One of my more enthusiastic teachers grabbed the book and turned to the "Tibetan for hypochondriacs" section, pointing out numerous phrases and begging me to utter them. "Nga tsa-wa gyay sha." *I feel feverish.* "Nga gyong may." *I feel nauseous.* "Nga gu yo kaw-giyt." *I feel giddy.* "Nga dar-giy." *I am shivering.* "Nga tro-gaw shay-giy." *I have diarrhea.* That one was worth remembering. "Nga chab-chen tan tu-giy ming-du." *I am constipated.* "Nga so na-giy." *I have a toothache.* "Nga gay-siy gya-giy." *I have epilepsy.* The list rather aptly ended with, "Am-chi lam sang gay tan-ah?" *Would someone please get me a doctor?*

I had to play-act a lot of what I was trying to say, for the phrase book was written in the dialect of the Lhasa district and key words were often different in the western region. I pretended to vomit and get an attack of diarrhea. The throng of Barga-ites had never seen an epileptic before, and thought my charade was a bizarre ritual dance. A young lad screamed, "Disco! Disco!" and jumped up to join me. Marcel Marceau, eat your heart out.

A group of three men appeared from somewhere off the plain and joined in the dancing and questioning. One tapped me on the shoulder and gestured for me to sit down with what had now become a sizable audience.

I couldn't believe it. Everything that had happened to me in the past week was reenacted before the hysterical crowd. Two men joined themselves together and became dear Budget. They imitated all his most unpleasant habits, and took off for the hills. The third man stood screaming, shaking his fists and weeping. A moment of truth. My journey to date was a complete farce and I couldn't stop laughing at myself. How on earth did these men know everything I had done? Ah—such is the mystery of the "Bush Telegraph," or in this case, "Mountain Morse." Eventually the crowd wandered off, and I went to the hotel manager's lodgings for dinner.

His wife had prepared a huge pile of "momos"—steamed meat buns—for her husband and me. She was anxious

about my journey and wanted to fatten me up a little. The
hotel manager and I spent the next few hours eating and
poring over my topographic maps.

He maintained that the southern road to Lhasa had been
cut by the swollen rivers and was subsequently impass-
able. If I wanted to get to Lhasa, I would either have to
wait a month for the floodwaters to subside, or trek back
along the route I had taken with the four-wheel-drive
team to reach Barga. That was dangerous; there was so
little water in those parts. Laboriously we plotted out an
alternative route. I could take the track back to Ali, on the
edge of the northern plateau, trek out as far as Gêgyai,
then veer inland to Yagra and cross the Gangdisê Ranges
in the south, eventually rejoining the main roadway at a
town called Parayang. It was a minor detour of some
thousand miles! I gave up the idea of ever reaching
Qamdo. Lhasa was far enough. The total distance of the
new route would be close to two thousand miles. An average of six hundred miles a month—provided nothing went
wrong—and I should be back safely in Lhasa before the
ravages of winter struck. For a heat-loving Australian like
me, Tibet's autumn weather was hard enough to bear.
Further drops in temperature were more than a threat—
they would mean a death sentence.

So much for planning. So much for Jigme's well-meant
instruction to stay on the road. After Gêgyai, there would
be no road at all until I rejoined the southern highway at
Parayang. Great stuff. My body tingled with excitement,
but my hostess quivered with fear. "You'll get lost! How
can you bear to do it all alone?" she intimated through
pained expressions and gestures.

First things first. One step at a time. We studied the
route to Ali, picking out a way to go other than the original
track.

During our discourse, an entourage of local officials
motored into Barga from Ali. The roadway was still in
reasonably good condition, but the rivers, they reported,
were becoming harder to cross each day. They pointed out

a couple of towns on my map and assured me I could get food there. There were nomads camped in the main Sutlej River valley all the way to Ali, but not too many. The officials claimed that they were hospitable and would be happy to help me in any way they could. They believed it would be all right for me to trek through the hills, but suggested, for my good, I keep the vehicular track no more than a day's march away from my own course.

While the men were chatting, I noticed one of the jeep drivers tapping his foot against the potbellied stove in the center of the room. Size ten sandshoes, good condition. I flipped through my phrase book looking for the words to express my desire to buy his footwear. I needed those shoes. My heavy climbing boots would be great for the Gandisishan Ranges but the bane of my existence if I continued to wear them on the dirt tracks and plains. But beginners and travelers were obviously not supposed to purchase footwear in Tibet. I knew how to ask directions to police stations and rug factories, knew how to ask someone to cure my warts and check my stools for worms, but buy a pair of shoes? Pantomime to the rescue. Exit the phrase book from my baggage.

Everyone in the room was laughing, but I felt like Cinderella in my new, perfectly fitting sandshoes. My feet felt fabulous; well, at least I knew they wouldn't get any worse. Life on the road would be a breeze!

After a really good night's sleep, I set out at daybreak to reach Mount Kailas. No one had ever climbed the holy mountain; to do so would be unforgivably sacrilegious. The summit was not for would-be Hillarys and Messners—it was strictly for the gods. Indians, Nepalese, and Tibetans ventured to Kailas to walk around the holy mountain, to gaze in awe at it and pray to the celestials on top. I had every intention of respecting the religious beliefs of the people. I could put my newly acquired mountaineering skills to the test on other peaks, in other years. For now, I simply wanted to walk around Kailas, to share the sacrament with pilgrims in order to understand them, and their religion, a little better.

By midday, it was raining and windy and the tent fly I held around me for protection from the elements flapped wildly and ceased to function as a raincape. A family returning from their pilgrimage to the holy mountain had stopped at the base of the Kailas Range foothills for a rest. Their yaks were feeding on the low, gray-green grass while they themselves drank tea with "zumpa," or roasted barley flour. Tibetans mix this to a soggy dough with yak-butter tea and it forms the staple of their diet. The family seemed to be oblivious to the driving rain, and sat listening to the tuneless chant of their father. I joined them.

I managed to put down a good three cups of Tibetan tea, without heaving once. Made with salt and rancid butter, "per-cha" isn't the easiest drink to get used to. Most westerners start feeling queasy when they so much as smell it. But it was time I started liking it; I would never be offered anything else more palatable, and it was awfully rude to refuse, even politely. If I wanted to understand Tibetans, I had to be one. In preparation for the race change, I had ruthlessly ditched half my instant coffee. But only half—if I became really desperate, I could drink it in secret in the inner sanctum of my little Western tent without feeling too guilty.

The mother and daughter of the pilgrim family from Hor had long earrings made from a thousand pearl-colored plastic beads, clustered together like the petals of a grevillia flower and studded here and there with coral or turquoise. A long string, looped around the top of the ear, held the heavy decoration in place. Dark patches on their cheeks also intrigued me. It looked as though dried blood had been applied to their faces and I wondered what purpose it served. A bizarre religious rite? A sacrifice? I summoned up the courage to ask just what the patches were. I could have sworn the elder woman answered "sugar," but since she used a questioning tone, I presumed

she had misunderstood my poor Tibetan and was consequently offering me some sweet additive for my tea. It
wasn't until a month later that I discovered the war paint
was actually sugar, melted down with butter and applied
in patches, lines, and concentric circles across the face.
The dark paint was not a symbol of spiritual purity, nor
the aftermath of animal sacrifice—it was just a western
Tibetan woman's answer to Helena Rubenstein.

After tea, I left the family and continued toward Kailas.
The foothills were home to hundreds of rabbits, who
darted in and out of their holes like the silver spheres in a
pinball machine. A well-worn foot track appeared on the
far embankment of a major tributary to the Sutlej River
and I sought the easiest section of the flow to cross and
reach it. My superior powers of judgment had me grip-
ping precariously to a slippery boulder, trying to stay
upright in the gushing, thigh-deep water. After three or
four attempts, I made it across—shaking with fear and
shivering with cold. I was drenched from the waist down.
It was still raining and impossible to dry out. I marched
on, to the small, weather-beaten settlement of Tarchen,
the starting post for the devotional circumambulation of
Kailas.

An old man beckoned me inside his small, river-rock
home, settled me down on a bed of twigs, and lit a small
fire. He sent his daughter off to find a teapot, then boiled a
strong, buttery brew. Small lamps burned at the rear of
the one-roomed dwelling, adding a glow to the otherwise
dingy, low interior. Upon his unpretentious altar, between
the lamps, lay dusty plastic flowers and spiraling columns
formed of molded rice and zumpa—symbolic offerings to
the gods who dwelled on Kailas. A water-stained set of
Buddhist scriptures lay on top of a few musty-smelling
woolen sacks filled with zumpa flour. The old man rubbed
his hands against the gooseflesh of my cold legs and made
a compress of sage for my soggy, smarting blisters. He
filled my tin cup with zumpa flour and moistened the
surface with tea. Eagerly I attempted to knead it into a

stiff dough, throwing puffs of flour up into my hair and nose and spilling most of the remaining mixture all over myself as I unleashed a mighty sneeze.

When I was warm and dry, the old man's son led me over another river to the ancient red-stone "gompa," or monastery, of Tarchen. Pilgrims, hushed by religious awe, were queuing to see a visiting lama from the Amdo region of eastern Tibet. I ventured through a maze of low, black corridors and climbed silently up shaky wooden ladders until I reached the lama's room. He sat in one corner, receiving the prayers of the faithful, and plying every one of them with a stodgy clump of fermented zumpa filled with "garum"—a solid, brown sugar—and shriveled dried apricots.

I accepted my clammy gift and paused for a moment longer to answer the lama's questions. He was thrilled to see a foreigner at Mount Kailas and astonished by what I proposed to do. Modern-day pilgrimages to and from Lhasa were usually wheeled affairs. The tradition of walking was slowly passing out of the Tibetan culture and twentieth-century truck rides were the custom now. Why was I, a Westerner, walking to Lhasa in the tradition of their forefathers?

The assumption made by most people at Tarchen was that I was fervently religious and my spiritual consciousness demanded it of me. Goodness knows what evils they thought I'd committed that required this ultimate penance! What about my family? My crops and sheep? Who would tend to them while I struggled to attain spiritual purification? It is hard to explain to a nation of struggling survivors just how easy it is to switch off the microwave, foster the dog, lock the front door, and hop on a Boeing 747. It was easier to leave them with the highly respected illusion than to totally confuse them with the truth of my nonreligious motivations. I quickly learned to mutter "Om Mani Padme Hum" with tireless reverence and prepared to walk around the sacred Mount Kailas; first rejuvenating my energy through sleep. I didn't stir until daybreak.

It seemed somewhat ironic that on that very day, most Tibetans would be celebrating—tongue-in-cheek—the twentieth anniversary of the official Chinese "liberation" of Tibet. In Lhasa, they would be setting off fireworks and parading through the streets with all the fanfare and color of a Mardi Gras festival. The liberation had robbed the Tibetans of their right to practice religious ceremonies for eighteen years. How nice it was to be a part of the resurgence of their religious sacraments! I felt honored. I wouldn't have swapped places with any tourist in Lhasa for all the world. Pilgrimages in Tibet will always be more significant and meaningful than any tinselly celebration of modernization and progress.

I slipped around the first corner of the four-sided mountain and strolled casually into a deep valley, listening to the hum of the river below and the shrill calls of small birds above. Massive rock walls fortressed the holy Kailas, enclosed and guarded it. From a distance, the mountain stands defiantly alone. Up close, only an occasional glimpse of its majestic peak is possible between the impenetrable walls. Now even those remained elusive, for Kailas was shrouded in rain cloud.

I stopped for an hour to listen to another lama chanting before the great mountain. His deaf-mute companion brewed sweet tea and borrowed my knife to whittle wooden knee and hand pads in preparation for his own pious journey. It would take him a full and exhausting five days to prostrate himself along the forty miles of track circling Kailas. He reached inside his cloth tepee home and pulled out a worn satchel of possessions—a framed photograph of his lama, two shots of himself in drab Chinese "uniform," a torn and battered slip of paper declaring his identity, and a postcard of the Potala. A wad of stale bread spilled from the top of a small leather pouch containing tea leaves and salt. That was all. The copper prayer wheel he spun while making the tea belonged to the lama. His scarred black hands revealed a life of toil and trouble, his eyes an unquestioning acceptance of his lot. I tried to wash away the lump in my throat with a gulp of his warm, welcome brew.

The lama struck a small meditation cymbal and stood to face Kailas again, blowing long, hard sounds from a white conch shell. The valley reverberated with its low, piercing note and the clouds above Kailas, as if magically provoked by the very gods themselves, burst forth with thunder, lightning, and torrential rain. I tried to cover myself with my tent fly, but again it proved a useless exercise.

It was too cold to sit still, so I set off, teeth chattering, into the head wind and driving rain. My sodden shoes turned my feet to ice. They ached with the cold. My fingers tingled and my ears burned. An hour or two later, I came to another battered tent, its flimsy calico cover protecting a motley collection of pilgrims from the elements. They had set out from Tarchen an hour before sunrise and Sonam, the oldest male member of the group, silently welcomed me with a cold cup of tea and a warm, sincere smile.

A final crash of hailstones ended the downpour. We dried out for a while in the ensuing sunlight and then pressed on, fording rivers and turbulent streams until we reached a patch of hospitable ground at 16,000 feet. I shared my tent with Sonam and Ani, a woman monk from Tarchen. Ani removed a Kathmandu gift shop bag from her Indian rucksack and pulled out an old set of Buddhist scriptures. Page after page she recited them, for hours and hours she was blissfully lost in their melodious sounds. Her tranquil rhythm filled my tent and rocked me gently to sleep.

My companions were up and about before first light. I peered outside the open tent flap and screwed my face up at the foreboding clouds. As well as a spiritually moving experience, this trek around Kailas would be a memorably wet one. I shivered uncontrollably and then started up the first pass behind my chanting, panting companions.

We were now at almost 17,000 feet. With hail and snow surrounding us, we had reached the highest and most sacred point on the pilgrimage route. We circled around the sodden pile of prayer flags and mani-stones which carry the inscription "Om Mani Padme Hum," then sat in the snow for a special cup of tea.

Ani removed a sack of dry sheep droppings from her rucksack and a bundle of wet sage twigs from Sonam's wool mesh satchel. Tashi and Draya, the other two women, lit a small fire and (with five teeth between them) whistled for the wind to keep it ignited. Whistling for the wind in circumstances such as this is a curious Tibetan custom with about as much scientific reasoning behind it as growing parsley to ensure the birth of a son.

I wondered how Alice had felt in Wonderland, sipping tea at the legendary Mad Hatter's tea party. The imaginative genius of Lewis Carroll was about to be challenged by reality. Ani was chanting. Sonam was meticulously counting out sweets and twisted, indescribable but edible things, arranging them in small conical piles—one for each of us. The two older women sat slurping tea and soggy zumpa from their rosewood and cracked-china bowls. Dressed for the occasion, one sported a bright green chuba, the other a technicolor dreamcoat of shining, blue satin over iridescent pink cotton with layers of black and purple robing beneath.

A procession of pilgrims in their more practical, grubby sheepskin armor, circled around the pile of mani-stones. The pilgrims came with horses, yaks, and flocks of sheep. Even the woolly, wandering minstrels carried a load of equipment and possessions, and waited patiently on the crowded pass while their owners paced three times around the central pile. The sheep bleated, the pilgrims chanted—a hymn from all reached out to the gods of Kailas.

Wonderland's March Hare, disguised as a maroon-robed monk, streaked past at a breakneck pace. I'm late, I'm late, I'm very, very late! His prayer wheel spun with electric speed. The paper roll of prayers inside the silver cylinder had been transformed into a whirring blender motor. He was trying to click up extra merit points by circumnavigating the holy mountain in just one day. The whistling women at the tea party had summoned up a hurricane, and hailstones fell forcefully, catching in their thick, matted hair. The ice tiaras made perfect crowns for these weatherproof queens. I was shaking and numbed into silence. Everyone else had climbed up and down the pass as quickly as possible but my insane friends were determined to linger on the exposed, sacred ground until the teapot was empty.

Completing the circuit, we reached Tarchen an hour after sunset. The day had continued with more tea parties, blisters, and unwelcome rain. I slept late into the next morning, and finally was shaken awake by my green-clad companion, who sought a Western medicine to ease her aching knee. I knew Hirradoid (bruise ointment) wouldn't hurt. It wouldn't heal either, but my magic massage worked its own spell and had her cured in minutes. Impressed by the miraculous medicine from the tube rather than the fingertips, she hugged me and scurried off to tell her friends. In the course of an otherwise boring day, I successfully treated thirteen cases of "Kailas-knee" with anything from toothpaste to sunscreen. Such is the power of the placebo!

Pilgrims from every corner of Tibet venture to the holy city of Lhasa, to pray and prostrate before the centre of their wheel of life—the great Jokhang Temple.

Above: Monks aged from eight to eighty chant all day in the monastery at Qamdo, photographed on my first visit to Tibet in 1984. This was the first such scene to unfold before my eyes. I was enchanted by the magic of Tibet.

Right: One of the 'extras'—a monk in ceremonial headgear for the filming of the television feature made in Gyantse about the ordination of a woman lama.

Pilgrims on the track from Burang to Barga make their way toward Mount Kailas. It is still spring and a touch of green dapples the vast Tibetan landscape.

Guess who? Yes, the notorious Budget, fully loaded with everything from bean-sprouting kits to musical instruments, stubbornly rooted to the ground not twenty kilometres from Burang.

The Yagra races—the riders thunder toward us over the plains.

Left: Nomad friends. Above all else, I will remember Tibet for her laughter, her uninhibited simplicity of expression.

Tsomo's daughter wears the infectious Tibetan smile during the goat-milking lesson.

At my first nomad camp, Tsomo and her sisters taught me how to rope goats together and milk them Tibetan-fashion. Later, around the evening fire in their large woollen tent, the family gave me an anatomy lesson in Tibetan.

Yagra horse races, and all the nomads in the region flock to the village in their finery to ride or simply to watch. Fox fur turbans are festive headgear for the men; for everyday use they wear less glamorous sheepskin ones of similar design.

Above: The horses are decorated with colourful felt and appliqué patches for the three-day Yagra racing festival.

Below: My nomad friend Dordrum leads me to the shelter of his homespun woollen tent at the foot of the Gangdise Ranges. A typical nomad tent, it has a front opening and a split in the roof for ventilation. Dordrum gave me flour, cheese and sweets for my journey.

Half-way across the Gangdise Ranges, we descended into a relatively snow-free valley. During the night spent here with nomads, I awoke in a pool of sweat, devoured by fleas, and found I was snow-blind.

Above: After a few days I recovered from the snow-blindness and was surrounded by a ring of smiling faces in my host's tent. In the rear, holding the baby, is Lobsang, the boy who accompanied our party through the Gangdise.

A Tibetan baby sleeps wrapped in a cocoon of sheepskins and an old woven zumpa (flour) bag, her head resting against portions of air-dried yak meat—dinner for the next few weeks.

Above: The village of Sakya, alive with song and activity as the villagers separate the grain from the chaff. The houses are painted mud bricks, the only ones I came across in western Tibet that were not whitewashed.

Left: Heading into the Gangdise foothills with Norbor (centre), Namgyal, Garma and a few of the pack-bearing yaks.

Below: Early morning in the main street of Gyantse, which led to the town's temple. It was here that a Beijing film crew were making a television feature about the ordination of a woman lama. Monks were 'imported' for the filming from Tashilhunpo monastery in nearby Shigatse.

Descending the last pass of the Gangdise Ranges with Gyardup and Chumba Tookten. Below, in the distance, are the snow-free plains leading to Parayang.

Mount Kailas with Lake Rakas Tal in the foreground. Pilgrims from India and Nepal receive this first glimpse of the holy mountain as they travel from the border town of Burang.

CHAPTER 4
The Valley of Ordeals

If only I still had Budget. My spine and shoulders were taking an age to get used to the weight of my backpack. They screamed out for rest to feet that functioned in spite of their cry. The rhythm of placing one foot in front of the other had long been set, and refused, against my own pleading will, to be broken before sundown. On and on they'd march across the wide plains, over rivers and mountains until they stumbled and crumpled beneath my weight at day's end. When the air was still, pure silence frightened me with its magnitude. The repetitious meter of my feet crunching over stones or crisp grass became a comfort. The wind created deceptive sounds; the heat, shimmering on the horizon, made all too deceptive images.

Occasionally an eagle sailed above me; with one awesome flap of wings, he would crack the silent air and wheel effortlessly higher into the vast void of sky. Gone. Taking my spirit which yearned to soar into a sublime dimension of freedom and weightlessness. Oh, to have wings, to have wings instead of blistered feet.

After three days, I surfaced on the roadway and entered Moincêr: a soulless mud-and-stone village about sixty miles northwest of Barga and 180 miles south of Ali. Three women dressed in Western fashion called me down to the pitiful stream, where they crouched washing dust from their children's clothes. I took off my shoes and soothed my feet in the water. We laughed and talked in a confusing mixture of tongues and limbs, Tibetan, Chinese, and the universal language of the body.

Later they led me to the Moincêr guest house where, for a paltry one yuan, I could rest upon an unmattressed, broken, bed frame and dreamily contemplate the similarly priced meal, just one hour away. Muesli and dry packet soups had sustained me from Barga and despite the low nutritional value, a bowl of white rice and a gray steamed bun seemed a very attractive alternative indeed.

Sharing my dank, dark room were a young couple from Qamdo in eastern Tibet and their sickly, tiny baby. I had seen them at Kailas where they had ventured seeking the help of the gods, in a desperate bid to restore health to their child. It was so sad. The little girl lay in a bundle of rags, coughing pathetically and gazing listlessly around the depressing room. Her thin, pale mother sat cross-legged in one dark corner, knitting a minute jumper sleeve on two twisted pieces of wire. I pulled out my Swiss army knife and filed away the blunt ends of her needles while she, putting on a brave front, retold her family's tale. Her young husband stirred a pot full of gruel, cooking slowly over the flame of a borrowed gas burner. He smoked the ends of discarded cigarettes, scrounged from the dust beneath a stationary military truck outside. With typical Tibetan hospitality, he offered me the longest of his collection of butts and a bowl of unappetizing gray sludge. The baby ate so little, her exasperated mother wept with frustration and turned to face me, eyes searching for an answer, a glimmer of hope. She glanced down at my feet and in an instant her woe was forgotten. She

jumped up and, holding my hand, led me quickly to the
village medical facility.

A chubby trio of white-cloaked Samaritans coated my
feet in gentian violet and painstakingly pricked the un-
burst blisters on my toes. We returned gay and laughing to
our room. It was five minutes to dinner time and I was
determined to treat my new friends to a more filling feast
in the compound's kitchen. I went to get my wallet from
my camera bag, and opened it then to find all but ten yuan
(about four dollars) missing. Oh God! I couldn't believe it!
I'd been robbed. I searched my pack thoroughly in case I
had absentmindedly transferred the wad of cash to
another place. Nothing.

My startled roommates turned their pockets inside out
to dispel all blame. I was deeply embarrassed, for the last
thing I wanted to do was to accuse them of the theft. The
dinner bell rang. But dinner could wait.

A child with pigtails said she would take me to the
village "detective." A smile lit the little girl's badly disfig-
ured face, a tapestry of hard, raised scar tissue and a sad
reminder of some fiery childhood accident. She waved me
inside a warm, large room and introduced me to the Sherlock Holmes of Moincêr. Come hell or high water, he
would catch the thief before midnight and return my
stolen money! I had the feeling that this was the most
exciting case he had had to solve all year. He put down his
bottle of Chinese "firewater," licked his lips noisily,
sucked in a breath of air, and vanished.

Miserable and tired, I dragged myself off to the kitchen.
Could I make it all the way to Lhasa on four dollars? I sat
down in the dust with the sun disappearing behind a low,
brown, lifeless ridge of mountains. I stared a hole through
my plate of cold, translucent vermicelli and lost my appetite somewhere in the process. The kitchen had run out of
rice and whatever the daily vegetable had been, cold vermicelli was all that remained. It was a small consolation to
receive the food for half the going rate—twenty-five fen,
or ten measly cents.

I returned to my room to find it securely bolted. A lot of screaming and crying wafted out through the cracks in the green timber door. What was going on? Someone showed me to another room—a better bed with two thick eiderdowns and all my belongings stacked neatly at one end. The same someone shut the door and begged me to stay put. That same someone returned five minutes later with her knitting and a candle and settled down to keep me company in the long hours that followed.

At 11:51 P.M., the mystery was solved. "Sherlock" had recovered my money. The gruesome sounds of sticks whipping flesh, blood-curdling screams, and hysterical cries flowing out from my old room, put all-too-vivid faces to the nameless culprits. I felt so hopelessly depressed and riddled with guilt. Hadn't those poor waifs suffered enough? If only they had asked for help. If only I hadn't dangled an unguarded carrot in front of their desperate noses. It was all my fault. The injustice of our world had left them penniless while I enjoyed a life of freedom, uncomplicated by comparative wealth. Why? It was so unfair. Engulfed in guilt, it was impossible to sleep beneath the cozy quilts, while others shivered and cried. Their child was doomed.

Morning came and with it the caustic chuckle of my successful detective. Justice, in his and most people's eyes, had been served. To his horror I wanted to give some money to the pathetic threesome, but he had banished them from the village in the middle of the night. I trekked out of town and cried all morning, unable to comprehend the selective process of the gods when they allot the riches of the world.

When dark clouds threatened yet another stormy afternoon, I stopped at a nomads' camp and welcomed their enthusiastic invitation to shelter with them for the evening. It would be my first night with nomads, and I was thrilled at the prospect of sharing and learning something of their unique lifestyle. More accurately described as

semi-nomadic, these people live in family groups and
move short distances within specific regions, seeking pasture for their herds of goats and yaks. Tsōmo, my beautiful dark-skinned hostess, stirred the ash and embers of the
central fire pit in her tent and ushered me to sit on a
grubby piece of sheepskin. Her small baby crept around
the earthen floor, sucking on bits of dry dung and twigs as
she scavenged them from the hard ground. I ate a huge
bowl of zumpa and a gallon of tea, a cup of fresh yak's
milk, and a handful of rock-hard cheese. Tsōmo thought I
looked hungry and as long as I kept eating everything (out
of politeness, of course) second, third, and fourth helpings
seemed unavoidable.

Strewn around me were the simple tools of the nomadic
trade. There were devices for spinning wool, timber saddles, and woven ropes for yak backpacks. When a nomad
wants to change address, his convoy of yaks carry everything on their backs with the aid of these crudely fashioned saddles. A broken clock held pride of place on a
heavy-looking wooden chest, next to a large, glassed picture frame filled with antiquated black-and-white photos
of Tsōmo's extended family. In the pictures everyone's lips
had been water-colored pink, and the cloth aprons of the
daily costume of the nomad women were striped with
yellow, green, and more pink. The origin of these photographs remained a mystery, but one could safely presume
a "trip to town" one year had been thoughtfully (and no
doubt expensively) recorded for posterity. A painted backdrop of the Potala peeped out behind the stiffly arranged
figures. They had never traveled far, had never seen the
real winter palace of their loving God-King, His Holiness,
the Dalai Lama.

Around the sides of the chocolate-brown woolen tent to
keep out draughts lay neat piles of clothing, bedding, and
the food reserves—sacks of barley and air-dried carcasses.
A fuel pile of neatly stacked, sun-dried yak turds doubled
as a shelf near the tent opening, and a couple of dented,
charcoal-covered pots and an olive green Greek-style plas-

tic urn sat upon it. A beaten brass ladle lay against six
squares of turf—freshly dug and ready to replace the
worn front doorstep when anyone became sufficiently mo-
tivated to make the household improvement.

Suddenly, a lot of bleating and trumpeting sounds carried into the tent on the wind. The goats were home and it
was time to milk them. I watched, amazed at the obe-
dience of the flock, as Tsōmo whistled and clucked commands of sexual segregation. She roped together all the
female milkers by the horns using a handwoven woolen
strap. Squatting down on my haunches, I grabbed the first
udder in line and joined the nomad women and children in
their afternoon milking ritual.

Easy to see I was city-bred! I spent the first half hour
searching for a second set of teats to squeeze. No one had
ever told me a goat's equipment was very different from
that of a Jersey cow.

The women sang while the children climbed all over the
goats, disappearing suddenly between the mass of shaggy
coats and legs, only to pop up with a squeal of delight and
surprise a few seconds later in another part of the herd.
The poor beasts stood quietly in line and, like patient
grandparents at a child's first birthday party, put up with
all the ear-pulling and beard-tugging and resisted the
urge to retaliate. Despite all their playing around, the
children extracted more milk from the little pink udders
of their flock in one hour than I could ever manage in a
year. I was far more at home squeezing the trigger of a
camera shutter, than the pink, floppy nipples of a goat.

With all the men and their yaks away from camp, it was
difficult to tell which children belonged to which family.
After the milking session, all of them piled into Tsōmo's
tent to further my education in Tibetan etiquette and in
their own western dialect. Over and over, bubbling and
giggling with the effervescence of a fresh glass of Coca-
Cola, they pointed to their eyes, noses, ears, belly-buttons,
and bottoms, delivering their animated anatomy lesson
with tireless enthusiasm. I sat in my seat of honor beside

the wooden chest at the "head" of the table-cum-floor and fell in love with every well-explored inch of their healthy little bodies.

Before bed, I helped Tsōmo rub butter (nomad moisturizer) into the skin of her weeny baby and then found myself being chaperoned outside the tent by a band of rosy-cheeked young girls. We squatted together for a moment and then, ablutions completed, they dispersed across the valley pasture to their respective tents—full of enough fantastic tales about the strange visitor to keep their mothers laughing till the early hours of morning.

With the full moon past, a million stars now filled the heavens. Content and warm in my sleeping bag, I watched them twinkle above the smoke vent in Tsōmo's tent. The clock on the wooden chest was not broken at all. It only required rewinding. Tsōmo had been thrilled by my mechanical expertise and couldn't thank me enough for repairing the timepiece. Now the minutes ticked by and I cursed my aptitude. Slowly, slowly, tick, tock, tick, tock. Long into the night, tick, tock, tick, tock. Pure silence shattered by the unbroken chant of harnessed time, hour after hour.

At sunrise, the smell of butter tea and smoldering embers stirred me from slumber. Tsōmo was outside the tent milking her goats again. I ventured out to join her and quickly immersed myself in the morning task. A truck passed above the valley on the narrow hillside roadway, laboring northward to Ali. A bright idea hit me. If I could put my heavy backpack on a passing truck and commission the driver to drop it off at the next nomad camp, I could walk unencumbered for the better part of the day.

I solicited Tsōmo's help, explaining my desire in animated gestures and the scant few words I now knew of her dialect. She seemed to understand. I pulled my camera gear over one shoulder, filled my water bottle, and headed off into the morning sun. A small crowd of children followed me to the roadway giggling and dancing around my

feet. They left me at the next turn in the valley and returned to their camp for another long day guarding their
flocks in the hills.

Morning wore on. The river valley beside which I
ambled deepened. From the plain, where one could see a
hundred miles in all directions, I now ventured between
hills, not knowing, but anticipating what lay beyond the
next bend. I reached a three-tent camp and called in on
the closest family.

Over tea and boiled sheep intestines I enquired about
my pack. No vehicle had stopped that morning for anything. I started to panic. Surely Tsōmo had understood I
wanted my pack left up-valley. My new host dragged me
outside his woven shelter and pointed to the north. More
nomads. He measured a distance with his hands, like an
amateur fisherman demonstrating the size of the one that
got away. Keep walking. This far. Over mountains. I
pulled my digger's hat low down over my forehead to
protect my eyes from the glaring sun, and climbed out of
the lime green vale.

Another long plain appeared—behind it a backdrop of
red, purple, orange, and terra-cotta-hued ranges. The colors faded to gray and blue in the distance. A few snow
peaks jutted out of the bare, mineral-rich mountain range.
I crossed over some low hills and approached another
camp. Dogs barked angrily. I held my distance. Three
women appeared at the entrance to their tent. A stream
separated us—I would not cross for fear of being mauled,
and tried in vain to shout above the gushing water and
loud-mouthed canines. The women couldn't understand
me.

I rejoined the roadway, anxiety increasing in my
thoughts and emotions. I walked for five hours. No trucks.
No nomads. I dragged my feet up another narrow pass and
gazed toward another endless, purple plain. Nothing. No
smoke from fires, nor dust from vehicles. A line of telegraph poles severed the barren, deserted plain. The dirt
roadway had vanished into the landscape. Fear welled

inside me. I tried to sing away my blue mood but only depressing songs came to mind. Leonard Cohen. Music to slit your wrists by. Someone send me a nomad! I have no tent, no food. The sun is disappearing. Somebody help, please!

I slowly picked my way down a rocky pass, completely dumbfounded by what lay at its foot. A half-constructed military compound came into view. Dismantled jeeps and 50-gallon drums lay strewn on the edge of the plain. A generator thumped a civilized tune from within the concrete enclosure. It was an ugly, yet welcome sight. I tore off my heavy climbing boots and raced toward salvation.

I caught sight of two khaki-clad soldiers roaming aimlessly behind the steel gates of their desert paradise. I whistled to attract their attention. Suddenly, four savage mongrel dogs leaped out from separate corners of the compound. One rabid-looking beast knocked me to the ground. Another ripped into the already damaged flesh of my heels. I screamed uncontrollably. The legs and seat of my ski pants were being torn to shreds. Flesh, blood. I couldn't feel any pain, just shock and confusion. A small stone clipped the back of my head. Another whizzed past my eyes and bit sharply into the mangy rib flesh of one dog. It released its grip on my arm, yelped, and retreated to its hiding place. More stones bombed the remaining attackers. They were gone. Seconds passed. I lifted my head and coughed out a mouthful of dirt, rolled slowly onto my side, and sat up on one elbow. My head felt like it had collided with a semi-trailer. Blood seeped from a long gash on my leg, soaking the torn white padding of my ski pants. Dust failed to hide the deep bites on my blistered feet.

Two cadres (young soldiers) lifted me from the ground, tongues clucking like those of sympathetic grandmothers. They picked up my camera bag and water bottle and lead me through the compound gates to the on-staff doctor's quarters. A small crowd gathered. While the doctor washed the dirt from my feet and leg wounds, I took swigs

of Chinese vodka (offered in lieu of anesthetic) from an
unlabeled bottle. My throat burned. The doctor's needle
plied its first stitch. I bit hard on the neck of the bottle and
tried to drown a spine-chilling scream. Eight stitches
later, the alcohol began to take effect. My brain now refused to register anything, least of all pain. The ordeal was
over.

Someone led me to a pale green room and gestured for
me to lie down on a bed. A plastic sheet covered the thick
quilt and mattress. I mumbled a "thank you" in Mandarin
dialect and wafted off to sleep. A few hours later I was
awakened by a vermicelli-stuffed steamed bun. My brain
felt fuzzy, sagging like wet wash on a clothesline. I bit at
the dangling gray bun and focused on its bearer. Bearers.
Had someone cloned an army of Mao Ze-dongs? I tried to
collect my scrambled thoughts and sat up to mime an
enquiry about my lost belongings. Truck, brooommm,
backpack—now that's a hard one—here, point at the
ground, today, point at the sky. It was hopeless.

An hour passed and a red-faced officer was summoned
to decode my mad ravings. He was clever and figured out
the bizarre charade in minutes. He, in turn, acted out a
little scene I interpreted with equal ease. He would be
traveling to Barga by jeep in the morning and offered me
a lift back to Tsōmo's camp where, with his aid, I could
establish the whereabouts of my precious backpack.

It was getting late. I was moved to another bed, then
another and finally, just after midnight, led to a private,
empty room at the far end of the sergeants' quarters. An
overweight, teenage soldier prepared a bed of green
greatcoats and blankets on the floor, then turned to face
me with a leering glint in his eyes. He formed a circle with
his thumb and forefinger, then slid his index finger in and
out of the symbolic circle. He grunted like a pig in heat.
Oh no, you must be kidding. I pretended not to understand
the significance of his gesture. It was a quarter past
twelve and the last thing I felt like doing was surrender-
ing my battered body to this inept, pimple-faced youth. I

felt repulsed. How dare he! The young soldier paid no heed to my polite plea of ignorance, and proceeded to dance around the room enacting his frustrated sexual intentions more elaborately. Enough. I lashed out with a smarting slap and shoved him out the door. The click of metal taps on his army boots echoed down the hallway. I bolted the door and collapsed onto what he had so arrogantly presumed would be our soft cloud of sin and pleasure for the night. Men! This one alone was enough to make avid droves of left-wing feminists take to the streets in angry retaliation. Enough to guarantee a frightened, over-exhausted woman alone in Tibet a sleepless night.

The red-faced sergeant summoned me at dawn. Breakfast and a hairbrush were delivered to my room by the token female on base. At 9 A.M. I climbed into the back of the sergeant's jeep and returned the way I had come. Oblivious to the familiar landscape, I watched the odometer on the instrument panel of the jeep slowly measure the distance traveled. Two hours and nearly thirty miles later, we reached Tsōmo's camp. Her husband had returned and ventured up to the roadway to greet my khaki-clothed companions. They shook hands and started talking. I limped down to Tsōmo and greeted her in the more traditional manner of banging foreheads. She ushered me inside for tea.

My pack? It had gone all the way to Ali by truck. Didn't I say I was walking to Ali? Well, yes—I had, but I didn't mean I'd cover the distance in one day! The misunderstanding hit me like a ton of bricks. All the way to Ali. What to do?

The sergeant wrote the truck driver's name and some other details on a scrap of paper and handed it to me. By early afternoon, I was back at the military base, having hitched a ride on an open truck full of Tibetan deaf-mutes and slaughtered marmots. I couldn't stay at the compound, despite the need to rest my stitched and aching feet. Yesterday's late-night scenario was still fresh in my mind. I felt uncomfortable. I would rather risk finding hospitable nomads at the end of the plain, than stay among ill-intentioned Chinese soldiers whose presence in this harsh, barren landscape seemed even more incongruous than my own. I walked slowly away from the compound without a moment's regret—my fear outweighing any gratitude I might have felt.

So the Tibetans believe I am a pilgrim. If I choose to adopt this guise, I must act like one and have faith. But faith in who? Myself or some unseen god?

Long ago I had rejected the doctrines of Western religion. Discos had replaced churches and Marxist philosophies, Bibles. Spiritual highs came not from Sunday sermons, but Saturday nights on the dance floor. I lived life hard and fast, and concentrated all my energies on tangible joys. I hadn't paused for more than thirty seconds during my late adolescence to seek the presence of a being greater than the men and women I could see and feel.

Traveling in Asia for two years meant an introduction to new gods and to more exotic themes of spiritual enlightenment. The perplexing hypocrisy of roaming missionaries in Asia strengthened my distaste of Western religion. Monasteries and temples paralleled churches. But monasteries and temples were not for the elite. You didn't have to wear a collar and tie, nor sign your name in a book on entering. I absorbed little of the theory behind Buddhist philosophy, but observed much of its effect on whole nations of people. Something stopped me from studying Buddhism further: fear of parental reprimand, my own pretentious suspicion of Buddha-conscious Westerners, perhaps an inbred response to all things organized or a disinterest in all games where one must play by the rules.

But as I walked away from the military compound, I did something I cannot explain. I clutched the thin red protection cord given to me by the Dalai Lama, which I wore around my neck, and prayed for safety to a god called Jesus. Om Mani Padme Hum. Amen. I found faith in a new trinity: God, Buddha, and myself.

For three days and nights I found sufficient food and

shelter along the river valley. Walking without my pack meant depending on other people for my survival at night, yet total freedom by day. I felt stronger and could walk farther without the cumbersome weight of trekking paraphernalia. My shoulders were singing, my feet dancing. Bites and blisters were healing. No mountain seemed too big. My trinity, the three musketeers, were winning.

In the tiny town of Gar, seventy-five miles southwest of Ali, I enquired about a shortcut route. The inevitable man with the "one-that-got-away" measuring expertise appeared and pointed northeast. This far. Good track. One day, maybe two. Nomads? Sure. I had come to accept a Tibetan's advice as gospel, choosing not to elicit a second opinion for fear of hurting the feelings of the first person.

I set off at daybreak, crossed the river, and climbed up a long winding pass. Morning turned to midday, midday became afternoon. I searched the horizon for nomads. Nothing. Not even a fresh yak turd on the track to raise my hopes. The familiar fears returned. I stopped to rest my weary legs and fell into a deep exhaustion-induced sleep.

Wave-like formations in the distant mountains beckoned me once again to the shore of my dream ocean. I stood alone at the water's edge, mesmerized by the incoming waves. The sea foam bubbled around my ankles, my calves, my knees. Was I sinking, or was the tide rising? The wind was blowing my hair into my eyes. I couldn't look toward the ocean any more. I turned to face not the familiar stretch of low, white sand dunes, but huge Tibetan mountains—close and threatening. Bare and ugly. The reality. The end of my dream.

I had to keep walking. To stop meant to freeze to death. The temperature was well below freezing despite the season, and I was inadequately clothed. The sun had set and taken all warmth from the earth with it. Move. Walk. On and on. The sky was clear—but my mind still clouded with fear. The god of night had emptied a secret hoard of diamonds across the black velvet void. Cold, semi-delirious, I walked by the ice-clear moonlight. There were too many falling stars, too many ghostly apparitions floating out from behind the cardboard cut-out mountains surrounding me. To combat fear and loneliness, I talked continuously to my camera. The mountain spirits were mocking me, their laughter echoed on the wind. Distant lights lured me beyond the limitations of my conscious will.

Shivering, I staggered toward Ali. A single light illuminated a low building in the marketplace. Through its frosted, dirty window I could just make out five men hunched over a glowing gas lamp, playing cards. I beat my frozen fists against the door. They had to let me in. A blanket appeared, a wooden seat at the card table. I glanced at the watch on a card player's wrist as he carelessly flipped the king of diamonds onto the cold, concrete floor. Seven o'clock. Only an hour to go and a new day would dawn above the whitewashed, newly constructed city of Ali. I had walked forty-two miles in 23 hours. Since I had invited myself into the card game, I supposed it necessary to take an interest in the proceedings. It was all I could do to stop from crying.

CHAPTER 5
Adventures—
for Better, for Worse

At 8 A.M. I stumbled from the card game into the cold dawn air. I forgot to thank the card players for their hour of hospitality. I wandered through the ugly, empty streets of Ali, re-familiarizing myself with its totally un-Tibetan layout. It was largely a Chinese, concrete town. I had stopped here overnight some weeks ago with the European four-wheel-drive expedition team. Jigme had given me the address of some old friends here, and a letter asking them to help me. Pemela—an old schoolfriend of Jigme—lived with her husband in a small mud-brick home across the road from the glass and green-tiled banking complex. He too worked for the Tibetan Sports Federation. The couple had been very kind to me, and after we had tea together, they had sent word to the Chinese officials in Burang that I would arrive there soon. It was also from them that I learned that I might buy a donkey in Burang.

My stay in Burang seemed like a century ago. Time had no meaning anymore—I had lost proper track of the days, the distances before and behind me. Numbers lost their significance for they did not ease pain nor make the way easier. Step by gradual step was the only way to cross Tibet, recording emotions, responses, meetings, rather than facts and figures, dates, and times.

Now I knew I would have to call on Jigme's friends again. I passed by the still half-constructed government store and slipped into the foul-smelling toilet block adjacent to the Ali Hotel. The huge, black pig who took care of Ali's waste disposal problems was still rummaging in the dirt pit nearby. She had recently been delivered of six scrawny offspring, three of which appeared to be stapled to her sagging teats. Oblivious to the piglets' ardent suckling, mother pig had her snout stuck in an empty tin can. She was hungrily trying to lick the lining from it, savoring each crystallized drop of mandarin juice pearled on its base.

It was too cold to stop and watch for more than a few seconds. I cupped my hands and blew warm air into them, turned on my heels, and continued my walk about town. I shot a few baskets with some track-suited athletes on the basketball court outside the town's stadium, and then stood freezing while the Chinese national anthem blared over Ali's loud-speaker system. The early morning broadcast stirred the small city into action. Like rats summoned by the floating melody of the Pied Piper's flute, the Chinese citizens of Ali swarmed from their nests onto the streets.

Truck drivers rose from their cabins near the river, cranking the engines of their vehicles into life. Bleary-eyed public servants emerged from their filing cabinet homes, scratched the dandruff from their scalps, and cleared their throats noisily onto the dust-laden thoroughfares. Mothers ushered children into school-bound processions. Simon says it's time to rise. Deng Xiaoping says it's time to work. Good morning China.

I wandered from the stadium to the home of Jigme's

classmate and her husband. They were older and slower to
rise to the call of the motherland. They greeted me with
both surprise and joy—hadn't I planned to trek the southern route to Lhasa? I sat on the sofa by the fire and began
to tell my adventurous tale. Pemela cut me short, cleanli-
ness first! My pungent odor, unnoticed by nomads, was
obviously offensive to the toothbrush-and-soap users of
urban Tibet.

I peered at myself in the cracked mirror above the
wooden wash basin stand. Was that dirt or suntan? Perhaps a bit of both. Hollow cheeks, gray hairs, two lifeless
oysters for eyeballs. I couldn't look for long—it was too
scary.

While I washed, Pemela churned Tibetan tea and arranged bowls of dry zumpa on the gaily painted coffee
table-cum-storage cupboard. She called across to me in
Tibetan, asking if I would prefer Chinese jasmine tea to
per-cha? Heavens no! The changes in me are not just skin
deep; the more rancid the butter, the better I'll like it!

Finally we were seated again. I was amazed at the
amount of Tibetan I had learned since my first visit to
Pemela's home. "Tor che-chay"—an ill-pronounced but
well-appreciated Tibetan thank you—was the only phrase
I had uttered then. Three weeks later, my vocabulary and
confidence in using it had extended beyond reasonable
belief. Jigme's friends were overjoyed by my eagerness to
learn and spent the next hour teaching me new nouns and
adjectives. Grammar was still confusing, but body language and facial expression cemented words together
firmly enough for them to carry meaning.

It felt so good to be warm and laughing and joking with
familiar faces. Talking with Pemela and her husband
sparked again the enthusiasm I had for my journey.
Laughter is a drug. In the light and warmth of day, it is
the sweetest, easiest pill to swallow. It cured the DTs I
suffered after overdosing on fear.

I ferreted around in my camera bag and found the piece

of paper detailing the possible whereabouts of my backpack. Pemela's husband made a few phone calls, then
motioned for me to follow him downtown.

We entered a hollow hallway and turned right into an
unlit office. The room was cluttered with high glass-
topped desks and rusting steel cabinets full of paper work.
More phone calls were made on my behalf, and Pemela's
husband told my saga to the attentive office workers:
branch directors of the famed Tibet Sports Service
Company.

Dorje, an enigmatic character from Tarchen, entered
the room. I had previously met him in the pilgrim's guest
house at the foot of Mount Kailas, and welcomed his warm
smile and handshake. Then, looking nervous and per-
plexed, the thin-framed, toothless Dorje spoke to me in
excellent English. Pemela's husband was having difficulty locating the truck driver entrusted with my backpack. His surname was Tsering, unfortunately a popular
choice in these parts. Phone calls had yielded butcher-
Tserings, baker-Tserings, butter-candle-making Tserings, but as yet, no truck-driving-backpack-bearing-
Tserings.

To fill in time, Dorje invited me over to his old aunt's
home on the outskirts of town. I stooped to enter the dark
living room of her small house, adjusting slowly to the
change from outside glare to inside gloom. Dorje's aunt
was blind. She sat cross-legged in the darkest corner of
the earthen room—comfortable on a long Tibetan rug,
moving her lips in silent prayer and fingering the beads of
her Buddhist rosary. A wry chuckle filled the room when
she learned she had a visitor, breaking (but only momentarily) the trance-inducing meter of her meditation. I
poured a cup of tea, and guided her soft, wrinkled hand
toward the cracked china vessel. Her middle-aged son
joined us in the tiny parlor, disguising his surprise with a
smile rivaling any I had received so far in Tibet. He took
my hand and led me to another low-ceilinged room.

A dismembered goat lay on the floor, its glazed eyes

fixed in a cold, blank stare. My host picked a selection of offal from the meat tray and turned to offer me a boiled, mahogany-colored kidney. We returned to the living room and Dorje's ancient aunt replaced her string of Buddha beads with a long, twisted sausage full of boiled and congealed goat's blood. Her meditation continued. She handled the sausage as if it were her rosary, fingering each section to the rhythm of her mumble, before grabbing it between what remained of her tusk-like teeth. Om Mani Padme, chomp, Om Mani Padme, chomp.

Dorje asked if I would take a photograph of him with his cousin, outside in the sunlight. To my surprise, he handed me a Nikon camera. A Nikon! How did a humble Tibetan come to possess such a camera? The truth involved an extraordinary coincidence. Apparently, the explorer Rienhold Messner had given it to him after the former's well-publicized trip through western Tibet—he was the first to traverse this region by car. Messner had in fact driven over much the same route later traveled by Hyo's expedition. The camera was Dorje's reward for the help he had given Messner.

I too had met Messner. During my first trip to Lhasa, Jigme had been able to arrange an introduction, and I had tea with this living legend, the greatest climber in the world, with a list of achievements almost as high as Everest itself. He was then organizing his expedition, and took time off just for me. What an inspiration. I shook even holding the camera he had once owned, and it wasn't until the third shot that I realized the shutter was jamming and the light meter didn't work.

Following a quick repair job, I peered through the viewfinder and focused on Tibet's answer to Harpo Marx. A blue baseball cap cast a shadow over Dorje's tuberculosis-scarred eyes. A huge pair of tortoise-shell spectacles balanced on his thin nose. Below, a few tufts of wiry hair suggested a mustache. A tweed patterned suit, at least six sizes too big, encased his slender body. The jacket's sleeves concealed his hands but the buttoned coat flaps failed to

hide a five-inch-wide pink, maroon, and white tie. Dusty
black lace-ups poked from beneath his sagging trouser
cuffs. A torn leather briefcase completed his business-
man's guise.

Dorje refused to smile. He didn't want the photograph to
reveal his missing front teeth, since it would be sent to his
older sister in India. They had not seen each other in over
twenty years. It was my job to record the still-youthful
features of Dorje's quickly deteriorating physique. Hence
the clothes!

His cousin stood by his side, decked out in more traditional Tibetan garb—a knee-length sheepskin chuba,
pulled to bare one tanned shoulder and belted at the waist
with a wide, woven band.

Photo session over, Dorje and I headed back to the sports
service office. My pack had been located and it was time to
begin serious discussions about my impending journey
from Ali to Lhasa. Snowfalls were already breaking long-
established weather patterns in the northern reaches of
Tibet and an early winter had been forecast for the central
plains region. The year 1985 was not the time to be out
trekking in Tibet. The weather conditions were too unsta-
ble. It could snow in Ali tomorrow, and it very nearly did.

I awoke the next morning in my room in the government compound to the howling tune of high winds. Dark
clouds obscured the barren mountain ranges surrounding
the town. Ice blew down from distant snow peaks, lightly
dusting the dirty streets and buildings. The freak storm
unnerved me. I spent the day poring over hand-sketched
cartographs and detailed topographic maps, plotting a
route to Parayang via the central plains settlement of
Yagra. The sports service company issued me an updated
travel permit and letters of introduction, aimed at soliciting aid from village mayors en route.

I had lunch with Pemela and her eight-year-old grandson, then returned to my mouse-infested room to rest. The
young Tibetan woman who shared it with me could not
comprehend why I wanted to cross her country on foot.

Perhaps the lack of understanding was due to her rather pregnant state. She found it difficult waddling the two hundred yards out to the toilet block.

Unfortunately that night, so did I. Awakened by a sudden attack of the Chinese-food-greasies I only just reached the compound toilet in time. On the second, almost predictable hit, I wasn't so lucky. I leapt from my sick bed and was ill all over the concrete floor. My roommate laughed. It wouldn't be the first or the last time she had to mop up after a belly-bugged babe. I felt too weak to apologize and crawled back beneath the thick eiderdown on my bed.

I sensibly delayed leaving Ali for another day. Laughter and fear pills aside, I took to popping bowel-cementing Flagyl and vitamins in an effort to restore my body to its former health. Late afternoon saw a flood of people enter Ali. A subtitled Japanese film was showing at the stadium and everyone with access to wheels had motored from as far away as Burang to see the acclaimed big-screen motion picture. I just had strength enough to greet a few familiar faces from the military base, then wandered back to my room for more luxurious—and hopefully uninterrupted—sleep.

Much to my surprise, my pregnant roommate and her husband had planned a small party to wish me success on my journey. Bottled beer from Beijing, oil-drenched Tibetan bread, a gray-colored stew of mutton fat and radishes. I popped in another Flagyl, picked up my chopsticks, raised my glass, and prayed for a miracle.

The following morning, feeling queasy but with insides fairly stable, I set out from Ali before the loudspeakers had a chance to wake the local populace. More of the vast unknown stretched before me. Again, heavy gray cloud covered the pale pink mountain ridges behind the town. A few drops of rain fell lightly on the brim of my digger's hat. After all those days of traveling light, my shoulders could not accommodate the weight of my pack comfortably. But my feet felt better. I had (no doubt prematurely) removed the stitches in my heels and legs before setting out, and it was heaven to walk without catgut threads pricking into unbroken flesh as they rubbed against woolen socks and cotton long-johns.

The fortress-like range on the right of the valley lacked character and contour under the foreboding sky. My route necessitated following the Shiquanhe River to Gêgyai along a partly constructed roadway.

By one o'clock the clouds had scattered and a fiery Tibetan sun burned high in the endless blue void. A jeep motored toward me and swerved to a halt. Two men hopped out and introduced themselves as friends of Jigme. They were driving two Chinese out to Mount Kailas. My good buddy and Tibetan mentor had told them to watch out for me, but where was my donkey? Wretched Budget, his memory would haunt me forever. The little band of jovial travelers produced a bottle of beer, stale bread from my favorite bakery in Lhasa, and two small bars of Chinese chocolate—gifts for the hungry pilgrim. I was touched by their thoughtfulness.

We sat together for half an hour, smoking unfiltered cigarettes and sipping amber brew straight from the bottle. A video camera appeared to record our happy meeting. From what I could gather, the men were on a reconnaissance mission to the holy mountain, collecting footage for a Beijing-based film studio. It was encouraging to learn of mainland China's interest in ancient Tibetan ritual. We parted company and I continued walking.

My eyes fixed on the bare parched earth beneath my feet. With every step, the weight of my pack sent shooting pains from my all-too-recently cracked pelvis right down to my toes. Why, why does my body ache so much?

I approached a road workers' camp, and stopped at a distance to absorb its significance. Two flimsy tents of stained cotton torn apart by savage winds and re-stitched a hundred times over. A road grader, symbol of man's endless fight to tame and change the structure of a landscape. It had obviously broken down.

The sky grew heavy with clouds. A thousand taps were turned on in the heavens. I was filled with respect for nature's awesome and unpredictable power, humbled through the recognition of my own fragility in its face and angered by man's continuous, predictable attempt to control it. It was a shame to see Tibet entering the twentieth century. Prior to external influences—welcomed or otherwise—Tibetans lived in harmony with the land, not fighting against it. No motor vehicles existed in Tibet before the middle of this century—the movement of wheels over soil was believed to release evil spirits from beneath the earth. Men came from the outside world, and told the Tibetans otherwise. Chinese engineers came with surveying tools and wooden peg markers. Chinese politicians came with lengthy legislation, and armies to enforce it. Pitchforks replaced prayer wheels. An ancient civilization had been condemned.

I jogged down to the riverside camp, startling a sheep tethered near the first, drenched tent. It sprang in the air, ran several paces, gathered momentum, then backflipped as the rope around its wooly neck yanked tight. A rather undignified landing in the icy stream followed. Formerly docile eyes met mine and glared a promise of revenge.

A young woman appeared at the entrance to the second tent and ushered me inside. She helped me remove my pack, then shook dirt and food scraps from a colorful rug, placed it near the fireplace, and motioned for me to make myself comfortable. Her husband and his teammate, grubby with dust, sat opposite, staring incredulously. I stared back. No one said anything. My hostess stirred the embers of the fires and sparked warmth. The fireplace was far more elaborate than those of the nomads. It resembled a pot-bellied stove. A chimney bent out and upward through the tent's smoke-vent and a blackened teapot rested in its crook. A battered cooking pot sat on the cast-iron griddle and a smell of burning rice filled the tent. My hostess stirred the congealed sludge and spooned a small quantity of it into a dirty enamel bowl. She woke her son and fed it to him, then offered her breast to the three-year-old for milk. It still surprised me to see Tibetan mothers breast-feeding toddlers. In lieu of other methods of contraception, the practice forestalls pregnancy. Among nomads, the nourishing of infants is a shared task—grandmothers and aunts included.

I darned my socks and examined a new blister on the tip of my big toe. The rain eased and I ventured outside to pitch my tent a few yards downwind of the road workers' camp. I climbed inside the domed, womb-like contraption and buried myself in my sleeping bag. I wasn't in a sociable mood. I pulled out the Polaroid photograph of Hyo and propped it up against my camera bag. I stared at it. Hyo stared back. Neither of us said anything.

My pelvis still ached in the morning, so along with the Flagyl, vitamins, and mineral tablets, I swallowed a couple of analgesics. A standard breakfast for the classic neurotic. My stomach rumbled and I burped halibut-flavored air. Vitamin A. It was time to move.

The Shiquanhe River Valley grew narrower as the day wore on. The mountains assumed characteristics which reflected my obsessive preoccupation with food. Honeycomb-weathered cliffs waited to be dipped in the chocolate shade of afternoon. At the next bend the rock wall became a row of exotic-looking artichoke hearts. On the left-hand side of the river, Turkish Delight-colored hills glistened temptingly in the sunlight. Behind them, dark Christmas puddings lightly dusted with icing sugar completed the Tibetan banquet. I stopped to slake my thirst at the bubbling river. Ahhh, champagne.

Late afternoon winds carried the scent of rain, offering a reasonable excuse to halt the day's march. I was covering good distances in spite of the terrain, for I usually found it difficult to stop for more than five minutes at a time. A restless energy fired my spirit until utter exhaustion extinguished its glow. Counterproductive midday resting bored me. It was imperative to keep moving until I dropped. Meditating—the art of contemplating nothing—

had always been beyond my understanding and ability. I could not derive any pleasure from inactivity. Even in sleep, my mind raced through oceans of fantasy and thought. In a day I could invent a thousand time-saving devices, write a hundred songs, plan a million dinner-party conversations, and ultimately solve a dozen of the world's major social and political dilemmas.

I settled on a beautiful lime green bank by the river and wrote until the pages of my diary were no longer visible.

In the morning I explored a cliff face pitted with small, dark caves. The roofs and walls were pitch-black from fire smoke. Prayer stones marked the entrances to caves and lined the precarious, narrow pathways that linked them. Long ago, monks used these isolated aeries for spiritual retreats, meditating and praying alone for months—even years—on end. Eagles circled above the cliff. It was not hard to imagine the deep-toned chants which once echoed within the lightless labyrinth.

Back by the riverside, warm sunlight filled the valley. I walked between mountains rough and encrusted with grazes, like kneecaps after a hockey match. They receded and the spongy, chocolate soufflés of yesterday lined my route. The valley opened—opened and dropped down to a flat, green plain through which the Shiquanhe snaked and fragmented into smaller, gentler streams. Nomad camps were scattered in the distance. The wheel track climbed away from the river and ran along the slope of the foot-hills. In the center of the plain, I felt the world expand beyond its three dimensions. The sky was too big, the landscape was endless. I felt as small and insignificant as a single grain of sand on a beach.

At the edge of the plain, the streams reconnected. I trekked down a dry creek bed to meet the main river flow and quenched my thirst with its ice cold water. Beautiful. Light danced on the water's jeweled surface. The glare was intense. I sheltered in the dry creek bed and admired the magic river, waiting for the winds above the bank to calm. Impatience overcame me. I struggled against the howling gale feeling as flimsy as a tissue in a hurricane and rejoined the narrow roadway. The still-swollen river zigzagged along its length. Not wanting to get my feet wet and chilled, I ventured by an abandoned village and on to the base of a red-colored cliff.

Earlier that morning I had heard three loud blasts thunder through the valley. Suddenly I realized the blasts had probably reverberated downwind from this very spot. This very cliff face. Fresh rubble formed the shaky surface beneath my feet. What if . . . ?

I quickened my pace. As I rounded the cliff, one hundred Chinese and Tibetan road workers appeared. They looked like an army of ants swarming all over the red-orange slope below the craggy mountainside. I bade them a carefree good afternoon.

Shovels fell to the ground and mouths dropped. Boom! Boom! Boom! The cliff fell away behind me, burying my fresh footprints in landslides of debris. The blast knocked me off balance. Loose stones ricocheted off the back of my pack. My ears were ringing.

I picked myself up, dusted myself off, and blushed before the confused blur of faces. This sort of thing happens to me every day, boys. I tried to appear nonchalant and walked off down to the river, hoping the men could not see the large wet patch between my legs.

A few miles away from the blasting area, I came to a row of uninhabited mud igloos, standing on a flat bare patch of earth halfway between the road and river. Sheep droppings littered the floor of two, and nomad odds and ends lay strewn about the others. I pitched my tent at the end of the row and marveled at the similar shape it held.

I collected some water from the river and sat down to write while it warmed for soup on my small fuel burner. All morning I had been thinking about my friends in Australia. Thousands of miles away—unreachable. My love for them had rarely been uttered. A great sadness overwhelmed me. Impulsive emotional outbursts—good or bad—were socially unacceptable these days. We mangle our minds with computer technology and in consequence, handle our personal relationships as passionately as programming discs. Our hearts function like silicon chips. The afternoon's near miss left me with an urgent need to communicate my unspoken feelings, my affection for all my friends.

Hyo, I need to love you, if only for the duration of this journey. There must be an end to the rainbow. There has to be. I must keep walking through my dream to find you—to find someone, something, at its end. I need to look at your photograph to gain strength, to pull me over and above every Everest I face. I started singing a song from a long-forgotten musical.

> Where is love?
> Does it fall from skies above?
> Must I travel far and wide . . .
> Till I am beside the someone who
> I can mean something to?

In the fading light of dusk, I wrote intensely emotional letters to everyone I cared about. It would be months before I came to a place civilized enough to find airmail envelopes and postage stamps.

Every morning, the Tibetan sun singles out one ridge on the horizon—smothering it in golden light while all the other mountains remain in shadow, or buried beneath cloud. Every morning I am stunned by the unsurpassed beauty of the light which falls upon this country. As I unzip and crawl from my nylon womb, the magnificent mountains, the awesome endless sky, and the vast plains below never fail to impress me. The thought of going back to bed, or sleeping in, does not exist once I have savored a Tibetan sunrise. I am addicted to dawn. A single sunbeam provides a greater rush of adrenalin than a thousand cups of coffee. Tibetan days begin in glory.

This next morning was no exception. As I started walking beneath a heavy ocean of clouds, a single ray of light lit

a fortress of rock upon a distant ridge. The jagged para-
pets of stone glistened like polished brass Buddhas on the
altar of mountains. The ridge was sacred, blessed by light
and warmth. One morning, one holy, sacred, blessed
morning perhaps the sun gods would shine their first rays
upon me—upon the width of my winding trail. Although I
didn't miss the jolting ring of alarm clocks, the tabloids
telling of world news, the frantic rush to meet over-
crowded peak hour trains, at times I surely missed Sydney's heat waves.

My hands and toes were numb. Winter had come early
to the plateau—the rumors were right. More nomad
camps appeared along the river's edge. I stopped to shelter from the icy wind behind a well-eroded mud hut, used
by the nomads as a grain storage shed. An old woman
pushed a crude wheelbarrow toward the building. She
stopped at the entrance, noticed me, and leaned back
against her cart in a relaxed pose. She started talking,
explaining the mechanics of the harvesting equipment
strewn around the storage shed. A huge wooden pole,
standing in the center of a cleared circle formed the axis
of a horse-powered thresher. As she spoke, she spun an
even thread from a thick bracelet of dark wool onto a
wooden spinning device. The long sleeves of her chuba
were rolled back to allow free movement of her gnarled
but nimble fingers. I laughed to myself, wondering what
amazing articles she could have in the belly pouch of her
garment. Special possessions, food scraps, tea cups, repair
kits, and clothing accessories are traditionally stored in
the pocket above the belted flap of a Tibetan chuba. Now I
imagined six snow-white pigeons, three decks of playing
cards, and a rabbit in a top hat. A chuba would make the
ideal gift for the cabaret magician who has everything,
but nowhere to hide it all.

An hour later, I came to another nomad tent and welcomed the offer of tea. A thin, toothless grandmother sat
by the dung-and-sage fire swishing a huge goat skin balloon full of fresh yak's cream. In several hours it would be

as solid as any mechanically churned butter and packaged in dried pieces of sheep or goat stomach lining for prolonged preservation. It was a far cry from my mother's kitchen—well-stocked with plastic tubs of polyunsaturated margarine straight from the refrigerated shelves of suburban supermarkets.

A bunch of low concrete buildings appeared around the next turn in the roadway. Gêgyai lay around the next bend, just two miles away. I had made it! I was alive, smiling, happy! This was remarkable, truly remarkable. I felt indestructible.

Gêgyai's basketball court and whitewashed housing compounds came into view. A dozen snotty-nosed little urchins raced down to give me a hero's welcome and escorted me to the village mayor. The townsfolk had learned of my impending arrival from Pemela's husband, who had apparently driven all the way out to Gêgyai on the eve of my departure from Ali to ensure I would be well received there.

The village goti (headman) shook my hand and greeted me by name. We walked over to his office, bypassed a pile of skinned pig carcasses and half-rotted apples, and sat down at a glass-topped desk laden with maps. He had worked out a route and plan for the next stage of my journey and was anxious to see if it met with my approval. I couldn't believe it! He had arranged for a horse and a nomad guide to meet me on the other side of the plain of Bumba. They would guide me to the small town of Shongba. The goti apologized for being unable to alert anyone beyond Bumba of my journey; the best he could do was add personal letters of introduction to those of the sporting company directors. The more paperwork I had, the better. We labored over maps, calculating distances and availability of water *en route*. Fantastic! This was going to be a piece of cake. Oh, how frequently I would eat those words in the following month.

After copious quantities of jasmine tea, the goti led me over to his residential quarters. His wife had prepared a gargantuan feast in my honor. Real food! Fish! Rice, vegetables, pork—food, food, glorious food! I had died and gone to heaven.

With belly bursting, I waddled away from the table to rest in the town's special guest room. I had overdone it—over-eaten. It was wonderful. What better way to end existence. Oh, the luxury of having stomach pains that weren't the result of hunger or bad food. I lay on the bed in an ecstasy of agony.

In the morning, I sauntered over to the goti's house. Another banquet! My hunger seemed insatiable. My host was busy organizing the town's affairs and trying to pack for an excursion to Ali. His wife put plastic curlers in my hair in an amusing attempt to make me look more feminine. At about ten o'clock, a white Toyota Land Cruiser pulled up outside his door. I raced outside to greet the occupants of the vehicle, and promptly scared the life out of them. Clad in my curlers and overalls, I was half-monster, half-suburban housewife. When they had regained their composure, the two Chinese army officers from the car entered the goti's home, sat at the table, and polished off the remnants of our breakfast.

Ten-thirty showed on the face of the goti's clock. Time for him to leave. Dozens of people milled around the dusty vehicle, inspecting the tires, headlights, and interior. The spacious rear of the four-wheel-drive was packed to the brim with little black vinyl suitcases emblazoned with the word "Beijing," sheep carcasses, blankets and cotton eiderdowns, spare tires, and reams of paperwork. The goti slipped on a fawn Woody Allen overcoat and dark glasses, and stood by the car shaking hands with all the doting villagers gathered to farewell him. He raised both hands above his head, like an Olympic medalist basking in the glory of success. A great man. The chauffeur-driven "limo" pulled away from the compound, the ensuing dust clouds settled, and the small crowd turned from the farewell site, dispersed across the compound, and resumed their morning activities.

Now what? Bumba. Twenty miles across a vast plain, nestled between two purple ranges. But I could see the base of those ranges. How could it possibly be that far? How can the naked eye see such a distance? It couldn't be, but of course it was. For this was Tibet, land of four, five, six, seven, eight-nine-ten dimensions. Incredible. Not one skyscraper, not one single tree to obstruct the mind-boggling vastness or give it some perspective.

With head low and back bent beneath the weight of my possessions and provisions, I battled on against the wind and marched toward Bumba. River gravel, rock, and sand—no earth, no soil between. I stopped only to relieve myself, to moisten the stony ground which no amount of water and fertilizer could transform. If I stayed on that same spot for the rest of my life, for a thousand years, it would not change. Tibet's stone deserts are dead. Stillborn. Not one nomad lived in this inhospitable tract of land. Not one rabbit, rodent, lizard, or beetle. Usually there is some form of life—some creature or microscopic plant form—attempting to wake the dead, silent landscape, attempting to resuscitate it. But not here. Not today. I had found the world's largest mortuary slab. And how cold it was.

Dark clouds and hail intensified the gloom. I ran to escape the grasp of ghosts and the wrath of angry sky gods. I ran, but Bumba was still too far away. Skeletons were rattling in closets. The hair on my neck was standing on end. Translucent apparitions were soaring from the opened lid of a Lost Ark. Indiana Jones was screaming, "Don't look! Don't look!" I regretted having watched too much television as a child and too many Hollywood horror epics in my teens.

Finally I came to the edge of the plain. A feeling of relief poured over me. Relief from the mind-bending desert, from the distorted visions and sensations it evoked. An old man appeared from nowhere and asked me where I was headed. He pouted his bottom lip, moved his head backwards, and mumbled something I guessed to mean, "Over

there, ten miles." My interpretation of his garbled utter-
ance was thankfully incorrect. I reached Bumba in fifteen
minutes.

A young woman dragged me into her low, mud-brick
home and poured cups of tea for me and the long procession of guests that followed close at heel. It felt like Bumba
was trying to break a long-held Guinness Book of Records
entry. How many people can you fit in a telephone booth?
Accost a foreigner, sit her down in one dark corner, and
start counting!

My hostess, Lahkbah, behaved as if she were entertain-
ing royalty. In doing so, her status among the villagers
would be exalted. Looking after the first foreigner ever to
visit your village ensured lifetime prestige. Lahkbah
would ever be Bumba's queen of socialites. We ate sweets
and dried yak meat and talked for hours.

> "Oh looking glass creatures," quoth Alice,
>   "draw near!
> 'Tis an honour to see me, a favour to hear:
> 'Tis a privilege high to have dinner and tea
> Along with the Red Queen, the White Queen
>   and me."
>
>   Lewis Carroll
>   *Through the Looking-Glass*

At nightfall, Lhakbah led me over to the new part of
town to the home of one Dorje Tsering. I should explain
that I met many "Dorjes" along my way—it is a common
Tibetan name, like Tsering. This particular one had been
expecting me, and together with his best mate was trying
desperately hard to scrape together a "Welcome to
Bumba" feast. The pressure cooker exploded and half-
cooked morsels of meat and potato landed (in part) upon
my dinner plate. Gêgyai's act would be a hard one to
follow, but I felt touched by their efforts.

Just when our conversation had lulled to a comfortable
silence, my appointed guide appeared and introduced
himself. We looked each other over. Pemma was a small
man, perhaps in his mid-thirties, with unusually round

eyes. He wore the navy blue trousers of the official Mao uniform, a pink shirt and sleeveless tan pullover, and, of all things, a golfer's beret. He was outwardly different from the Tibetan nomads I had met and befriended so far, but I warmed to him instantly when a smile ignited his wide, round face. I smiled back, shaking off my last reservations about sharing my challenge with others. Even if we couldn't communicate fully in words, it would be a great comfort to know I wasn't alone out there. We agreed to start out at nine o'clock the following morning. With that, I went off to my room, fiddled with the radio for half an hour trying unsuccessfully to get a clear reception, and subsequently drifted into dreamland.

Pemma, my new traveling companion, materialized at 9:30 A.M.—our packhorse at ten. I was curious to see the kind of horse the headman at Gêgyai had chosen. The gray stallion had been held up in the shoe store, and now proudly paraded before me in his new shoes. He belonged to a nomad from the district who was happy to offer his beast for a small part of my pilgrimage. The owner handed me the reins, flipping back his long thin plaits and smiling broadly. The horse was soon loaded and Bumba-ites came out in force to see me off. Away we went, into the sun. For the first time in days the sky was free from cloud and wind.

We wandered past a large nomad settlement, tents obscured by ten-foot-high piles of baled wool. The anxious nomads were awaiting a Buddha-sent vehicle so that their produce could be transported to one of Tibet's few trading posts before winter really took hold. I waved and my companion smiled. What a glorious day!

We headed merrily down the valley between pale yellow, bare, rounded hills. How good it felt to be walking without my pack and without fear of its whereabouts. At one turn of the long valley, huge sandstone-colored cliffs met the river. "Om Mani Padme Hum," written in nearly seven-foot-high script, graced one sheer stone wall. My companion stopped and clasped his hands in prayer. Bless the jewel in the lotus, and us too, if You will.

The horse was fantastic. Unlike cantankerous Budget, he moved when he was told and required only the occasional tugging of reins. And he didn't stare holes through the back of my head, or backfire, or otherwise disgrace himself.

More nomad camps dotted the dry, barren river valley. We took an extended tea-and-zumpa break at one tent, then moved to a tiny castle-shaped dwelling belonging to a semi-nomadic herdsman for dessert. The shepherd's wife scooped a large bowl of yogurt made from sheep's milk from a cauldron-sized pot and passed it to me. It was still warm, and indescribably delicious.

This Lilliputian castle was a curious sight. The roof was constructed from sheepskins, twigs, juniper roots (goodness knows where they came from), twisted goat horns, and yak pelts, all woven together with woolen rope and supported by large beams of Nepalese hardwood. Old pictures of the Panchen Lama and insipid posters of Deng Xiaoping riding a horse and shaking hands with other Chinese dignitaries were stuck with butter to the circular mud walls. Happy little Chinese cherubs wrestled with a cherry-cheeked panda bear on the back of the sheet-metal door. The decoration did not reveal support of the Communist regime but rather showed the characteristic Tibetan love of color. In other dwellings I saw fruit tin labels and magazine cutouts adorning walls.

A domestic altar filled half the space of the round house. Upon it, small brass vessels held butter candles and by their light I saw two smart tape recorders sharing pride of place with a framed collage of lama and deity portraits. Such affluence! The herdsman asked me if I had my own player, and I had to admit not. His four handsome children watched my every move with complete fascination. After about half an hour, we moved to yet another tent. (And I thought progressive dinner parties were a Western social phenomenon!) We drank more tea, then rescued our horse from pasture and moved from the valley into hill territory.

The hill slopes were steep and sharp; loose gravel covered them. Our trail was often no more than four inches wide and slipping seemed inevitable. In the warmth of afternoon light, we rounded the base of a massive hill and climbed another cleft in its lee side. The angry barking of savage mongrels echoed in the hillside amphitheater. Nomads. Not just any old nomads though, for this was my companion's family.

We let the horse free to roam after untying our luggage and Pemma's mother took my hand and led me to the fireside. Two other sons returned home with their flock and two daughters strolled down from another tent with their grubby little babies. We gave the family presents of discarded clothing, sweets, and cigarettes, scavenged thoughtfully the night before in Bumba. We all sat smoking—women included—laughing and teasing each other into hysterics. Someone produced a deck of playing cards and a bizarre game began. It was impossible for my poker-and-cribbage-sophisticated mind to comprehend. Cards were held, flipped, thrown away, stolen from other players, bent, twisted, and even torn in half. And all the time laughter, bubbly and carefree—contagious, despite my lack of understanding.

Slowly the sun descended and the hills behind us cast great shadows over the camel-hued humps in front. The sky turned pastel blue; horizon clouds turned pink and gray. The brothers went outside the tent and playacted cowboy scenarios, lassoing wayward sheep and rounding them up into the steep, rocky slope beside the camp. The fattened flock stood quivering in fright on the craggy hillside. "Bullets" of revenge were shed over their pursuers below. More laughter. The goats were herded outside the tent opening and my now-experienced milking fingers went to work. The chill of evening set in.

In the morning I declined the customary offer of tea and brewed a dry packet of soup for myself. Mum was curious, and asked if she could sample the murky yellow broth. No more than a miniscule amount passed between her lips. She gagged as if poisoned, retching until she was blue in the face. She rolled over and kicked her arms and legs in

the air like a dying dog. I guess Continental Pea and Ham
will never take off in the wild, wild west. Her crazy sense
of humor followed us out into the sunshine. Her laughter
rang in my ears for hours.

Yellow-green hills stretched forever. We picnicked after
a few hours on the remnants of last night's meal—boiled
mutton and fried bread. It felt good to be sharing the
landscape—its beauty and its ugliness—with someone
else. It was wonderful to be able to depend on someone
other than myself for survival—for water, food, and guid-
ance. Free from the thought of getting myself irrevocably
lost, I could better appreciate the mountains around me.
They were no longer threatening. No longer inhabited by
leering, evil spirits. I felt incredibly calm. Four musketeers—two heavenly and two human—and a horse. Perfect. Way in the distance I could just make out another
camp. We rested on the trail halfway, then beelined down
the hills, across the valley, and approached the new camp
without hesitation. Afternoon clouds showered us in hailstones the size of golf balls and a whipping wind thrashed
us toward our destination. We were welcomed to the camp
by an army of children and collapsed in exhaustion inside
their parents' tent.

After a short rest and a gallon of tea, I attempted to help
the menfolk soften sheepskins for their wives' new chubas.
I sat on the ground with my legs extended, pressed my
boot soles against those of my host, and rolled my edge of
the fleeced skin around a thin, dark antelope horn. He did
the same and rhythmically we bent forward, as if rowing a
boat, pulling the horn implements across the spongy, soft
underside of the pelt. After ten beats, we paused to catch
our breaths. Beads of sweat trickled down my temples. It
was hard work. Ten more counts and I was out, exhausted.
My forearm muscles ached as if I had crossed the English
Channel by canoe, using teaspoons for oars. No rower nor
Tibetan tanner will I be.

Garma, my hostess, looked up from her own handiwork
and laughed at my panting, hunched pose. She looked a lot

like Tsōmo, the first nomad woman with whom I had
stayed, near Barga. One of her children rearranged some
other sheepskins by the fire and she motioned for me to lie
down. I marveled at the speed with which she plied spun
wool from two balls onto a single spool. The thumb on her
right hand was deformed or was I seeing double? No,
indeed, she had two thumbs, two perfect thumbs joined
together as one.

I must be jinxed with animals. In the night the horse
broke its woolen tethering rein and vanished. Of all the
lousy, Budget-bungling things to do! No one at the camp
seemed too perturbed by the disappearance and it wasn't
until an hour and a half and a gallon of tea had passed that
anyone went to look for the beast. Such a task was men's
work—I was instructed to stay at the camp with Garma
and just enjoy the sunny warmth of the morning.

I sat outside the tent and watched the men disappear
over the hills. Garma's two young sons, Zumpa and Sonam, came out to play. Fancy calling a child Zumpa—
barley flour! The boys made a new tent for themselves
from an old corduroy chuba and clucked around playing
mummies and daddies. Zumpa dragged huge rocks over
to the cubby house and placed them in a ring around the
base of his imaginary tent. Sonam was too little to aid his
brother and toddled around in the dust, dragging behind
him a piece of goat's horn tied to a string. A dirty piece of
purple cloth was knotted at one end of the string and a
three-inch ring of metal tubing clanged against the
twisted horn. In the course of the morning, that simple toy
became a truck, a doll, a glamorous pony, a lasso, and a
best friend. I thought about the single-purpose electric
gadgetry we give our children in the West. How quickly
they tire of a battery-operated model Porsche, a plastic
Barbie doll. How quickly they demand we buy them a
newer model Fiat, or Barbie's boyfriend, Ken.

Garma came outside, sat down, and pressed her feet
against a solid lump of turf. She tied an assortment of
woolen ropes around her midsection and tensioned herself

against two wooden stakes pitched six feet away. The warp threads of the complicated loom she had created pulled tight. Quickly she raced a spool of weft thread backward and forward between the warps, stopping to beat each row down with a roughly crafted wooden reed. The woven fabric, once completed, would be used to make sacks for flour and large bags for household odds and ends. Garma's brother sat nearby, twisting and pulling another sheepskin. He coughed perpetually from too many cigarettes. His two nephews mocked his racking, spluttering cough as they played. The sound of Garma's hands beating dust from the tense warp threads, the noise of Sonam's clanging horn dragging through the dust and gravel, the thud of Zumpa's rocks striking the ground, the coughing, the squeals of innocent delight when thrown stones connected with camp-dog flesh harmonized together in a special symphony; composed by the mountains and conducted by the breeze.

At midday, the men returned, horseless. There were just enough hours left in the day to walk to Shongba. As much as my hosts longed for me to stay another day, they agreed I should take advantage of the good weather and try to reach Shongba by nightfall. I listened intently and with confidence to their directions, hitched my pack upon my back, and ambled away from the music of nomad domesticity into the still, silent valley, alone.

Shongba came as some surprise. In the latter stages of the afternoon, my mind had wandered off to meet new mountains, greener pastures, saner cities. Twenty miles had passed beneath my feet, unnoticed. I searched in my pack for my letters of introduction.

These were passed around with some confusion; no one in Shongba could read Chinese. The headman or goti, to whom the letters were addressed, was out of town. The townsfolk held a quick meeting and decided I should remain in the village until the all-seeing, all-knowing goti returned. And to make sure I wouldn't disobey their rule, the door of the tiny, cold concrete room they poked me in was bolted from the outside. I was too stunned to think straight, too tired to protest. I sat on the edge of my mattressless bed frame and lit a small stub of candle I had found on the rammed earth floor. I curled up inside my sleeping bag for warmth and reached inside my backpack, fingers searching for an antidepressive: the photo of Hyo, a few stray sultanas. I drew out the bar of Toblerone chocolate I had been saving for one particular festive day in December. Merry Christmas, Sorrel. Merry Christmas, Shongba. I wiped a tear from the corner of my eye and tore away the chocolate's foil wrapper. It was still September. My dreams were dying.

CHAPTER 6
Arrest and Attack

The village prison wardens had overlooked my basic needs. I had no food, no water, no toilet. I could get by without food and water for a few more hours, but not the toilet. No! I badly needed to empty my bursting bladder. I tossed and turned inside my warm sleeping cocoon, trying to push the desire into the furthest recess of my mind, but it wouldn't stay there. Finally, in desperation, I got up and squatted on the floor! I looked like a randy chicken waddling around in circles trying to disperse the flow. I tucked my hands under my armpits and moved them like wings, quacking romantic overtures to further strengthen the courtship implication of my bizarre dance. I was glad no one in the village saw my pre-sunrise performance. It would have surely been construed as madness. I knew better. It was medicine for my sinking spirit. Adrenalin for my dying dream. Don't let them get you down, Sorrel. Laugh! Laugh until your seams split.

My door was opened at 10 A.M. by the tall young chap who had so kindly locked it. He took me down to his room at the far end of one whitewashed row of house-boxes and made me sweet tea and a plate of noodles. I could show no gratitude. My sense of humor and state of depression had passed. I was angry. Okay buster, what's your story? Why are you locking me up like a convict? I really do have permission to pass through your village, you know. And whether you like it or not, that's exactly what I intend to do. Pass through. I'm not staying another second locked up in your cell on this godforsaken plateau.

Oh madam . . . the door . . . the lock . . . oh, of course. The door doesn't shut from the inside. I am sorry. Tenzing had locked the door to keep out the cold plateau wind and over-curious children—he had not meant to lock me in. What a simpleton. Then I'm free to go? Free to leave Shongba? Now? Well, ahh, no madam. Please stay in Shongba. But do not feel like a prisoner. Here's the key to the bolt lock. And here's another cup of tea. And another bowl of noodles. Tenzing was sweating and shaking like a leaf.

House arrest in Shongba. I could wander to the toilet block, walk out onto the plain, walk around the two old rows of house-boxes and up onto the hill behind them. I had to wait for the goti. If I left without his permission and aid, the villagers would suffer. If something happened to me between here and Yagra—the next village on my route—they would be held responsible. And what might happen? Well, madam, there are wolves out there. And you wouldn't know where to get water. And your pack's too heavy. And the nomads, they might eat you too. Come on guys. You were winning with the wolves and water— but head-hunting nomads?

I decided to stay. Perhaps the goti would return in the morning anyway. I spent the rest of the day writing and talking to the locals, eating, and planning the next moves on the chessboard of my life. Chessboard? Snakes and Ladders seemed a more appropriate analogy. Moves dictated by dice throws. Ladders to climb.

But the goti didn't come and my journey down the spine of a snake was a long one. It was six days before he returned to the village. Physically and emotionally, I was back at square one. I filled in the long hours of each day in much the same way as I had my first in Shongba. Noodles and tea. Writing. Talking. Walking around in circles.

Maydor, the woman next door, kept me relatively sane. She chatted to me over the fence of firewood that separated our miniscule front lawns. (Of course we didn't have real front lawns, just seven-by-ten-foot dust bowls, demarcating individual territorial space.) She plied me with tea and leftovers from her family's evening meal. When I looked as if I needed cheering up, Maydor filled my pockets with sweets and Kashgari apricots. Each morning she would raise my hopes by saying, "Maybe goti comes today. Maybe goti comes tomorrow." Then goti's wife, who lived on the other side of my cell, would duck her head around the corner and say "Maybe goti never come back at all!"

I started channeling my energies into writing children's books. Wombat and Emu were the two central characters, who explored countries such as exotic Thailand, Japan, and of course Tibet. I wrote the stories in rhyming verse— an attempt to keep my sanity. Wombat and Emu became my best friends. We explored each others minds and experiences; plodded over old ground and new. They were the only people in the settlement who could speak English, and it didn't matter a bit that they were merely fictitious.

I toyed with the idea of sharing Wombat and Emu with Drula. Drula was about ten, a pretty little real live girl with a heart of gold. Each day she would come and knock on my door, or cough loudly to get my attention when I was sitting in the midday sunshine, and she would pour little sweaty apricot kernels from her tiny soft palm into my own. She would blush and smile and run away, or, on bolder days, sit beside me for hours on end, twisting the ends of her pigtails. Often a ruddy-cheeked little sister would trail behind in Drula's shadow—hiding from view. Sometimes Drula would take my hand and walk with me out onto the plain. We never talked. Just enjoyed the silence and the hugeness of the sky together. One morning I heard her mother chastise her for spending so much time with me. There was work to be done around the house and Drula should have been lending a hand. There wasn't much else for a child to do in that place.

On my fourth day in Shongba, three of the five families living in the settlement had to move from their old row of house-boxes to new concrete ones, built on the other side of the toilet block. Emu and Wombat gracefully retired to the prison and I danced off to help Drula's family with the big move.

We scavenged wheelbarrows from around the town and loaded all kinds of paraphernalia into the carts, racing them to and fro across the uneven dust and gravel pathway. It was amazing to think so much accumulated junk had actually fit into such a tiny house. Bags broke and cupboards collapsed. Tins of petrol split and old toys were discovered with glee and discarded with shocking ruthlessness. When new loads failed to fill my barrow, I poked Drula's little sister into the remaining space and jiggled her slowly down the path. She squealed with exquisite pleasure and excitement as we gathered momentum. On the return journeys she clung for dear life to the edge of the metal cart—her knuckles white from pressure, her lips blue with fear. Her little bottom bounced and her stubby legs quivered beneath torn and dusty overalls. I had obviously missed my calling in life. I should have been a roller coaster operator. A ride in my barrow was the ultimate thrill.

It was starting to get cold in Shongba. Each morning, before my neighbors awoke, I sneaked out into the frosted air and stole twigs from their wood piles. I had not yet perfected the art of starting fires with sheep dung and the like, and needed good old-fashioned paper and twigs to get mine burning. My diary got thinner. Wood piles got mysteriously smaller. Billowing clouds of telltale smoke rose from my chimney long before dawn. In the afternoons I roamed the windswept plains collecting dry horse and yak

dung to keep the home fire burning in the evenings. Maydor used to soak a few pieces in kerosene for me. A single
match—whooosh, warmth and singed eyebrows.

Hailstorms generally preceeded sunset. While I waited
for the smoke to clear from my room (it always took half
an hour to find its way up the narrow, blocked chimney
vent) I would climb the hill behind the settlement and
gaze into the vast space above and around, then watch
with awe as clouds raced toward me from the northwest—
clouds on an invisible conveyor belt, moving from the
factory of their genesis toward the distant southern snow
ranges. Oh, how I loved those Shongba skies! The clouds,
the hail, the wind. With a small concrete shelter as a
retreat, the elements were never more than an idle threat.
It was pure joy to spit in the eye of a storm and escape the
rains of revenge. From the summit of my hill I called to
the sky, challenged it. Send me a storm! Drown me! And
when the clouds fell from their production belt and shattered, I would run for cover, laughing.

One morning as I was filling a bucket with icy water at
the village well, the Chinese film reconnaissance team
whom I had met on their way to Mount Kailas motored
past and pulled up with the customary screech of brakes.
What are you doing here? We thought you'd be in Lhasa by
now! Ahhh. Good question. I explained my predicament as
best I could and accepted with good grace another loaf of
their stale bread and more condolences.

From the rear of their Land Cruiser tumbled a rather
rattled round ball of hitchhiker. Well, well, well. It was
Tashi, one of the pilgrim women I had picnicked with on
Mount Kailas. She was equally surprised to see me again
and reached for my hands in greeting. She looked radiant
beneath the dust, her smiling eyes filled me with hope.
When the film crew left to return to Lhasa, I helped Tashi
pitch a cotton lean-to and when I saw its flimsiness, I
begged her to share my room for the duration of her stay
in Shongba. Despite my lengthy insistence, she would not
accept the offer.

I did not challenge the sky that evening. I knew my audacity riled the storm gods and tonight, with Tashi so vulnerable in her pathetic little shelter, I prayed their fury would abate. Instead of climbing the hill, I sat inside Tashi's lean-to, munching flat bread and blood sausage while she taught me the outmoded art of spinning wool on a chopstick.

Tibetans are the most generous people on earth. Whatever they have, they will share. It doesn't matter who you are. It doesn't even matter if they have next-to-nothing. Half of next-to-nothing isn't very much, but it's yours. A twisted nob of blood sausage and a piece of stale Tibetan bread may not, in all honesty, satisfy the belly, but the love, the caring, the innocence and unselfishness which flow as condiments with the meal, make the heart replete. In a materialistic sense, Tashi had nothing more than that cotton lean-to, a bag of zumpa, and a swag of mantras. But spiritually, she had everything. When she wasn't looking I tucked a ten-yuan note between the last few pages of her mantra. She would never have accepted it from me.

The next morning the goti arrived, full of apologies for his delayed return. There had been a big meeting in Ali, of all the headmen, and Gêgyai's representative had already warned Shongba's headman about my probable presence in his village. The goti's wife made a mutton stew and rice and we feasted for an hour, discussing plans. It would take a day or two to get a companion and a horse organized. But there was plenty to do in Shongba, the town's resources were formally at my disposal. Plenty to do? If it weren't for Emu and Wombat, I would have needed a straitjacket and an ambulance to take me to Yagra! The thought of having to spend two more days in Shongba was a bit too much for me to stand. I twitched, itched, ached to be forging onward. Patience will never be one of my stronger virtues. I was born two weeks late and, for the rest of my life, I will be burdened by congenital guilt. Always hurrying—trying to make up for fourteen days of lost time. I am sure if I had been born prematurely, the weight of eight, long days in Shongba would not have been so heavy.

Wombat and Emu went to Paris. Suddenly, a beautiful black stallion galloped down the Shongba Champs Elysées, under the whip and call of a handsome herdsman. The reincarnation of Napoleon Bonaparte, a nomad named Yarbo blew into town on the wind. However, his enigmatic face belied heroism, and his two thin plaits were a far cry from shining locks. He wore an ancient felt hat and when he smiled, his missing front teeth put an end to my romantic notions. I left Emu and Wombat beneath a moonlit Arc De Triomphe, savoring snails and French champagne, and ran to my cell to collect my possessions.

We had the horse loaded and raring to go in under half an hour. I hurried around and farewelled everyone in Shongba, then Yarbo and I started walking to Yagra. Drula followed us with a gift of apricot kernels and a smile. I was free. It was almost too good to be true. The sky was clear and I felt like singing. Halfway across the plain, I turned to face Shongba for the very last time. My dream had not died, just slipped into a temporary coma. The speed with which it had regained its clarity was miraculous. Eight days melted away in eight minutes.

Yarbo grew tired after five hours of walking. He mounted the already heavily weighted stallion and left me to follow at a steady pace, alone. He was a garrulous man, and a strange silence hung on the early evening breeze behind him. I ambled along, feeling a new freedom from burdens. No pack upon my back. No nagging fears of being lost. I crossed the edge of a dry salt plain and caught up to my companion on the edge of another long plain. There was water ahead. A river. A hundred "jung"—wild Tibetan donkeys—were standing on the distant bank. The sun caught their forms; the reflection of the light on the water dappled their underbellies. They were the links of a golden chain, suspended beneath the breasts of mountains. As we approached, the chain fragmented. The links went wild and danced away to safer ground, disappearing between folds of soft velvet pasture.

Yarbo pointed to anything that moved and named its species in Tibetan, mimicking appropriate movements and sounds to make sure I understood. An endearing sandy-colored lizard named "apuchee-poo" quickly became our favorite creature. Whenever Yarbo saw one, he tested my skill at recalling its name, keeling over with laughter as I pretended to unleash a mighty sneeze. Ah, ah, ahpuchee-poo! The tiny reptile would invariably scuttle off in fright. Yarbo would laugh some more and keep riding, eyes riveted to the bare earth, searching for more victims.

We reached the camp of one Ama Samgee, and hobbled our horse by the riverside. She shooed us inside her frail tent and poured endless quantities of tea into our cups. She and her daughter talked. And talked and talked and talked. The younger woman's face was comically adorned with sugar makeup. Lines and circles exaggerated her many facial expressions. Two thin lines swayed between her eyebrows, across the ridge of her nose, and over her eyelids, terminating on either side at the temple. When she opened her eyes wide with surprise the painted lines contorted, eyeballs bulged, and a sister was born unto Marty Feldman. When she smiled, her colored cheeks swelled and she became a delicious plum pudding. When she gasped, one could almost pop a ping-pong ball down her throat, mistaking her for a laughing clown at a fairground sideshow.

Ama Samgee and I wandered down to the river to collect water. The sun had set and the western sky glowed with pink and blue shafts of light. Tonight I would see my second Tibetan full moon. With water vessel full, I turned to help Samgee to her feet, accidentally spilling half the pot of icy liquid all over her huge sheepskin coat. She just laughed, cackled like a hen, and slowly refilled my big saucepan. She steadied herself on my arm and we wobbled awkwardly back toward the camp. A string of bells around her middle jingled as we moved. Suddenly she stopped dead in her tracks. I could almost hear the hairs on the back of her neck stand to attention. Samgee held her breath and motioned for me to do likewise. She closed her eyes, and I mine. Suddenly there was music. For a number of seconds, there was music. Apollo was playing the lyre at a banquet of the gods. The muses were smiling. A camp dog barked in the distance and the music was gone. I had either gone completely crazy or just heard the Pythagorean philosopher's song of the spheres. I looked at Samgee. She had heard it too. But she *was* a little mad. Her bells and her laughter rang all the way back to the camp.

My night was plagued by fear of madness, eerie dreams, and absurd visions. Ama Samgee and her daughter talked incessantly, on and on and on. The goats outside sniffed and snorted. Yarbo snored. A single dog yawned and trotted off across the pebbled ground. With all the logic I could muster, I tried to dispel the music I had heard—had not heard, I had imagined—or not imagined. I couldn't sleep.

As the dung embers of the fire began to fade, I reached over and gave Ama Samgee a photograph of the Dalai Lama. When she realized what it was, she gasped and quickly, respectfully touched the portrait to her head. Her daughter did the same, then returned the photograph to Samgee, who bounced it up and down on the crown of her sleeping grandson. She reached up and slipped the picture under a rope on the roof of her tent. She prostrated before it, her weathered hands oblivious to the hot ashes she touched. One hundred and eight times she thus expressed supplication to her god. Exhausted, she sat down silently and fingered her Buddha-beads. She smiled at me in the light of a moonbeam, falling through the smoke vent of her tent. Her mind, body, and soul were as one. In perfect harmony. Perhaps that was the music I had heard.

In the morning, Ama Samgee leapt up from beneath her

heavy bedding and began dancing around in a small circle, laughing hysterically. She was naked except for a pair
of boots and a sheepskin tied around her bottom. She
hopped from one foot to the other, puffing warm air into
her cupped hands. She was anxious to get a pot of tea
brewing on the fire, but had kicked over the saucepan of
water, spilling all that had been collected the previous
evening. I was fully dressed beneath my sleeping bag, and
volunteered to make the dash to the stream. When I returned, Samgee was still undressed, still hopping around
in her circle. Her cheeks were ruddy under a mask of dirt.
Her daughter had set a new fire and leaned above it,
striking a piece of flint against the metal edge of her
tinder box. Outside, Yarbo emerged from a mound of
sheepskins. Ama grabbed her heavy chuba and wrapped
it around her body, suddenly shy and self-conscious. Yarbo
coughed and entered the tent.

Nomad men nearly always sleep outside, under the
stars. The comparatively warm enclosure of a woolen tent
becomes the domain of women, children, and the elderly
after dinner. The nomads sleep in an absurd position—
crouched with backs arched, and knees drawn up beneath
the chest. Foreheads touch the ground and arms are bent
forward, shielding the face and body from the falling
debris of imaginary bombs. Women—mothers and grandmothers—invariably tuck a small child or baby in the
space between their head and kneecaps. How they escape
suffocation is beyond my comprehension. The entire body,
head and all, is covered in undone chubas and sheepskin
blankets. It is not hard to mistake a sleeping nomad for a
pile of dirty laundry.

Ama Samgee and her daughter resumed their midnight
conversation—talking, talking while the sun rose and the
water boiled. Yarbo caught the stallion and loaded it with
all our baggage. We finished our tea and prepared to
leave. Samgee clicked her heels in the air and cackled
"Teshi delay!" Good luck! Off we went toward the sun,
toward new mountains.

An improved-formula infection in my big toe had me going slowly for the duration of the day. We reached the base of the mountains at midday and Yarbo pointed upwards and frowned. We had to climb—slowly, slowly over rough rocks and around boulders, along a dry stream bed and up to a 17,000-foot pass. About halfway up the steep mountainside we crossed a small trickle of water and paused for a drink. A thick layer of ice covered the many small ponds of the broken stream. The ground was a mass of hedgehog-shaped islands of yellow-green turf and we hopped from one to another trying to keep our boots dry. On top of the pass we rested again. The wind raced around us, cooling the sweat on our cold, clammy bodies, instilling a chill right through to our bones—I grabbed my down jacket from the load on the horse. I gazed over the vast landscape sprawled below. It seemed a mass of mountain ridges. The enormous plains which took hours to cross were insignificant, narrow valleys, snaking between the massive, sculptured mountains. Ridge after ridge, row after row they stretched—like some giant pastel meringue, bleached by the intensity of the sun to hues of light yellow, pink, and blue.

Yarbo handed me a bone to gnaw on, and a piece of steamed bread his wife had prepared for our journey. I started to shiver and signaled to Yarbo, let's get going.

On the other side of the pass we entered a steeply descending valley, running with the wind down precariously steep slopes. Down, down, down, until we were walking along a deep cleavage between the domes. We crossed another river, then turned with it and entered a second long vale. We met some yak herdsmen and sat with them briefly, trying to get sound directions to the next nomad camp. Yarbo pointed at the sun and ran his finger in a short arc toward where the giant orb would eventually set. We'd reach a camp in about two hours. It was so lovely to be traveling with someone whose wristwatch banded the sky.

Yarbo mounted the horse again and I trailed behind its

swaying rear, trying to concentrate on its hypnotic rhythm rather than that of my pulsating toe. I strained my eyes, trying to see the camp. Nothing. We walked on and on. Nothing. Yarbo pointed to another mountain top and sighed. Up we go again my little tired pilgrim. Yarbo reached the summit on horseback, and collapsed with fatigue in the saddle. Sheep droppings marked a trail down the lee side of the mountain. Five nomad tents dotted the valley below us. We headed for the closest tent, and reached it in just over an hour, limping slowly over rocks and the streams trickling from the main river. Yarbo was completely done in. Although he had volunteered to take me all the way to Yagra, he would prefer to return to Shongba if we could find a substitute guide. We talked to a young boy at the first tent and he directed us to the last camp, nestled beneath a natural outcrop of rock at the base of a snow-covered peak. The nomads there had horses, yaks. And they would be more than happy to take me the rest of the way to Yagra, he thought.

So we walked. And walked some more. I could not look toward the camp for fear of it escaping farther into the distance. We must have covered over thirty miles that day, starting at sunrise. A full twelve hours.

I looked up. Yarbo, in excited relief, was greeting a tall thin nomad. The latter shook my hand and a smile creased his warm face from ear to ear. Four teeth divided the huge dark void of his mouth. What an adorable man! His small eyes sparkled with so much love and happiness. His wife stood by the doorway of their tent, her thin, Bo Derek plaits gray with age. The last of the sun's rays caught her wiry, matted hair and turned it into a gentle halo. I greeted her, touching hands and foreheads lightly and together we entered the tent. I collapsed on the ground before the old couple's youngest daughter had a chance to put a skin down for me to sit on. Everyone laughed—the infectious, simple laughter of the nomads.

Yarbo tried to pull me to my feet and our host slipped a small, worn lambskin under my bottom. The old nomad

smiled at me again, pointed to himself and said "Apa."
Just call me Dad. I've always wanted another daughter! I
took off my shoes and socks to warm my feet by the central
fire. My toe was swollen with puss and throbbing. Apa
produced a bottle of antiseptic he kept for healing punc-
ture wounds and scratches incurred by his family and
livestock. He dabbed the liquid all over my toe with his
long, arthritic index finger. My toe glowed nicotine-yel-
low. I baa-ed like a goat to show my gratitude. He laughed
again and rumpled my hair in a fatherly way, sucked the
air out of his cheeks, and smiled. Operation over.

     After dinner, I pulled out my battered topographic map
and pinpointed our location on it. Apa was fascinated by
the colorful document. I pointed to Burang, Barga, Mount
Kailas, Moincêr, Ali, Gêgyai, and Yagra—showing Apa
and his family the way I had walked to reach their camp
and my intended journey beyond it. The map wasn't big
enough to show the route all the way to Lhasa. Apa looked
at me, took the map from my hands, turned it upside
down, turned it over, looked at me again, and said,
"Where's Australia?" He had no idea, no conception of the
world at all beyond his narrow valley. Australia, like India, was just "over there" somewhere. Over a few mountain ranges.

     And the rest, Apa? How do you explain to someone who
has probably never seen a plane before, perhaps never
heard a radio, never seen a television nor spoken on a
phone, the mind-boggling magnitude of Planet Earth?
The continents! The oceans! Ah, yes Apa. Australia is just
over here. Just off the map. About ten million miles—ah—
six days' ride on a yak from Lhasa. I hope to goodness my
friend never comes looking for me! The farthest Apa had
ever ventured beyond his valley was when, many years
ago, he made a pilgrimage to Mount Kailas. As the crow
flies (and the experienced nomad goes), Kailas wasn't so
far away. He had teamed up with his father to make the
journey. They had trekked a shortcut route over many
ranges and reached Kailas in ten days. I had obviously

taken the long way round, since I had left Kailas more
than a month ago. But then Apa said, his journey was
made a long, long time ago. And this place—this place is
bigger now. Comforting words.

In the morning, Apa went off on his own tan mare to
round up his yak herd from an adjacent valley. Ama
walked off into the distance, destination unknown. One
daughter led the family's sheep and goat herd away to
greener pastures. Chō-Yin, Apa's youngest girl, helped me
to wash my hair in water so cold it froze, and made a
cardboard wig of my lackluster locks.

Chō-Yin and I went down to visit Tsōmo (this was a
common name for nomad girls), another daughter, for the
day. My hair quickly softened and dried by Tsōmo's fire.
Apa wanted Tsōmo to braid my hair so I would look more
Tibetan, more like his daughter. It was not long enough to
plait, so when it had dried, Tsōmo rubbed rancid butter
all through my hair. Her husband Shō-Sum passed me a
plastic-rimmed mirror, about the size of a powder com-
pact, and I peered at my reflection. For the first time in
weeks my hair had been clean and now, just seconds later,
it hung lifelessly, caked in pungent grease. Tsōmo and
Shō-Sum thought I looked beautiful. How reassuring. Perhaps I should have photographed myself for the cover of a
girly magazine or an advertisement for the latest in alternative shampoo and hairspray products. Yak butter—the
styling gel of the future.

After milking the goats, Apa's wife and two daughters
joined us by the fireside. Yarbo and Apa were deep in
conversation, discussing new plans for my passage to Yagra. I strained to keep my ears and eyes open. While Apa
spoke, he rolled small balls of white flour dough between
his palms and tossed them into a pot of boiling meat juices
on the fire. His wife hacked off strips of meat from a
sheep's carcass and added them to the thick, soupy stew.
Apa pointed at the evening meal. "Togba." He pointed at
my aluminum cup. "Puru." He pointed at his hollow mouth
and said, "Apa so ming-du." Dad's got no teeth. I dissolved

in laughter. When he finished making flour balls, he wiped the sticky globs of dough from his hands and reached behind the domestic altar at the end of the tent, directly opposite the doorway. He pulled out a small cloth bundle and slowly, carefully, undid the knotted string holding the precious parcel together. A pile of letters lay between the dusty rags. He unfolded each one, as if it would disintegrate beneath his fingers. He beamed with pride. Letters from India. Photographs. Blurred portraits of exiled relatives and recent Polaroids of His Holiness the Dalai Lama. He could not read the words on the thin airmail pages and asked Yarbo to translate the script into dialect. Apa listened intently to every word. He had had those letters a few months now, waiting for a literate visitor to read them to him. His face glowed. I remembered how my mother used to read "The Night Before Christmas" to my brothers and sisters and me. "Twas the night before Christmas, and all through the house, not a creature was stirring, not even a mouse. . . ." We hung on every word, like the baubles on the tree itself; eyes sparkling, hearts racing, anxious to hear the next page and the next. It was a wondrous tale, and the infrequent evenings on which it was read are the most cherished of all my childhood memories. I looked at Apa. At Ama. At their two lovely daughters. They were my family. Yarbo read the special letters with the passion and warmth of my incredible mother, over and over again. A tear formed in the corner of my eye and trickled unnoticed down my cheek.

I was amazed that the letters and photographs, sent from Dharamsala, had escaped censorship on their journey through China. And how they actually found their way out to Nomads' Land was completely mystifying.

Shō-Sum was hard at work constructing himself a new sheepskin chuba. A pile of skins had been laboriously softened and using a tiny Chinese penknife, he cut sections of the skins and maneuvered them into place before sewing. I watched as he carefully measured sleeves and yoke

sections with the span of his hand, wiping charcoal from
the firepot onto his fingertip, then on the skin, thereby
marking the exact point at which to wield his blade. A
needle was threaded with thick-ply wool, and Shō-Sum
deftly stitched the garment together. It would be finished
by nightfall. I took several photographs and vowed to send
them to Pierre Cardin at a later date. Yarbo was anxious
to return to Ama Samgee's, and galloped off on a black
stallion, planning to make the trip in a single day.

Tsōmo made a rice and mutton stew for lunch, then
organized kitchen implements around the fire for making
fresh barley flour. She heated a deep-sided dish half-full
of coarse, black, river silt. She tossed presoaked barley
into the sand when it was sufficiently hot, then quickly
picked up the dish (using woolly bits of sheepskin for pot
mitts) and tilted and jiggled it so the sand and barley
blended evenly. As the vessel moved, the barley roasted
gently in the river silt. In a matter of seconds the grains
popped like corn in an oiled skillet. Tsōmo sifted the sand
from the barley through a handmade sieve fashioned from
a flat piece of tin punctured by hundreds of nail holes. The
river silt passed through it efficiently.

Then she knelt down on the ground and dragged a
heavy, stone grinding wheel onto a tightly woven piece of
calico cloth. The grinding device looked like a squashed,
gray hamburger bun. The stone slabs, half a yard in diameter, were sandwiched together and the popped grain
fed through a hole in the center of the top slab. Tsōmo
turned that slab against the bottom one using a handle so
that the grain fell through the hole, was crushed between
the two grinding stones, and spilled as flour onto the calico
sheet.

Sō-Num, her twenty-month-old son, delighted in steal-
ing handfuls of the warm, popped barley and tried to poke
his tiny, fat fingers in between the grinding discs as his
mother worked. He disappeared behind her shoulders and
popped his head up occasionally as if playing a game of

hide-and-seek. His deep saucer-shaped eyes sparkled, his teeth flashed, and his cheeks dimpled. A long curly mop of matted hair bounced and bobbled like an ill-fitted wig as he wobbled around the tent distributing his treasures, scavenged from his latest dig around the family's fire-pot. Chō-Yin received a piece of wool on a stick, Shō-Sum, a long-forgotten piece of flat bread.

The day wore on. Outside, the wind howled and fresh snow swirled around the tents in billowing clouds. Chō-Yin and I returned to Apa's tent to prepare a fire for his return. Ama had gone visiting, and wouldn't be back for several days. I hoped she had reached a camp before the blizzard had struck. Chō-Yin's other sister came back with the sheep and goats just at sunset, and Apa finally returned with his yaks an hour after dark.

We sat around the fire, silently absorbing its warmth. Apa emptied his knapsack, handing us each a lump of boiled mutton. He pointed at his mouth again and laughed. It is not easy to chew tough meat with so many teeth missing. He gave me a few gifts then, for my journey—a small block of dry Tibetan tea leaves and a huge lump of hard butter, preserved in a tight-fitting shell of dried goat-stomach lining.

He reached behind the altar and grappled in the dark for a small calico bag. Chō-Yin lit the butter candles on the altar. The tarnished bronze candle holders shimmered in a golden hue of light. She spooned a small quantity of sage onto a metal disc. Apa lit it and the perfumed smoke wafted gently around the tent. Apa started chanting, softly whispering the mantras of his faith. He removed a conical lump of clay from his calico bag and placed it on the palm of my hand. He closed my fingers around the tiny mountain and gestured for me to put it in the pocket of my backpack. He took out another clay peak and broke off minute fragments, handing them to his daughters and to me. The girls silently slipped the clay particles into their mouths and I did likewise. Apa continued chanting. He put a piece of the clay under his own tongue and smiled at me, saying quietly "Strength. Mount Kailas. Great strength."

Apa took a flat, dented piece of tin and scooped a piece of smoldering horse manure from the fire. He sprinkled sage onto the ember and passed it to Chō-Yin. She lifted her braided hair and tilted her head to one side. The sage smoke entered her young soul through her earhole. Apa took the sage-covered ember and let the smoke spiral up into his nostrils and then under his armpits. The wind had died down and the only sound was that of his melodious chant. Not a creature was stirring, not even a goat . . .

I let the smoke rise into my own ears and passed the ember on to Apa's other daughter. Chō-Yin prostrated herself a few times before the framed pictures of His Holiness. The candlelight reflected on the glass of the frame and for a moment the gentle, flickering glow brought the Dalai Lama and the other postcard deities to life. The curious ritual ended. I said nothing. I was overwhelmed by a feeling of acceptance—an unspoken bond of intimacy. The whole world, the universe, had been sucked into that tent. The entire solar system was no bigger than an ember in the fire. There were no answers to the dilemmas of the heart, for tonight there were no questions. Only acceptance. Closeness and security. Ah, this was Tibet. More than the mountains, and the vast, endless skies. I had found the soul of the country at last, found it in the smell of burning sage, the chant of "Om Mani Padme Hum," the warm and loving smile of Apa, and the flickering of a candle flame.

Shō-Sum arrived at the crack of dawn, looking like a handsome model from the fashion pages of *Nomad's Weekly*. His new chuba was smashing. A number of scarves were tightly wrapped around his neck to keep out the frosty, morning chill and an old felt hat was pulled down low over his brow. He had been about a mile away, visiting his best friend, Gyardup. The latter had decided to come with us to Yagra and we would collect him on the way. We loaded up Apa's horse. It was hard to say good-bye, and hello to lonely mountains and sky again. I took photos of Apa and his daughters standing outside their tent in the golden glow of sunrise. Chō-Yin had plastered fresh sugar makeup on her face for the occasion. Shō-Sum and I walked off into the mountains and Apa's warm eyes followed us until we were out of sight. We climbed a ridge and crossed over into another valley, reaching Gyardup's camp in under an hour.

We had tea with his wife and young children—all six of them. They were a wild-looking dusty band of ragamuffins, not unlike prehistoric cave dwellers. Wild, matted hair, tough, bare feet, bodies swathed in roughly crafted sheepskins. Gyardup put saddles on another two horses and redistributed the weight of our collective belongings, then led the three horses down to the ice-covered river.

I hadn't ridden a horse since I was seventeen and had totally forgotten how to mount one. Something was missing. Ah ha! Stirrups and a saddle. My small black mare had neither. An oblong of Tibetan carpet was draped across her back and secured with a woolen rope. My pack had been separated into two portions and they were tied on with a second strap near her hips. Gyardup gallantly offered his knee as a stepping stone and I clumsily straddled the beast. I was petrified. What if she throws me? Takes off into the wild blue yonder? Oh God. Panic set in. I clutched onto the reins around my horse's neck and crossed the river behind Shō-Sum and Gyardup. The horse stumbled. I screamed. Shō-Sum and Gyardup laughed. Oh dear, it was going to be one of those days.

But by the time we reached the end of the valley I was riding like a seasoned professional. Provided the horse didn't bend forward, tilt to one side, attempt to trot or worse still, canter, I felt completely calm and in control.

Shō-Sum taught me how to yodel like a nomad and Gyardup entertained us with jokes and fantastic tales I only half understood but fully enjoyed. We stopped at every camp in the valley and took photographs and shopping lists. Going into town, are you, Shō-Sum? Just pick me up some tea and sugar, there's a dear. Buy some sweets for the children will you? Here's a fleece to barter. "Kali-pay!" Goodbye!

For a while I felt like a real cowboy, roaming the West. While the men yodeled, I sang. But after a while, I started to get a touch saddle sore despite, or perhaps because of, my lack of saddle! My bottom became the butt of Gyardup's jokes. The riding game became agony, sheer agony. Gyardup laughed. He rode up alongside me and whipped my poor black mare to make her trot. I bounced out of control, up and down, bang-bang-bang. Even an orthopedic specialist would think twice before referring to that mare's spine as a backbone.

By the time we reached Yagra late that afternoon, I was walking again, more awkwardly than ever. I felt like a lady of ill-repute after a very financially successful weekend.

Shō-Sum and Gyardup hitched the horses onto the guy rope of a large white marquee pitched just outside the town. They told me to go inside and rest while they unloaded the beasts. I wandered through the opening of the large tent and stood for a few moments readjusting to the internal gloom. Eyes stared. I moved over to introduce myself to the group of men huddled over something in the far corner of the tent. It was a mah-jongg board. Empty Chinese whisky bottles lay strewn on the ground. Empty whisky bottles. Cigarette butts. Money. No tea. No women.

Suddenly a crazed Goliath rose from the circle of gamblers. His sword flew out from its long sheath. He yanked the thick red tassel looped around his forehead, and let it dangle loose from the end of his single matted plait. His face tensed with anger. His lips parted and a spine-chilling scream severed the uncomfortable silent air. I turned and ran. Oh my God!

My legs wouldn't work properly. I tripped outside the

entrance to the tent, fell heavily, face-first into the dust, and rolled over onto my back. A flash of silver . . . Oh my God . . . oh my God. The sword slashed through the collar of my down jacket and caught on a metal stud. My heart felt like a punching bag, splitting beneath the repeated blows of a boxer's fists. Round two took place in my head.

Goliath towered above me, his forehead dripping with sweat. He was screaming. A feather from my torn collar lifted gently on the breeze and landed on my upper lip. Oh God, oh God . . . don't sneeze Sorrel. The blade of a sword is an inch from your jugular vein. Don't even breathe. I suddenly thought, "Do I have clean underwear on and ten cents in my pocket for a phone call?" Oh, my mother was a wise woman. How well she had prepared my psyche for danger. Ten cents. Ten cents. Concentrate on that feeble, useless coinage.

Screaming, screaming. My own silent screams somehow reached the ears of others. The attacker was pulled away, his sword dislodged from my neckline. It wasn't her fault! She didn't know! Or words to that effect. The wild, inebriated giant turned to face Shō-Sum and Gyardup. They were scared witless. The color had drained from their cheeks. The attacker yelled again. Five men tried to hold him down. I focused on the veins in his arms, the blood vessels bursting with fury and throbbing above his white-knuckled fists. I thought the handle of his sword would crush beneath the pressure of his anger. He screamed still, raving like a possessed lunatic. I had entered the domain of men, unwittingly ventured into forbidden territory. Someone had to pay.

It took an hour for Shō-Sum and Gyardup to appease my attacker. I was still shaking, although the sword had long been returned to its sheath. What could I say? I really hadn't known. How could I pay? Not with my life, surely. Shō-Sum stopped quivering and brushed off the incident as pure folly. A drunken misunderstanding. He led me into town, away from the marquee, to the domain of families—women and children. To mothers who could well understand the importance of clean underwear and ten-cent pieces.

I had letters of introduction for Yagra's goti, so Shō-Sum took me straight to his house in the central mud-brick compound. As I half-expected, he wasn't there. He was out of town. I sensed the Shongba chapter of my life was about to be repeated. A crowd gathered. A handful of over-curious souls swelled to a dozen, two dozen, three, four, five dozen. Eyes grew wide all around me. Dozens of wide, staring eyes. I felt completely naked. Stripped. Bare and vulnerable. The goti's wife appeared with a key and led Sho-Sum and me to a minute, rammed-earth room. She opened the door and ushered me inside. Chairman Mao leered down at me from the cobwebbed wall. Shō-Sum dumped my pack in one corner, shook my hand, and departed. I turned to face alone a sea of soul-searing eyeballs.

People were standing on their toes, straining their necks, climbing on each other's backs in an effort to get a better look at me. I might have been an intergalactic being from some unknown constellation. Help! Beam me up, Scottie!

I closed the door, but the eyes found cracks in the timber and tiny patches in the window, free from dust and grime. I jammed my hat into the largest hole in the door. I hung my torn down jacket over the window frame and tore out pages from my diary, stuffing them in every tiny orifice I could find. Then I sat on the edge of the raised, dirt sleeping platform and cried.

Stones bounced off the door. It heaved and wobbled as bodies tried to push it open. A rock shattered through one of the small glass window panes. Laughter and footsteps, running away on the wind. I sat for half an hour, my patience growing thin—my nerves brittle. People gradu-ally moved away, but only to recruit brothers, sisters, uncles, aunts, and grandparents.

The stones hitting the door were driving me mad. I

leaped up and threw the door open. The crowd shuffled
backwards and fell silent. Aha! A lesson from Goliath! I
screamed. Aghh! The crowd laughed. I tucked my tail
between my legs and went back into the room. Chairman
Mao smiled. Those terrible posters! One had adorned the
wall of my cell in Shongba too. Mao—the picture of innocence—rosy cheeks, smiling eyes, hands raised ready to
applaud his red-book-reading comrades. That picture will
haunt me forever.

A soft little tap on the door interrupted my thoughts. It
sounded friendly. Friendlier than pelting stones. I opened
the door an inch and peered out. A gentleman cleared his
throat and asked me if I would like some tea, gesturing
with an imaginary cup to his lips. I sighed. If you can't
beat 'em, join 'em. I accepted his offer and locked the door
behind me. The crowd followed close at heel.

Dorje Tsering (another one!) and his wife were kindness
itself. They had made tea and prepared zumpa, a tin of
candies, and a plate of fried breads to welcome me. I
greeted Mrs. Tsering and sat down on a Tibetan rug
draped across a bed in her claustrophobic home. The
crowd edged inside the door, but held their distance. A
child of no more than eleven years of age sat on the floor
puffing away at a cigarette. I said something inane, like
"You're too young to smoke." Dorje gasped. "Per-gay sing-
giy du gay?" Yes. I do speak Tibetan. "Nyung-nyung." A
little bit. My audience applauded. I launched into my
long-winded tale. They were captivated. "I once had a
donkey . . ." And on and on it went.

At the end of my story I showed Dorje Tsering my map
and asked him how far it was to Parayang. Parayang was
my next port of call after Yagra and lay on the other side
of the Gangdisê Ranges along the banks of the Tsang Po
River. The crowd debated their calculations. Somewhere
between a hundred and a thousand miles. Not bad. I decided to wait and hear the goti's estimation before panick-
ing.

My body ached and my spirit felt heavy with too many

emotions. I could not recall ever having had such a confusing array of intense feelings in a single day. Love, acceptance, security, joy, pain, fear, insecurity, alienation, anger, hatred, compromise, and exhaustion. I walked back to my suffocating room, locked the door, and collapsed on my bed, despite the relentless crowd outside.

Later that evening, a white sheet was hung on the wall outside my room, and an old Chinese "Western" film was subsequently shown on it. Everyone in Yagra had brought along a chair, and efficiently arranged themselves in neat rows, just like the seats at a real movie theatre. Mothers brought along their knitting and fathers smoked cigarettes. They sat, one eye on the silver screen, the other on my door, waiting for it to open. They knew I would have to surface sooner or later to go to the toilet. What a sensible, even subtle way to get another glimpse of the frightened little Martian! I take my hat off to them.

I appeared alongside China's answer to Clint Eastwood at about 10 P.M., stood for all to see for a full three seconds, then fled to the toilet block. Seven little girls followed me in. I squatted over a hole and grinned at them. They grinned back. I pulled up my overalls and turned to leave. The little girls raced over and crouched around the hole, peering down the dark void trying to see if anything was different. They ran back and reported their findings to attentive mothers and grandmas. I saluted Clint Eastwood and returned to my room. Yes, it really had been one of those days.

CHAPTER 7
Nomads' Land

There are good kids in Australia and bad kids. Obnoxious and precocious kids; kids who kick footballs through the walls of greenhouses, bend car aerials, and dare each other to shoplift bubble gum and cigarettes from unguarded store counters. There are kids who huddle in the corners of news agencies, poring over the pages of soft-porn magazines and kids who ride their skateboards into crowds of old-age pensioners on walking sticks just for laughs. But fear not, mothers—you are not alone with your delinquent youths. For every little Western ratbag, there will always be an Eastern equivalent. Even in Tibet. Never in a nomad's camp, but always in a village.

I sat for an hour against a compound wall beneath a hailstorm of stones and devilish laughter, waiting for my juvenile tormentors to tire of their vindictive game. But Tibetan kids, as I had learned earlier, don't bore easily. Patience unrewarded, I tried scaring off the little beasts with one of my bloodcurdling screams, but it only made them war against me more enthusiastically. I could not surrender and retreat to my room—it was too cold in there and the noise of their stones hitting my part-metal door would have driven me crazier still.

Eventually two young women, Lu La and Dra Drung, came to my rescue—dragging me off to a small, warm room for tea and zumpa. The earthen walls of the room were covered in dirty white paper and lengths of floral cotton fabric. A tin-pot stove, identical to the ones in Shongba, sat just behind the door leading into the room. Opposite the door were wooden chests, set up like nomads' altars—only a big magazine picture of Lu La's favorite Chinese movie star held pride of place. Two peacock feathers framed the actress's portrait, and below it stood a large but portable radio tape deck with a white khata, a Tibetan scarf, draped respectfully over the tuning and volume dials. Two vases of purple silk wisteria sat on either side of the player. Narrow bench beds, covered with Tibetan rugs for padding, butted up against the walls on either side of the modern-day altar. At the foot of one sat the fire-stove and at the end of the other, a makeshift wardrobe and a table covered in boxes, bottles, books, and beauty aids. A piece of gaily colored cloth was fastened like a curtain around the legs of the table, turning the space beneath into a food storage cupboard. A shelf behind the door held an array of big black cooking pots and utensils. The two girls were dressed in their best black chubas, plastic jewelry, and brand new woven aprons.

Lu La moistened the earthen floor of her tiny room with water from a second teapot, then swept the bits of paper and food scraps which littered it out the door. Within fifteen minutes, the wind had blown half the debris back into the room and passing neighbors and friends had carried the other half inside on their boot soles. Lu La swept again. And again and again. Between sweeping and pouring cups of tea for Dra Drung, myself, and other transient guests, Lu La redecorated the altar and covered a second small table before it with strange foods and plates of cigarettes and sweets. The tape deck was moved onto the table near the wardrobe and a row of bottles—whisky and beer—arranged in its place. I was thankful Lu La refrained from hanging a khata over the assorted alcohols.

When the room was tidy, she asked me to retrieve my camera and join her and Dra Drung in the compound courtyard. An icy wind was blowing outside but the sky was endless blue, drenched in mid-morning sunlight. Everyone else in town was dressed in his or her best clothes too. The men roamed about the courtyard in gorgeous turquoise, green, or tan knee-length satin chubas and huge fox-skin turbans. They were knotting colorful ribbons and appliquéd felt panels into the manes and tails of their horses. The women were rounding up their freshly scrubbed children, repolishing their halos, and banging the new layers of dust from their bottoms. The ringleader of the notorious "gang of four" stone-throwers was dressed in a miniature military uniform with red stars on the shoulders and another in the center of his ill-fitting cap. He screwed up his face and poked his tongue out at me. It was no courteous greeting, and neither was my response to his insolent gesture. I turned to Dra Drung and asked her what was going on. "Korang hako ming-du gay?" Don't you know? It was Yagra's annual three-day festival. She reeled off a lot of words I failed to understand, then with Lu La, broke into mime to explain what was about to happen. The girls neighed and whinnied like horses, then, on the count of three, took off across the compound, wielding imaginary leather whips. Aha! A horse race!

I followed Lu La and Dra Drung to a spot on the plains about two miles away from Yagra, before the snow-covered mountains. All the women folk and the children of the settlement were assembled. We sat down in the middle of nowhere and awaited the men.

Finally they appeared in a cloud of dust, straddling their glamorously costumed horses. The colorful dust ball became larger and louder as it grew nearer. The men screamed and laughed as they raced their horses in tight circles around the crowd of women and children. Dust and laughter, laughter and dust. It was a miracle no one got trampled to death. It was as if we were on an out-of-control merry-go-round at the fair. Horses, colors, lights flashing, squealing: faster and faster, around and around. It was dizzying. Then suddenly the ride stopped. The men took off across the plain, and the women and children coughed out the dust from their throats and sat down in a neat huddle again; eyes riveted to the fast-dissolving blur of horsemen galloping toward the distant mountains.

We waited. Someone passed me a handful of sweets. A few of the men who had stayed behind argued noisily as they attempted to focus a pair of Chinese plastic binoculars on the horizon. Finally the men screeched and pointed. The race had begun. The crowd jumped to their feet in excitement. The horsemen appeared, stretched across the plain. They were flying toward us on their mounts, screaming like Hollywood Apaches bound for battle, whipping their horses' flanks with narrow bamboo twigs and leather. First, second, third, and fourth flew home. The crowd went berserk. The horses sweated and heaved from exhaustion. Not-so-fit stallions trotted in behind the winners. Ponies all but collapsed on the finishing line. Everyone was singing and laughing and the winning rather misshapen mare was festooned with a garland of ribbons. Her rider was shouldered triumphantly by a dozen smiling men. The jockey received a paltry wad of cash for his prize, then remounted his horse and led the men back to Yagra. The women and kids all followed on foot. The Melbourne cup was over and Phar Lap had won again.

All along my way, I continued to compare Tibetan experiences with Western images. Perhaps this behavior was a way of placing an alien world in a familiar perspective, for the sake of understanding and sanity. When everything inside and around me was so different, I guess I couldn't cope or comprehend it all until I could put it in a Western frame of reference. As I walked back to Yagra with Lu La and Dra Drung, I realized I could never really be a Tibetan, for my mind would always be utterly littered with foreign-ness. I could try—create an illusion—but Western I would always be. I drank the Tibetan barley beer and thought of champagne. I ate the twisted fried breads and thought of donuts. And I smoked dry seeds in neatly rolled strips of newspaper and thought of Benson and Hedges.

In the afternoon, the men formed themselves into teams and had a basketball competition, then everyone joined together for a few hours of singing and dancing. Tibetan dancing is hardly a strenuous affair. Hands are held and feet are shuffled to and fro in monotonous rhythm. To the uneducated ear and eye, all the songs sound the same and all the dance steps look alike. I was quickly initiated and educated in the art of Tibetan music and dance, and now I *know* all the steps and tunes are the same!

After a while Lu La asked me back to her room with a few of her close friends. They locked the door, pulled the curtains and Dra Drung put new batteries into the tape deck. Chinese disco music filled the room. "Dance! Dance! Teach us how to do it your way now!" Oh, God, strike me down with instant paraplegia! Suddenly self-conscious, I tried to excuse myself from the party. The girls pleaded for me to stay and teach them, which meant a moral dilemma for me to solve. If I taught them, would I be adding to the destruction of their culture? If I didn't, was I denying them the right to learn what they want? Oh heavens—may all the purists forgive me—in the end I bumped and jived with glee, as I had done unabashedly in the Lhasa disco with Jigme. The forces of change, sadly, can't be denied.

The next two days were a repeat of my first in Yagra— but the horse races got longer and the basketball competitions more professional. The Yagra team was nearly ready to take on Harlem's Globetrotters. One afternoon, foot races and a rifle-shooting competition were added to the festive program. The gun-toting competitors were either drunk or seemed quite blind (or both) and in consequence few of the empty beer bottle targets were smashed.

On the third day, Yagra's goti came to tell me a nomad friend with a horse had volunteered to guide me to Parayang, and would be ready to leave on the following morning. The goti had returned to Yagra for the start of the festival, and had read my letters of introduction that evening.

I sat in the sunshine for an hour, protected from the wind, writing down my thoughts in my diary. Four days to Parayang. Only a hundred miles or so to reach the southern route! As I wrote, I noticed a toothless man in his fifties eyeing me from a distance. Behind him stood the Khampa—the east Tibetan—who had drawn his knife on me. My heart started pounding with fear as the older man approached. His eyes were bloodshot from alcohol and his words slurred to an unintelligible mutter. He reached into his coat. My muscles tensed. He withdrew a thin, battered wallet. Relief. He handed me a crisp five-yuan note. This was his winnings from the mah-jongg gambling and he wanted me to have it. Without words, he gestured his admiration for my journey across Tibet. I was flabbergasted. Here was a man, dressed in a worn sheepskin chuba and torn black lace-ups, giving me the only money he had in the world. He didn't even have long pants or socks to stop the wind numbing his legs. No, I gestured. Please—I can't take this. You keep it. But he wouldn't take it back, and gave me a sad look of rejection, clearly suggesting I had hurt his feelings. He claimed I needed it more than he. I protested. I have plenty of money for my journey. Please keep it. He laughed. If I had money, I would be taking a truck to Lhasa, like everyone else. I was a pilgrim. Guided by the gods and fed by the people. The five yuan, he gestured, was for food when I reached Parayang. He returned to the half-hidden swordsman and they disappeared from sight.

Compared with Tibetan wallets, mine was bulging. Compared with Tibetan hearts, mine was empty. I could never be a Tibetan, but I had so much still to learn from them, so much about giving and caring. I went back to Lu La's room and tucked the five yuan into my camera bag. I would never spend that money. It symbolized precious wisdom and knowledge. Perhaps in time, there will be a son or daughter to pass it on to.

I fiddled with the tuning dial of the radio on Lu La's tape deck and finally got a crackly reception of Radio Moscow. I was ecstatic! It was the first English-speaking voice I had heard in weeks! I sat with my ears glued to the speaker, listening to a report about a disarmament convention in Geneva. A hopeful sign! I was so happy, I grabbed Lu La and gave her a hug, then waltzed her around the room, banging into furniture and laughing. I translated the gist of the report for her, then went back to the tape deck to listen to some more. Wow, English. I started talking back to the announcer. Lu La doubled over with laughter, and suddenly I realized why. I was speaking to Radio Moscow in shortwave Tibetan.

In the morning, I had breakfast with Lu La's neighbors: the proud parents of the ringleader of my small persecutors. The incorrigible brat proceeded to dismantle my camera bag and pulled out an assortment of lenses and bits and pieces for all to see. There were a couple of long-forgotten tampons in the pile, which as one could well imagine, created a great deal of curiosity—especially since they had tumbled out from my bag along with a collection of trinkets and lucky charms. I held the conical clay icon Apa had given me, and said, "Mount Kailas." I held up a tampon in the other hand, and said, "Australia." All heads nodded in complete understanding.

I had taken the easy way out of a potentially embarrassing situation, yet there was a certain amount of truth in my comparison. The pointed clay dome stood for Eastern spiritual consciousness, my token tampon—Western social awareness. Never the twain shall meet. The female organs of my body had long ceased to function in the high altitudes of Tibet and so my tampons were merely talismans of former femininity. It was absurd to cling to such symbols in a world of higher planes, both physical and spiritual, but cling I did. They were the only reminder I had in this harsh environment, that I was, at one time, capable of functioning like a woman. I closed my eyes and imagined myself in a candle-lit room. I was dressed in a glamorous gown and high-heeled shoes, and I smiled across the elegantly laid table at my faceless beau. I am a woman once more and proud of it.

I came down to earth again, gave the clay mountain to my host, and crammed all my Western odds and ends—my security and sanity—back into my camera case. But my host tapped me insistently on the shoulder and held out his hand, saying, "Australia, Australia—guchi guchi?" So I gave him the tampon which he solemnly placed on his family's altar. I hoped to goodness he would never try feeding it to his children for strength.

The goti came in to tell me the horse was all ready to head south, but Norbor, the requisitioned nomad guide, was somewhat hesitant about the whole business. He was pleading everything from a sore finger to complete insanity before a crowd of chuckling local inhabitants assembled in the compound courtyard. He was an old fellow with very short, gray hair and sad, puppy-dog eyes. His nose—by Tibetan standards, was bulbous, and, wrapped up in his thick sheepskin chuba and knee-high felt boots, he looked exactly like a performing bear from a Russian circus. When he saw me, he bit his bottom lip and quivered. He tapped his index finger to his forehead, rolled his eyes and mumbled, "madness." He reached across and rapped his knuckles on my own skull, held up two fingers on his other hand, and uttered, "double madness."

We eventually waved goodbye to everyone in town and led the heavily laden mare through the compound gates. We got as far as Norbor's worn, calico tent on the other side of the ice-covered stream bordering the settlement, and stopped. Not bad, 200 yards. Time for tea.

While Norbor packed a couple of extra leather satchels with supplies. I fanned the fire into action and made a

rich, buttery brew. Norbor patted me on the head. I wasn't
so bad after all. I casually asked him if he would like a
picture of the Dalai Lama and his face flushed in total
disbelief. I reached into my camera bag and pulled out one
of the photos and passed it to my new friend. Norbor's
voice quavered. His puppy-dog eyes went watery and a
tear leaked out onto his left cheek. He couldn't speak for
several minutes, just stared from the photograph to me
and back again. Finally he cleared his throat, wiped away
the tell-tale teardrop, and found his voice.

Norbor told me how he had been shackled in a Chinese
prison for seventeen years because he had refused to de-
nounce the Dalai Lama. Every time he had muttered "Om
Mani Padme Hum," a soldier had struck him across the
back of his neck with the butt of a rifle. Day by day, year
by year, he had grown physically frail and weak in the
hands of his oppressors. Many of his cell mates had died
from the inadequacy of their pathetic prison diet and from
injuries from torture. Many had yielded to the Communist
doctrine in an effort to diminish the physical punishments
inflicted. Norbor had clung to his faith like a dying moth
to a candle flame. They had whipped and beaten him
continuously, but he refused to let his spirit be broken. He
pulled down one sleeve and turned to show me his right
shoulder. It was covered in long, ugly scars—a constant
reminder of seventeen years of pain and suffering. Seventeen years. At the age of twenty-four, that is not easy to
comprehend, but I got an inkling of what Norbor must
have experienced in those terrible times and I wept as he
told me his story.

He put his ancient arm around me and his glassy eyes
sparkled. He touched his heart and kissed me on the forehead. I had given him compensation for all those long-lost
years—understanding and a portrait of his God-King.
Norbor had heard so many conflicting stories about his
leader's fate, but now I had brought the truth to him. The
Dalai Lama was alive! I had seen him, touched him,
spoken to him, and brought recent photographs to distrib-

ute to his people. And now, Norbor said, he was with us. Bitter memories vanished with a final tear. Mysterious ills and accusations of insanity vanished with a short giggle. We loaded a second old mare and in silence, walked across the plain, hand in hand. Norbor had the picture of His Holiness safely, respectfully, tucked beneath his woolen balaclava. I had my fraying protection cord around my neck. Four days to Parayang. The jewel in the lotus was glistening.

Early in the afternoon, two of Norbor's young friends caught up to us. Namgyal, a handsome, pigtailed nomad, trailed behind a herd of yaks, while Lobsang, a precocious, chain-smoking eleven-year-old boy, rode in front on a pony without a saddle. As we walked alongside them, it became apparent they were joining us on the march to Parayang.

When we all reached a camp on the far side of the plain, another two men and thirteen horses arrived. I took a head count. My expedition comprised twenty-four yaks, seventeen horses, six humans, and, momentarily, a dog. The days of Budget and me alone were long passed. I tried to visualize our troop's arrival in Parayang and hoped the villagers there would not mistake us for an invading army of marauding mountain tribesmen.

We unloaded the animal contingent and crammed inside the single small tent by the riverside. We were all well-received by the living fossil who owned the tent, an arthritic woman named Dolma. She was quick to entertain us with a dozen cups of tea and as many wild tales of days gone by. While we listened to her stories, a baby yak blundered into the tent and proceeded to smother our hostess in wet, sloppy kisses. Dolma had recently become the calf's surrogate mother after its natural parents had both died up country in a blizzard. I took a few photographs of the kissing couple and Dolma shooed her charge out of the tent. Putting a baby yak in a crowded nomad's tent was like putting an epileptic in a shoe-box full of fine bone china. We all pitched in to clean up the post-party mess the calf had left in his wake. All the tea cups, cooking pots, and utensils had been upturned. A layer of dust and ash covered all and sundry.

When things were more or less back to their former semblance of order, I ventured outside to pitch my own tent. Norbor came out to help, and when the dome was erect, he promptly crawled inside and fell asleep.

I went to bed down with Dolma and her young grandson and the other men retired to a place beneath the stars, alongside their dozing yak herd.

In the morning, we pushed on. Norbor and I went ahead with the horses. By midday, the weather had turned foul. An icy wind blew us across another plain and dark clouds dusted the distant foothills of the Gangdisê Ranges with icing-white snow. I fumbled around in my bag for a last remaining piece of chewing gum to give my chattering teeth something to do. We came to Norbor's family tent after a mere ten miles, and decided to call it a day.

Norbor's wife had been sent to work on the roads when he was imprisoned, and was hit on the head at some stage by a large lump of rock. The accident left her without sight in one eye and the Chinese road-gang guards had thrown her with her tiny child to rot in a prison camp somewhere in Tibet. But somehow they survived. When the daughter grew big enough to hold a spade, she was taken back to the road camp. Alone, half-blind, hungry, and in a constant state of fear, Norbor's wife spent the next seven years praying to her gods for peace of mind. How their family was reunited after the end of the Cultural Revolution I will never know. My faith in miracles was strengthened. But seventeen long, empty years of separation had weighed heavily on the relationship between Norbor and his wife, and now they greeted each other as coolly as two acquaintances. Norbor's daughter and son-in-law lived with them, and all the old man's affections clearly flowed out to their son, his only grandchild. While we huddled close to the fire inside the family tent, Norbor cradled the small child on his lap and mumbled stories about the old kingdom of Tibet into his little pink ear.

I picked up a piece of bone from the fireside and sawed it down to an inch-long cylinder, on which I planned to etch with a needle the words "Om Mani Padme Hum." Amazing, the things one can find to do with a Swiss army knife. Norbor wrote the Tibetan characters for me in shaky print on a piece of paper and for the next few hours I sat absorbed in my task, listening to the family discussions and Norbor's animated reports of the horse races in Yagra. He unbandaged his swollen finger to show his daughter. It had become infected and a red line trailed from the edge of the nail all the way down to his wrist. I put down my prehistoric handicraft and wriggled closer to Norbor to get a better look at his finger. It was a mess. It took me half an hour to scrape the dirt out from under the nail and beneath the cuticle and finally I made Norbor soak his pointer in cooled, boiled water and salt. I slashed the side of his first finger joint and drew out what seemed like a cupful of puss and watery blood. Norbor was delighted with the extent of his injury and pretended I was hurting him every time I stopped picking and squeezing at his wound. When I did actually hurt him, he traded in his mock-moaning for some legitimate and serious chanting.

I painted the old man's finger in gentian violet, then bandaged it in a sheath of surprisingly sterile gauze I found wedged in the bottom of my pack, inside a pair of forgotten cotton socks. I tied a small plastic wrapper from a bag of muesli around it for protection from further grime and dust.

Half an hour later, the whole thing had come unraveled and I had to admit to a certain lack of prowess in the art of bandaging. Norbor looked down at the ground like a naughty schoolboy, and admitted he had helped the gauze to unwind while trying to see if his finger was still purple from my "medicine." It was. And dirty again, too. Norbor whined as I washed his finger again, and smiled when I reapplied the horrid purple stuff. I took a photograph of his prized dyed finger and said I would send it to him later, so that he could look at it forever—if he promised to leave my good doctoring alone. He agreed and a big smile spread across his face. I remembered what it was like to go to school with a big plaster cast encasing a broken arm—it was the stuff heroes were made of, and the day the cast came off was always one of gloom. Norbor could boast and brag about his battle wound forever, if he had a photograph of it. I couldn't imagine how I could ever post it to him, but that didn't seem important.

When the tea ran out, there was a dearth of volunteers to trek down to the riverside for more water, so we all got comfortable around the fire to sleep. The wind was blowing a gale and I hoped the other men in our party (who had continued farther down valley with the yaks and unroped horses) were safe. I rolled over and asked Norbor when we would reach Parayang. He giggled and held up four bent fingers. Four days to Parayang. We were not, apparently, making any progress.

The wind did not abate and, by morning, a fine veil of snow covered everything in sight. Norbor and I set off, albeit reluctantly, and met up with the yaks and their masters inside an hour. They had sheltered at another camp and now the various occupants came out to welcome and invite us inside for tea. The horse drivers had charged ahead with their stock to reconnoiter a route for us. Norbor and Namgyal discussed the weather as they unloaded our horses and Lobsang led me into a stained calico tent, then disappeared.

A withered old woman sat alone by the fire-pot, kneading dough. She was quite surprised to see me towering above her, near the doorway, but she dusted the flour from her hands and eased herself up to greet me. I bent low to touch the side of her forehead with my own, and she laughed. Namgyal and Lobsang had told her a "pilgrim woman" was coming, but had failed to mention my Caucasian origins. I sat down to help her with the bread-making and pulled back the sleeves of my down jacket. My hostess's eyes grew wide and she ran her floury fingers all over my forearm in absolute amazement. I thought she deserved a second thrill, so I rolled up my overall-trousers and let her goggle at my hairy legs. I too was stunned by how long the hair had grown in recent months and I was not at all surprised when she renamed me "Ai-ni gya gung-ba"—"The nun with the bearded legs."

Despite the severe wind which whistled through her tent, the old woman had removed her right arm from its snug sheepskin sleeve, baring her thin shoulder and bony chest. An old, coin-sized portrait of the Dalai Lama swung like a hypnotist's pendulum between her breasts as she worked. I gave her one of my card-sized pictures of His Holiness and she abandoned the bread-making for the suddenly more important task of chanting. Without pausing for more than the occasional breath, she gathered together a collection of religious items from around her tent. She polished up a brass candleholder and poured some melted butter into it. She made a wick for the small, shining vessel from a wad of special cotton and unwrapped the dusty cloth tied around her thick pile of Buddhist scriptures. A battered tin drum with a torn, oil-stained "Marvello Margarine" label on it, formed a simple altar.

While she prostrated herself before the photograph, propped up now against the butter candle, a short, balding ball of mirth waddled into the tent, leaning on a polished walking-stick. In one hand he balanced a round china plate, piled high with freshly ground barley flour and a stodgy cone of sweet cheese. The cheese was decorated with red-dyed butter motifs and shriveled-up apricots as dry and wrinkled as the old man himself. He smiled and handed me the plate, welcoming me to the valley. I helped him sit down by the fireside, thinking how easy life would be for aged nomads if Tibetans had invented the armchair. Fortunately, the old man's legs were so short, he didn't have far to bend before his bottom hit terra firma.

His name, he told me, was Dōrdrum. His mouth was completely devoid of teeth and a pair of gold-rimmed glasses balanced on the edge of his narrow nose. They were purely for effect, for every time he looked at me or at my hostess, he peered over the top of the lenses rather than through them. The top of his head was as shiny and smooth as a brass bowl and long gray hair spread out from beneath it like the fluted collar of a clown. He held my hand in his lap and asked me to tell him the story of my journey. He kept turning and tilting his head at an awkward angle. When I eventually realized why he was doing this, I got up and moved to his other side to shout my remarks in his less-deaf right ear. Halfway through my tale, Dōrdrum interrupted and asked me to follow him to his own tent, so I could meet his crippled wife and thus share the story with her. My hostess was still chanting and prostrating herself reverently and there seemed little reason to bother her by excusing ourselves, in the Western manner, from her tent. The wind was blowing a gale again, and transporting Dōrdrum the fifty-yard distance between camps was no small challenge.

Norbor and Lobsang were crouched over the fire and wriggled up to make room for Dōrdrum and me. The old man's wife was ladling soaked barley from a cooking pot into calico feed bags for our horses. She looked up through a hazy screen of smoke rising from the fire-pot, and smiled. The personalities of the aged couple were woven into every fiber of the tent.

The last time I recall seeing such an impressionably personal decor was when I was about four years old, visiting a family friend with my mother. The house was cluttered with the memorabilia of all-too-numerous years, its air was permanently perfumed with the owner's distinctive scent and that of the frangipani trees which grew outside her window. She had sea horses in a small fish tank and wind chimes made from shells hanging in her front garden. No one else I knew had sea horses or wind chimes and no one else I knew had that particularly sweet aroma. When you entered this house, you understood the old lady herself. They were as one, inseparable.

Old Dōrdrum's tent was claustrophobic with collected odds and ends and heavy with a smell equally as distinctive, but not nearly as sweet, as my childhood friend's perfume. Nomads are not great bathers and since it is invariably too cold to remove one's clothes in the higher regions of Tibet, body odors are not exactly pleasant. When combined with the ever-present smell of rancid yak butter and burning dung, a comparison with frangipani and eau de cologne clearly borders on the ridiculous.

Dōrdrum's domestic altar was an old chest covered by a stained canvas sack. Upon it, framed portraits of various spiritual leaders and an unopened tin of Chinese mandarin segments stood behind a row of cheese and butter sculptures similar to the one the old man had presented to me earlier. He explained that they were offerings typical of the Kharmapa sect of Tibetan Buddhism. A set of four posters and prints of painted deities hung above the altar from a thin string.

Dōrdrum showed me some ancient, stained books, illustrated with fast-fading watercolor sketches, and I spent a lively hour trying to pry intelligible tales of Tibetan folklore from my toothless companion.

The scouting horsemen returned with their unruly charges and delivered a rather depressing weather report. Snow thinly covered the foothills, and presumably the higher we ventured into the Gangdisê Ranges, the thicker it would become. The men did not think it would be possible for horses to cross the snowbound mountains. My heart sank. But what about the yaks? We had twenty-four of them—surely we could make it. They were fitted with four-wheel-drive gear boxes, and were not so apt to sink in inhospitable terrain. Norbor decided to take the horses as far as possible before rearranging our expedition plans. We wandered outside to start again.

Namgyal had thrashed my pack horse down the river valley in pursuit of the horsemen and now the mare was sweaty and tired. Norbor tried to fasten the saddle onto another beast—a black-as-night stallion with a lightning-bolt temper. He motioned for me to mount the fiery-eyed animal and I gulped back my fear and swung my leg over. I got up, but I didn't stay there for long. Nightmare bucked and reared up on his back legs as if he were auditioning for a Hollywood western, and I came flying off and landed headfirst on the hard earth. Minor injuries: a chipped tooth, grazed chin, bruised hip, and very crushed pride. Norbor realized, at last, why I preferred to walk rather than ride.

My baggage went back on the gentle, tan mare and Norbor straddled his own short, gray mount and off we went into the wind. It was unspeakably cold. The wind tore at my clothes and tried in vain to blow the horses sideways into the icy river. They stumbled and tripped continuously, yet battled on like stoic veterans. Norbor rode on, and I dragged my throbbing hip alongside him. He "Omed" relentlessly, trying to warm his spirit and body through prayer. Lobsang had galloped ahead with the horsemen, and Namgyal trailed behind with the four-legged Land Cruisers. I don't know what had happened to the dog.

The valley narrowed, widened, twisted, and turned. We floundered over two short passes, and viewed—with trepidation—the seemingly ever-receding Gangdisê Ranges. Halfway down the second pass, Norbor produced a pair of binoculars and asked me if I knew how to operate them. I focused, and scanned the horizon for camps. A third of the way up what appeared to be a hillside gully were two white dots and a black one. Two sheep and a yak, or, perhaps, three very, very distant tents. I showed Norbor the direction in which to point the binoculars. At that moment, a great gust of wind, moving with the speed of a Tokyo-to-Osaka express train, threw Norbor off balance, and he toppled off his mount and rolled, screaming, down the steep embankment. Both the horses reared in fright, then bolted.

Disaster. Their retreat caused a landslide of rubble, which fell like shrapnel around the still-tumbling body of Norbor. He reached the bottom of the earthly roller coaster with an audible thud. My heart was racing. I peered down. Norbor wasn't moving. Oh God, no! Come on, this isn't fair. Not Norbor, not now. The landslide was fast threatening to bury him.

I moved several yards to the left and began a rapid, zigzag descent down the slope. I kept slipping. My legs were like half-set jelly. Norbor is dead, I thought, you've killed him. Norbor is dead. It's all your fault. Over and over inner voices cursed me. I wiped the tears from my eyes and looked again. The only thing moving was my horse—galloping, still laden, far off across the plain. Norbor's gray mare had vanished.

I stopped a few yards short of Norbor's body and stared. He lay on his side, his eyes in a fixed gaze toward the horizon. He was half-buried by the loose debris. Blood clotted on his left temple. The wind stopped. Time stopped. A small apuchee-poo darted over the old bear's torn boots. I crouched down over Norbor and wept. Oh, Norbor. The tears rolled on like the waves of an ocean. I closed my eyes. Black, black, black.

"Om Mani . . . Om Mani Padme Hum." Agh! Who was that?

"Om Mani . . . Om Mani Padme Hum?" Norbor rolled over onto his back and stared up at me with a look of confusion, then smiled cheekily, as if to say, "What took you so long? Did you miss the shortcut?"

"You old devil! I thought you were dead!" Even though I screamed at Norbor in English, he understood what I was saying, feeling through my intonation the accompanying flood of tears and joy. "You old bear!" (This in Tibetan.) "Are you hurt?" He thought about that for a while, then a serious frown creased his forehead. He wriggled his hand beneath the small of his back, and pulled out a mangled set of binoculars. "Yes. I'm very hurt. Look."

I helped Norbor to his feet and banged the dust from his sheepskin coat. By my own methods of evaluating heights from which people fall, I estimated Norbor's plummet to be a good nine-and-a-half elephants' worth! His thick chuba had functioned like a Niagara Falls thrill-seeker's barrel. Save for the cut on his head, he was unscathed. He asked after the horses, and I pointed to the tan mare on the far side of the plain.

We heard a low snorting and shuffle of hooves and Namgyal—who had taken the route around the base of the low mountain we'd traversed—appeared with the yaks. He was clearly distressed. He signaled for us to join him. Ten yards away from where Norbor had landed, we found the gray mare, lying on her side, panting. She had broken a leg. Oh no. Tears of sorrow and pain returned. I squatted down and cradled the mare's head in my arms, stroking her blaze to comfort her. Norbor forgot his brave façade and cried. There was nothing we could do. Namgyal slowly removed his homemade rifle from its sling across his back.

The old bear started chanting between sobs, and walked off, with a directionless, drunken gait. Namgyal motioned for me to fire the gun. I clutched onto the horse's sweaty neck and drenched it further with my tears. It had to be done—the poor beast had to be shot—and since it was against a Buddhist's tenet to kill any living thing, it was now my responsibility. It was true that nomads now killed their own livestock for meat, rather than relying on an "untouchable" as they had in past decades. But a horse, a dear friend, was different.

I couldn't do it. I tore myself away from the mare and ran blindly after Norbor. I reached him and took his hand. He was staring into nothingness, lost in thought and chanting. Boom. The rifle shot pierced the windless silence. Norbor's grip tightened on my hand and he stopped dead in his tracks. After a minute or two, he resumed his

chanting and continued walking. We didn't turn back.
Namgyal and the yak herd caught up with us. He had tied
Norbor's leather satchels and saddle over the lead beast
and the stirrups clanged from the last yak's load.

Lobsang came toward us on his pony, leading my still-
frightened mare. He was puffing on a seed cigarette and
laughing—unaware of the events of the past half hour. Too
young to be aware of our silent mood, he went on cracking
insolent jokes about my lack of horse sense. Norbor's voice
quavered and he briefly told the boy what had happened.
Lobsang went a deathly gray and shut up. He helped the
old bear into my mare's saddle and we continued on across
the plain.

Half an hour passed and low clouds raced between us
and the distant camp, obscuring it from sight. The clouds
brought snow and the winds returned to make the last leg
of the day's journey more miserable than ever. My chewing gum, vaguely tasting of soap and grit, provided little
comfort. My hands and feet ached with cold. Namgyal and
Lobsang made camp near the river with the horsemen,
and Norbor and I continued on to the nomad's tents, arriving, thankfully, seconds before the worst of the snowstorm
broke.

While we warmed ourselves by the fireside, our new
host took the tan mare and tethered her farther down the
gully. A row of healthy-looking children, sitting opposite
me, shifted inch by inch until they were close enough to
touch. I pulled out my camera, fitted the zoom lens, and
passed it around the kids, showing them how it worked.
They were amazed. In a world sadly devoid of wonderment, where pleasure rarely comes without a six-figure
price tag, it was always a joy to see Tibetans fascinated
and entertained for so long by something so comparatively
simple which we Westerners take for granted. The camera
went around and around the tent a dozen times, from big
old hands, to small new ones. I attached the flash unit and
another hour of fun followed. The first few times it fired,

my host family reacted with screams of fear. The children hid their heads between their fathers' legs or buried their faces in the deep folds of mothers' chubas. One old man covered his eyes with his hands and yelled, "Ahh! I'm blind!" Then quickly, and with surprise added, "Oh! No I'm not! I think I can see better now than before! Whoah!" And so the day ended in laughter. The next morning the sun came out in full, glorious force and I was keen to take advantage of the weather and walk as far as my legs would carry me. But Norbor did not share my enthusiasm. The journey was wearying him. He played dead again by the fire, and only occasionally stirred from his hibernation to drink hot tea.

Finally at midday, Namgyal and Dōrdrum's handsome grandson arrived with fresh mounts for Norbor and me. Suddenly fearful at the thought of having to lead Nightmare, the black stallion I had tried to ride the day before, I retreated inside the tent and buried myself beneath my sleeping bag.

Dōrdrum's grandson coaxed me back into the sunshine, promising the horse had been rightfully reprimanded for his bad behavior and swearing on all the Buddhist mantras he knew that Nightmare would not cause my days to end prematurely. Foolishly, I believed him. To all extents and purposes, the stallion appeared to be well chastised and quite tame. But I envied Norbor. The horse they had selected for him was indisputably docile. And short. But the exaggeratedly concave spine was a bit of a worry, and, when Norbor straddled the mare, her underbelly very nearly touched the ground.

We left the nomads and headed up the gully and over the hills behind their camp. Nightmare really was okay. He trailed obediently behind me at an even pace, and only once in eight hours did I have to tug gently on his lead rope to make him move.

By sundown, we had reached the end of nowhere. Perhaps it was the middle of somewhere, or even the begin-

ning of everywhere. I was past caring—exhausted from
the day's march, and far from thrilled by the knowledge
that it was *still* four days to Parayang.

After a substantial breakfast of raw meat and cold,
stodgy rice (which Norbor had apparently carried all the
way from his family's camp in the chest pocket of his
chuba) we made patty cakes of tea leaves and zumpa to
feed to our horses. While I dismantled the tents and
packed up my troubles in an assortment of old kit bags,
Norbor wandered off to fetch our mounts and Namgyal,
Lobsang, and Dordrum's grandson, Garma, prepared the
yaks for travel. The other horsemen had decided to abandon the expedition, and had left earlier with their stock
and Lobsang's pony, to return to Yagra.

Our horses were frisky. Nightmare was tiresomely reluctant to be saddled but finally my load was upon him. He
was breathing like a steam train and his eyes flared like
headlights in fog. I was scared. I knew something unsa-
vory was going to happen.

We started off. A minute later, Nightmare went berserk. He bucked so violently that the lead rope I held
twisted around my gloved hand yanked tight, and I somer-
saulted twice through the dust and sharp gravel. I held
onto that rope for all it was worth. Nightmare charged
around and around in circles, bucking and neighing in
fury. I spun with the grace and control of a break dancer
in a Chicago gutter, around and around, screaming for
mercy. The rope snapped and Nightmare took off for the
river. He succeeded in loosening the saddle with his jerky
movements and soon my pack tumbled to the ground. Just
at the edge of the river, Nightmare caught his front leg in
a stirrup and went crashing head first into the ice-covered
stream. The ice broke in an instant beneath his weight and
the horse sank. Namgyal and Garma went charging down
to rescue the floundering beast and Norbor waddled off
slowly, chanting of course, in pursuit of his own horse
which had also bolted in sympathy.

I sat up and eased the woolen glove off my right hand.

Oh joy! Three mangled fingers. My middle and little fingers were obviously broken and the one in between was dislocated. At first I thought the finger was missing its nail, but quickly realized—after wiping the haze of dust and tears from my eyes—that it was intact. My finger had just rotated 180 degrees and the nail was obscured from view. I bit hard on my pathetic piece of chewing gum and wrenched the digit back into place. This was a terrible way to start the day. But at least it couldn't get any worse.

While Namgyal and Garma quieted Nightmare, I noticed two men with half a dozen yaks approaching them from another branch of the main river. I shouted to Namgyal, and they waited on the bank for the herdsmen. Norbor returned with his horse in tow and sent Lobsang down to instruct the boys to let Nightmare go free. He was of no use on our expedition. If my hand wasn't hurting so much, I would have been turning cartwheels for joy. No Nightmare—no more nightmares! Or so I thought.

With my baggage distributed among our yaks, my fingers artfully bound up in a sheath of dirty sheepskin, and my girlish tears suppressed by an unconvincing smile of courage, we made a second attempt at leaving the valley-side camp site. Namgyal hid Nightmare's saddle and broken stirrups behind a large rock. He would collect it, and presumably Nightmare, on his way back to Yagra. The two herdsmen and their six charges joined us, welcoming us to shelter at their camp for the evening.

For several hours, they talked about the abysmal weather conditions at their high camp near the foot of the Gangdisê Ranges. If we walked continuously for the remainder of the day, we could reach their tents by sunset.

Norbor soon grew tired of walking and raced off on his horse. I wandered behind the yaks, learning how to keep them together and under control by whistling and throwing stones. It was a simple process to which I added a certain amount of Western panache. Every time I whistled, my gum flew out of my mouth and landed in Garma's plaits, or worse still, in the dirt. Every time I threw a stone, it clipped the back of precocious Lobsang's little round head. (I swear I was truly aiming for the swinging backsides of our bovine contingent. . . .)

By late afternoon, the valley we were following met at a right angle with a deep, fast-flowing river—behind it were the Gangdisê Ranges, looking formidably impenetrable. My experienced companions hurled themselves onto the backs of the closest yaks at hand and charged across the river. I stood watching, amazed at the highly skilled spectacle, and then took a running leap at the last remaining beast. I missed. The boys—the herdsmen and Lobsang—stood on the far side of the river, laughing hysterically. Unfortunately I did not find my predicament amusing. I was so furious with my lack of aptitude for any and everything, I wanted to cry. Garma yelled across the loud, angry river, instructing me to take my clothes off and wade across it. Respecting the modesty which had suddenly surfaced as a result of his command, Garma turned his back and led the others up the steep river embankment. I stripped off my shoes, socks, overalls, and long-johns and wobbled—petrified—through the river. The water gushed about my thighs. I had my pants tied around my head, one boot balanced in each hand (the right one just dangling by the shoe lace from my only undamaged finger), and my camera bag tied high across my chest. Thank God they weren't looking. If I looked half as ridiculous as I felt, their laughter would have weighed like a life sentence on my slowly diminishing credibility and pride.

I will not describe the temperature of the water, suffice it to say that had I stayed in midstream for more than a minute, I would have been an interesting case for scientists of the future when I thawed out centuries later.

I dressed, jogged up the embankment, and welcomed the sight of a pot of tea on the boil. After half an hour, we pressed on again, up a precariously steep pass I thought would never end. The world was closing in around me. Huge, bare, pudding-shaped mountains threatened our

hungry party. Up and up, on and on. The sun vanished and
the wind and clouds left a heavy dusting of powdery snow
on the hills. We reached the top of the pass and the herdsmen pointed out their camp, nestled at the far end of the
narrow valley below. Behind their camp, the landscape
was completely white. White mountains, white snow, thin,
white, blizzard-bearing clouds.

Had I been a clinically diagnosed masochist, I would
have viewed the scene in a state of ecstasy. As a self-
certified coward, I looked toward the mountains in a state
of unadulterated panic. It seemed the pseudo-adventuress
had taken on a bit more than she could chew. If she didn't
perish in a snowstorm she would surely choke to death on
the misconception of her abilities. Norbor had arrived at
the camp a good two hours earlier and quickly eaten the
nomads out of house and home. When we got there, he was
trying to lasso a sheep for our supper. It was quite dark,
and given Norbor's age-induced lack of agility, his repeated attempts were a delight to behold, but far from
successful.

Namgyal, Garma, and Lobsang led our yaks down to the
river and I trekked up to the camp with the herdsmen. We
stopped to help the old bear with his circus act. There is no
sound more pathetic than the desperate, pleading cries of
an animal cornered for slaughter. The last few bleats are
delivered with such awesome understanding and fear they
never fail to send my body into a quivering mass of goose
bumps. The most barbaric ritual I had ever taken part in
was the sacrificial killing of a piglet at a tribal New Year
celebration in the hills of northern Thailand. We had to slit
the scrawny, wriggling morsel from the throat right down
to its belly and drain all the blood from it before its small
heart stopped beating. The piglet squealed and squirmed
frantically while its life-sustaining fluids gushed out into
a deep enamel dish. Its high-pitched cry echoed now,
around and around in my head, as I held down the twitch-
ing legs of our future meal of mutton.

In any other part of the world, Buddhist practitioners

abstain from eating meat. If the devout Tibetans followed suit, they would very quickly die out. Man cannot live by bread alone . . . nor even zumpa.

After dinner, while I warmed my numb, broken fingers by the fire, Norbor told me he would not venture farther into the mountains with me. He was worn out. Predictably enough, it was still four days to Parayang and he did not, in all honesty, believe he could make it that far. He relinquished his responsibility to Namgyal, Garma, Lobsang, and Renzin—our present host. The old bear had grown a little too lecherous for my liking in the past few days, so I quickly agreed he should return to his wife and family. In spite of his frequently groping paws, I dearly loved and respected old Norbor and was quite saddened at the prospect of having to bid him farewell. The hardest thing about traveling is having to say the inevitable goodbye to new friends. The often uttered "See you later" is voiced through habit, in hope rather than truth. The chances of Norbor's path and my own ever crossing again were a million to none.

With the yak contingent depleted to a mere dozen, we met the snowline at midday and began climbing. I was glad I had dragged my cumbersome boots halfway across Tibet, for here I would have suffered without them. The dearth of complaints from my sneaker-soled companions amazed me.

I tried to sing inane songs like "The Hills are Alive with the Sound of Music" and Cliff Richard's "We're All Going on a Summer Holiday" to forget my miseries, but boisterous vocalizing is not uplifting at high altitudes. It was physically exhausting just to walk and breathe at one and the same time. Inexplicably though, I found chanting a comfortable way of evening out a breathing pattern, and I "Om Mani Padme Hum-ed" my way up to the top of the pass. Since that took no less than four hours, I considered myself worthy of ordination on the summit. The others had made it in three-and-a-half hours and lay, still as dirty laundry strewn across a carpet of snow, looking over the pass.

The view completely spoiled my mood. I could not believe what I saw. Exhilarated by my achievement, I had honestly expected to see the sparkling waters of the mighty Tsang Po River, snaking through wide, southern sun-drenched valleys all the way to Lhasa. I was speechless. The top of the pass was nothing more than an insignificant point on the edge of a vast, undulating snowfield—a white crater encircled by still-higher peaks and still-vaster plains.

Renzin himself was clearly shocked to see so much snow. The weather was obviously worse than he expected and he now expressed fears of getting over the pass.

Despite my ardent protests, he insisted on calling this massive football field for legendary yetis a "pass." To me, the word implied an end, a route to go down, and unfortunately, here, I could see none. This was No-man's—as opposed to Nomads'—Land. Arguing over what label the godforsaken place should bear wasn't going to make it any easier to traverse, but at least the sit-down debate gave me an opportunity to rest. There was really only one practical way to solve the question of the passability of the pass, and all too soon we began walking again.

To add insult to injury, a bank of clouds rolled over the plain toward us. How does one greet a blizzard at 18,000 feet? I cursed. Renzin, Namgyal, and Garma chanted. Lobsang buried himself beneath a sheepskin blanket on the back of the only ridable yak in our herd. We kept moving, mile after mile through the whiteness.

The wind drove the fine snowflakes into my bare cheeks and eyes as if needles were being rammed into my face. By the time we surrendered to the elements and made camp, utter exhaustion chose our tent site. It was surprisingly bare of snow. Nomads had long abandoned the area for lower pastures, leaving behind a low pile of sun-dried yak dung and sheep droppings. It was soggy, but with a great deal of huffing and puffing, we eventually ignited it. At some stage of the afternoon I had developed a raging fever and sore throat. My perpetually leaky nose was now gushing like a broken fire hydrant. My hand was throbbing, my face itching, and my feet burning with the cold. I felt miserable and limp, like a wilted flower. I found my tent in the pile of junk outside the men's haphazardly erected lean-to and struggled in the wind to pitch it, one-handed. I was sure I had seen the resulting half-hour scenario on an early Laurel and Hardy film, only without Laurel, it wasn't nearly as funny, it was pitiful. I gave up trying to get the guy rope pegs hammered into the frozen ground, and crawled inside my tent, hoping my weight would be enough to hold it down. Apart from my sanity, I was also losing weight rapidly. I didn't doubt the wind had strength enough to hurl me through space if it so desired.

Being inside my tent was like being inside a miners' cave during an earthquake. The whole thing shook violently while I hung on, waiting for it to collapse around me. I didn't return to the "safety in numbers" shelter of the men. I was in a miserable, self-pitying mood and wanted to be alone with it. I got even worse as the night hours rolled by. I shivered and tossed and turned in my sleeping bag and cursed the wind which forced great mounds of blizzard snow beneath the floor of my tent. I don't know how I ever managed to fall asleep, but eventually I did.

When I awoke, I noticed my five-gallon water bottle had frozen solid. An upturned cup of pea and ham soup looked like freeze-dried vomit on the side of my pack and sleeping-bag cover, and my climbing-boot uppers had mysteriously turned from soft, pliable leather to unmalleable lead. The blizzard was still raging. I forced myself through the doorway of the dome tent and peered out into nothingness. I could barely see my companions' tent (just ten yards away) through the snowstorm. The sun had come up again somewhere, but certainly not to warm our little inhospitable part of the world. At that moment, I

hated Tibet and all the crazy dreams that had brought me
there. I looked hard at two of our yaks, standing guard
like stone Mycenaean gate lions. Their black coats were
white with snow. How hungry they must have been. There
wasn't a blade of grass in sight. I raced over to the men's
tent and quickly thawed out by their blazing fire. No one
was in a hurry to leave, and it wasn't until the fuel ran out
that we did.

For some peculiar reason, I trusted my companions'
sense of direction more than my yet-to-be-used compass. I
hadn't studied my maps since leaving Shongba, and didn't
have the faintest idea where I was. For the next two days
we walked blindly through the relentless blizzard—trudging through mile after mile of knee-deep snow. Up down,
up down. My face was a mass of bleeding grazes. The skin
on my cheeks had blistered and the water beneath them
had subsequently frozen. They soon became maddeningly
itchy. Like a crazy dog tearing hunks of fur from its body
in pursuit of parasites, I scratched the flesh from my face
until it was red-raw. My eyes were bloodshot from the
needling snowflakes and my lips split in a dozen places
from windburn. No amount of Helena Rubinstein would
ever cover the scars. I gave up my childhood dream of
appearing on the cover of *Vogue*, and satisfied myself with
the new ambition of gracing silver screens across the
globe in *Exorcist 3*. Linda Blair would be out of a job and
so too would the production team's makeup artist.

"Om Mani Padme Hum" underwent serious reconsider-
ation. Instead, between tears, I mumbled "Oh, Mummy,
take me home, oh Mummy, take me home"—a pathetic
plea to the powers of hearth and home.

After three days of unending blizzard, we came to the
remnants of a recently abandoned fireplace. The wind had
swirled the snow around but had not yet covered it. Hope
lifted in my heart. I smiled. "We must be getting close to
civilization! At last!" Garma bent down in the ashes and
sifted out a strip of gym-shoe fabric. My heart sank. It was
part of the scraps from Renzin's boot, repaired two days

earlier. We had walked in a complete forty-mile circle. Even Garma's ever-present smile had vanished. I was speechless with despair and frustration.

We made camp in silence. The yaks appeared to be holding up quite well under near-starvation conditions, but I began to fear for them. Even four-wheel-drives don't move without gas. The men had food enough for three more days, yet even if they ran out in two, or stretched it to four, it wasn't at all appetizing. I still had my faithful piece of chewing gum to chew whenever my stomach roared. The men were down to their last bag of yak turds for the fire, thoughtfully carried all the way from Renzin's camp, and if nothing else, warmth would have to be rationed.

We clearly needed another miracle, but alas, I had forgotten how to pray. It seemed as if Buddha and God—my faithful musketeer brothers-in-arms—had temporarily deserted me. I refused to believe they had abandoned me for good. I didn't have the energy to battle against the wind and space-age technology of the Vau De Tent, so I opted for sleeping in with the men. I was so exhausted, even fear of dying in the wilderness failed to keep me from slumber.

At some hour the following morning, I was jolted awake by the shrill screams of Lobsang. "Sun! Sun everywhere! Look!" And indeed there was. It was still piercingly cold but the wind had died down and the blizzard abated. Renzin spent a good half hour detailing a route to Namgyal and Garma. He had had enough and wanted to go home. (So did I.) We divided up the food and yaks and soon were on our way.

Three hours later, with the aid of Garma's binoculars, we saw a flock of sheep trudging through the snow toward lower ground. We were going to make it! The sun was intense on the snow and to reduce the glare, I knotted my short plaits over the bridge of my nose, as Namgyal had done—far more successfully—with his. The other two lads had old snow goggles. I couldn't for the life of me remember where I'd lost the American sunglasses Jigme had given me prior to my departure from Lhasa. My eyes were already stinging from the blizzards and I would have given anything for Lobsang's goggles or Namgyal's longer pigtails.

The snow cover gradually got thinner as we descended and by late afternoon, we reached an inhabited nomads' camp. There were real, live mongrel dogs snapping at our feet, sheep bleating, old women baring their breasts, toothless grins, and everything! Even a stream which wasn't a solid road of ice! Granted, it wasn't Parayang, but it sure felt like Paradise!

Namgyal stayed with the nomads, and Lobsang, Garma, three of the stronger yaks, and I pressed on. We climbed over another long but snow-free pass, and gazed over a wide tan-colored vale. My eyeballs were itchy, but I could see sheep and wild antelope cavorting. As we climbed down, I was singing. Singing for Hyo, singing for all the people who believed I could make it. We met up with the flock of sheep and followed two shepherds on toward their distant camp. It took another three hours, but it felt so good to be alive, I scarcely noticed the aches and pains which begged to tell me otherwise.

A half-dozen ragamuffin children came out to welcome us and to lead us proudly to their parents' camp. The tea tasted better than ever; the meat stew tasted fresher, and, to round off the delicious feast, lashings of warm yogurt was served. Ah, angel's food. Blissfully satisfied, I crawled inside my sleeping bag and nestled down by the glowing embers. I closed my stinging eyes and listened to the happy sound of the family around me. Garma had gone to another tent but Lobsang had unfortunately remained behind. He was showing off his hoard of cigarettes to the nomad children and boasting about how brave and clever he was. I had long tired of his cocky, insolent manner, his constant interruptions and interjections into adult conversations. He really irritated me. I would be glad to see the last of him.

In the dead of night, I woke in a pool of sweat. My eyeballs felt as if they were on fire. I fumbled blindly with the zip on my sleeping bag, trying to get some ventilation. Someone—presuming my lightweight, down cocoon to be as warming as a cotton sheet—had covered me in at least a dozen thick sheepskins. I tossed them off, and lay back again, panting. I couldn't see, not a thing. Snow blindness. The dreaded ailment of foolhardy mountaineers. The pain was excruciating. I cried silently, continuously, until the stirring sounds of my host family intimated the dawning of a new day.

Someone asked me what was wrong. "Nga-rang mig min-du. Mig-chu mung bu mung bu." Literally, "I haven't got any eyes. Many many tears." Paraphrased to better express how I was feeling, "Leave me alone, and don't you dare take advantage of my blindness by staring for any longer than you normally do at my Caucasian person."

My spirits were at the lowest ebb imaginable. Suddenly I started to feel little prickling sensations about my midriff. I scratched the flesh thinly covering my rib cage. It felt like a page of Braille. Fleas! The sheepskins added to my bedding had left my sleeping bag infested with parasites. I scratched and I cried, and the tears made my eyes hurt even more. Someone passed a cup of hot tea into my hands. I didn't bother to thank them. Revolting Tibetan tea. All the romance of being a nomad was wrenched from me as I choked on yet another sheep dropping floating in the liquid.

I screamed in English, "I hate this place! I hate you! I hate everything! Oh God, someone blow these mountains away!" And the tears fell in torrents down my tortured cheeks. My outburst met with a chorus of clucking tongues and whispers. "Stop staring at me! I know you are—even if I can't see you, I can feel your beady eyes burning into me." And then, in Tibetan, "Mig par der. Mig par der!" Turn the other way!

I buried my head in my sleeping bag and wept again, oblivious to the searing pain of tears. I hate being a nomad, I hate it! Living day after day on zumpa and rancid tea. Putting up with runaway donkeys, blisters, dog bites, freezing nights, lonely days, detonator blasts, crowds staring, madmen wielding knives, broken fingers, blizzards, bloody noses, frost-bitten cheeks, fleas, and snow blindness. Ever since I left Yagra, I'd been told, "Four days to Parayang." It had been a full ten days now, and it was *still* four days to Parayang! I began to doubt the place even existed. I had a bizarre vision of wandering for the rest of my life in search of Parayang. All the people I would meet—the good, the bad, the ugly, the wise, the rich, and the insane—would have the same nightmare message for me. "Four days to Parayang!" They would wear the message on T-shirts. Some would wear Chairman Mao caps and wander around and around in circles with the message emblazoned on white billboards. Wise men would point to the southeast and say nothing; just hold up four rigid fingers on their hands and smile. Four days to Parayang. Ha.

I stayed like that for a further thirty-six hours: blind and bitchy, irate and itchy. Then the Devil stopped branding my eyeballs with his red-hot trident, and my two musketeer partners dropped by to see how I was getting on. Buddha sat quietly contemplating his navel and God gave one of his eloquent sermons from the mount. His opening gambit terrified me. "You ungrateful child, Sorrel! Look at you! Sitting there feeling sorry for yourself, abusing people who are trying to help you, swearing like a common fishwife." (I think God borrowed that expression from my mother.) "You ought to be ashamed of yourself." (This from my father.)

The voice didn't say any more. It didn't need to. I felt like a scolded puppy with my tail drawn between my legs. Over dinner, I apologized to my blurry host family. They were acting as if nothing had happened, as if my appalling behavior had gone completely unnoticed, and they could not comprehend why I had to say, "Sorry." How sweet it is, to be accepted for what you are, at any time. I scoffed down my zumpa and tea and happily choked on the goat hairs which had found their way into my cup.

I decided to do some more engraving on my piece of bone, and fished around in my camera bag for my Swiss army knife. It was missing from its sheath. Lobsang coughed, and quickly started talking. I interrupted him and asked the family if anyone had seen my knife. The parents stared blankly and the kids all shrugged their shoulders in believable innocence. Oh, come on. If it is back in my bag by the morning, I decided, I won't ask any questions. I sensed the straw about to break the camel's back, and switched off the anger buttons in order to stop myself from cracking up. I faced the kids, drummed my hands on my knees and started to teach them some cute little songs I knew. We got "Ging Gang Goolie Goolie" and "Frère Jacques" down pat in an hour and a half. The smoke from the fire was playing havoc with my eyes and eventually I had to abandon the singing lesson. I stumbled outside and pitched my own tent for a bit of privacy. I could hear my host parents putting the fear of God into the children about my knife. The culprit had eight hours in which to place the knife back by the fireside and if it wasn't there by daybreak, all of them would suffer in consequence. It was quite a threat. I hoped Lobsang thought so too.

The oldest daughter in the family brought her bedroll outside, and asked me if she could sleep in my tent. We sang together for a while longer, then she drew a stick figure sketch of me on a page of my diary, turned off the flashlight, rolled over, and went promptly to sleep.

My pocket knife did not materialize with the rising sun. I turned everything I owned inside out three times, then proceeded to do the same to everything inside the nomad's tent. Nothing. The parents pestered me to tell them who I suspected of the theft. I felt like God on Judgment Day. I knew Lobsang had taken it. He was the only one who even knew I had it. Mother lined up all the kids, and father rolled back his chuba sleeves, ready for action. The kids were scared. They looked away from me toward Lobsang. He was puffing on a cigarette, looking as if he owned the whole world. Okay. Time for truth and accusations. I named Lobsang as the thief. The kids danced off into the sunshine, and Lobsang took off for the hills. I went back inside the tent, feeling terrible.

Half an hour passed, and Lobsang came flying back into the tent. I have never seen a child so mortified and angry. He was screaming at me and crying. He stripped off his chuba and shook it wildly. "I didn't take it! I didn't! Look!" He kicked me in the shins and stood howling like a dog at the moon. His performance and denial were so convincing, I questioned my own judgment. But it was too late. The sentence had been handed down and was irreversible. May I never be called to serve on a jury. I *thought* Lobsang had taken my knife, but did I *know*, beyond a shadow of doubt? Yes, well, no. My two new traveling companions were ready to leave camp. I said goodbye to Garma and all the other nomads. Lobsang stood defiantly alone, staring out toward the mountains, seething with hatred. And if I was wrong, who could blame him?

By now I was used to unpredictable occurrences and unexpected landscapes. Consequently, it came as no surprise when we entered into a second series of snow-covered ranges. My companions, Gyardup and Chumba Tookten, assured me the route would lead to Parayang and, forever faithful, I believed them. When we reached the snowline, after trekking upward along a gorgeous river valley, my friends blindfolded me by pulling my Nepalese beanie right down to the top of my lip. It was such a shame to have the beautiful zebra-striped mountains obscured from view, but it was for my own good. I could not risk being blinded again.

Chumba took my hand and led me clumsily along, or sometimes I rode one of the three horses we had saddled for the expedition. Riding blindfolded was pretty weird. Each minor wobble or stumble was a major upheaval. I felt as if I was on a camel, crossing the Arabian desert—

not on a tame mare wading through soft, powder snow. Just before nightfall we made camp in a quiet gully, sheltered from the wind. I removed my mask, and collected some bits of soggy dung from near the river. High up on the snow-bound mountainside, a few wild yaks watched me from a safe distance. In the light of the setting sun, this valley was clearly the most beautiful I had ever seen. Even the snow was beautiful. When the stars came out, they were beautiful too. But was it cold!

We spent hours coughing and spluttering from smoke inhalation, trying to get a fire started. I burned half of my topographic map in an effort to make a big enough flame for the dung to catch alight. Nothing worked, not even my solid fuel tablets. Eventually, our brew of tea reached boiling point on the strength of half my diary and our constant puffing and flapping. I felt as if I had exhaled enough air to fill a thousand balloons and stepped outside the tent in an attempt to stop my head from pounding. When I went back inside, I found a layer of ice had formed on my cup of tea.

Gyardup and Chumba told me many tall tales that night and showed me all their little curios. Chumba unwrapped a small cloth, and on it lay a fish bone, a few scales, a dried-up eye, and a tiny hollow sac which, he said, was a stomach. He explained how many years ago his father had ventured to Mount Kailas and caught a fish while swimming in the holy waters of Lake Manasarovar. Chumba now carried its remains for good luck.

In the morning Gyardup jolted me awake with the news that my horse had mysteriously vanished during the night. I couldn't believe it. What is it about me that animals find so offensive? My smell? The color of my skin? Chumba was rolling all around the tent in an uncontrollable fit of hysteria. Gyardup smiled and told me it was all a joke. If I bothered to look outside, I would see my tan mare content and ready to go. I felt the color return to my cheeks and laughed. One good practical joke deserves another, but I couldn't think of any on the spur of the moment. Perhaps the altitude was affecting my sense of humor.

Unfortunately it was a glorious day and I had to be blindfolded again. I couldn't resist sneaking the odd glimpse of the landscape and took a lot of photographs when the blindfold was off, so that I could appreciate the scenery at length some day in the future. It took hours to reach the top of the pass—and not just because of my imposed blindness. The snow was so thick the horses sank in it up to their bellies, necessitating a lot of digging and pulling to free them. We collapsed at the top, exhausted. Another massive wasteland of snow. Another daunting football field for the yetis. Ice rivers . . . acres of virgin white snow . . . acres of cerulean sky above.

We went on and on, up and down. I rode my mare for a while. On and on, up and up. We were moving slowly along a gully toward another summit. I removed my blindfold again and dismounted. I could see Gyardup and Chumba standing on top of the ridge, peering through their binoculars. I quickened my pace to join them.

Euphoria replaced every pain and ache in my body, melted through every fiber of my being. It was truly the most wondrous sight I had ever seen. A pot of gold at the end of a very, very long rainbow.

Below, thousands of feet below, were the vast yellow-brown plains of southern Tibet.

CHAPTER 8
The Long Road to Shigatse

Just for old times' sake, Gyardup and Chumba decided to camp the night three-quarters of the way down the pass, in the snow. They were as exhausted as I, yet seemed oddly nervous. The sunset had turned the plains below into a sheet of tarnished copper; the sky was a vat of pastel-pink fairy floss, swirled by invisible high winds. Behind us, the top of the pass was obscured by ominous dark clouds. The snow cover up there would be growing thicker by the minute. Gyardup and Chumba had to get the horses back across the ranges before another snowfall. Another foot of powder snow would render impossible the route back to their family camp. According to the men, it was still— yes—four days to Parayang. Twice four is eight, plus two is ten. Ten days. It was possible for a foot or more of snow to fall in ten hours. I didn't think much of their chances. In fact, they clearly needed a miracle.

In the morning, we reached the base of the range and stopped. There were three choices. Left, right, or straight ahead? Gyardup wasn't sure. Chumba wasn't sure, and, of course, I had burned the relevant section of my map a few days previously and didn't have a clue which way to turn. My musketeers had temporarily disappeared again. We trekked up a comparatively low hill on the edge of the plain for a better view of the situation.

Gyardup scanned the horizon through his binoculars, looking for a nomad's camp. He pointed left. Chumba also scanned the plain, and pointed right. I strained my blood-shot eyes across the desolate plain. Then, to the right, I saw a rock outcrop jutting from a distant ridge. Suddenly, I felt I had seen this scene before—danger signals flashed loud and clear.

Just before I left Lhasa, I had received a letter from my mother. She had had a recurring dream about me, lost among rocks. She described the scene in great detail and urged me a dozen times to remember it. Of course I hadn't given it a second thought, passing off the vision as a typi-cal parent neurosis. (Would you believe that someone whose survival kit in the face of danger was ten cents for a phone call and clean underwear had prophetic powers?) But here they were. Here were her rocks. I sided with Gyardup. Two against one. We went to the left and began to cross the wide plain.

After four or five hours, I saw some white spots shim-mering on the horizon. Horses? Houses? Hallucinations? We continued on. Gyardup and Chumba mounted their horses and rode ahead. I straggled behind, dragging my feet and my reluctant beast of burden across the stony fields. Clumps of dry, thorny vegetation began appearing, and finally a river. The white blobs became tents. I would never doubt my mother again.

I crossed over a second shallow stream and paused. My companions had reached the camp and now stood as still as soldiers cast in bronze, at some distance from the first tent. I sensed something was wrong. Normally nomads usher guests—invited or otherwise—inside their tents for tea and attend to the horses themselves as a gesture of hospitality. It was a full ten minutes before I reached the camp and neither custom had been followed. The wind was howling again and flat, gray clouds rolled across the sky.

Chumba and Gyardup were talking with a thin, wild-looking nomad and an attractive teenage girl. Actually, Chumba and Gyardup were talking, the thin, wild-looking nomad was screaming, and the teenager was silently spinning wool, completely disinterested.

Chumba unloaded my horse. The nomad went three shades redder and his voice grew three tones angrier. I felt tired and confused. Gyardup pointed to the sky. There was snow in the clouds above the Gandisê. Buckets of it. They had to get the horses back across the last snowbound ridge before sunset. They mounted their beasts, roped mine, then retreated in a cloud of dust. Just like that. Gone. I turned to face the fuming wild man. He was tearing my pack apart, screaming, scattering my belongings from one end of the earth to the other. I turned to face the diminishing figures of my friends, rolling like tumbleweed across the plain. Abandoned. What to do? I felt sick. I looked at my imaginary wristwatch. Time for an emotional breakdown.

I threw myself down onto the ground and cried. I smashed my fists against the hard earth until they were numb. I screamed like a child. I wept and wailed with the passion of a widowed Hindu at her husband's funeral. And I went on crying and screaming. This was the end. I wanted to die. The wind circled around me, throwing icy daggers between my layered clothing. The dust was choking me, my tears blinding me. I rolled myself into a fetal ball and rocked sideways, over and over like a demented child. Tibet, you have won. I surrender. No escape.

An hour passed. I was still rocking from side to side. My fingers ached from self-inflicted pain. My voice was raw and croaky. My nose was bleeding and my head throbbed. The dust on my face had turned to mud, so many tears had been shed. I looked at my imaginary watch again. It was time now for Clark Kent to turn into Superman—in a hurry! I struggled to my feet and pitched my tent. Time was running out. I had to get inside it before I cracked up completely.

The fuming nomad peered out from his tent at my half-erected dome. Curiosity overcame him. I breathed a sigh of relief. He didn't look so angry any more. He wandered over. I reached out my hand to greet him. He refused to shake it and spat at my feet. The wet mucus balled in the dust and vanished. I swallowed hard. A few kids climbed through the doorway of my tent, giggling. Then the nomad asked me over to his own tent for tea. Jekyll and Hyde!

Over tea, the nomad managed to be pleasant. So did I. Various weather-beaten women came in to offer words of encouragement and tolerable friendliness. Dr. Jekyll asked to see the passes and permits I supposedly possessed. He held them in his hands upside down and pretended to read them. I offered to pay him money if he led me off his godforsaken plain and into Parayang, or even just told me the way. But he didn't want the money. He simply didn't want to help, didn't want to leave his camp. Apparently all the other men had gone to Parayang a few days earlier to trade their fleeces for zumpa, and he had remained behind with the women and children, to more or less protect them. The women hissed at him. *They* didn't need protecting. They were stronger than six men, wiser than six mountains. I had the feeling old Jekyll was henpecked. The women were badgering him into guiding me to Parayang. They were on my side.

Eventually the situation was resolved. Jekyll would reluctantly bury Hyde and lead me to a point where I could see the southern roadway. And all he wanted for his troubles was my disposable yellow Bic lighter. Earlier, after watching him struggle with a piece of flint and his tinder box, I had produced my lighter and showed him how to operate it. He had become obsessed by the twentieth-century toy and had flicked it into action several dozen times during the course of our conversation. He was fascinated by the bright-green "Come On Aussie" slogan emblazoned down one side of the gadget, and he was thrilled to bits when I agreed to the exchange. A guide for two days and two horses for a miserable little lighter. No prizes for guessing who had scored the better half of the deal. I would have paid a king's ransom to be off his detestable plain and on to Parayang. I asked him again how far it was to town. Two days. At last I had apparently made some progress.

That night the wind swirled violently around my tent. The dogs were howling. The yaks were restless, dragging themselves to and fro like wounded Spanish bulls, snorting and bellowing as if choking on their own blood. I reached out in the dark and felt around for the knife Hyo had given me. My silver sword. I would probably never have the courage to draw it in combat, but it was reassuring to have anyway. I rolled over and fell back to sleep instantly. And then I entered a nightmare world.

I dreamed of a crazy, kaleidoscopic circus. I stumbled through a crowd of fat ladies, dwarves, trapeze artists, acrobats, bears, camels, and even sequinned yaks, seeking an elusive someone who couldn't be found. Where was the clown? Where was my hero? Where was Jigme? They circled round me, closer and closer, chanting, "He's dead, you're mad, he's dead, you're mad." The procession quickened and the circle tightened. "He's dead, you're mad." I awoke, panting and sweating and looked outside my tent. A new day. I felt shattered.

The winds had brought snow down from the mountains and the morning frost. My tent had been converted to an igloo. Jekyll was stirring. His children came out to help me pack. The women of the camp came forward with mounds of zumpa to add to my load. As they tipped their gifts into my cotton flour bag, they stared long and hard into my eyes. They would not smile. They just stared, as if looking for the answers to a thousand questions. More children came. They were pulled away. It was all right to look at the stranger but taboo to touch her. I felt strangely alienated. I looked around at the plain. Barren. Desolate. Worn out. Just like me.

Jekyll didn't want to walk. He insisted we ride his saddled horses. Having already experienced the Hyde side of his nature, I quickly agreed and mounted. I did not, under any circumstances, want to upset him again.

A few hundred yards from the camp, Jekyll actually flashed me a smile. He laughed and reached across to shake my hand. He whipped the flank of my horse and we broke into a trot. He whipped again, and we were off at a canter. We raced together across the plain, laughing at nothing, laughing at everything. Jekyll asked me why I had cried for so long. He asked me why I had my fingers bandaged and why my face was covered in so many thick, ugly sores. He asked me if my bottom hurt, bouncing up and down in the saddle and he laughed at every answer I gave in response to his questions.

By midafternoon, we were approaching a low pass between the mountain ranges on the far side of the plain. A caravan of yaks were approaching from a different direction and my guide suggested we speed up in order to meet them at the summit. He presumed they would be going to Parayang. There was nowhere else to go but Parayang. If he could pass me off to the herdsmen, he could return to his family camp before nightfall—to protect the women.

We met the yak drivers, Garma and Perma Renzin, and stopped for a smoke. They looked me over, and reluctantly agreed to take me to Parayang. My pack was added to their bales of wool and camping paraphernalia. Jekyll smiled contentedly. He pulled out his "Come On Aussie" lighter and beamed with pride at the herdsmen. He lit Garma's pipe, then flicked the toy at his own. It wouldn't work a second time. He must have been playing with it all night, for it had run completely dry. He face reddened with embarrassment. He popped the lighter back into his chuba, and promptly changed the subject.

During the half-hour "smoko," I had remained uncharacteristically silent. A smile here, a nod there. Consequently, the herdsmen were quite surprised when, ten minutes after Jekyll and the horses had left, I began telling of my experiences of Mount Kailas and the Gangdisê Ranges ordeal. To further shock them into realizing they had inherited someone vaguely useful, I began whistling and chucking rocks to keep their large herd together. Garma let out a hearty "Yabo-du"—Tibetan for "This is good!" Yogi Bear couldn't have said it with more enthusiasm. I was touched. The yaks were moved—literally. We crossed the pass and made camp in a narrow vale, beside a well-situated lake.

While the men unloaded their gear and pitched a tent, I exercised my dried dung- and water-collecting skills on the lake's edge. Perma had earlier assured me we would reach Parayang by midafternoon on the following day and I was riding high on a wave of excited anticipation. I tried to visualize Parayang and the warm reception I would receive from the town's goti. For days I had been fantasizing about the great southern highway: a six-lane freeway, lined with secondhand car lots, pizza parlors, and hotel-motels. I could smell the rain-wet asphalt and see the endless strands of colored lights and billboards reflected on its slippery surface. Parayang, I imagined, would look like something out of a glossy magazine; the goti would live in a two-story house on a tree-lined street and welcome me with hot coffee and croissants. I would sit by his built-in aloha pool, sipping piña coladas and reading *Time* magazine, until the cows came home. Beyond Parayang, there would be nothing. I would need to go no farther. I had been to hell, survived, and now I welcomed the prospect of spending time in paradise. Parayang. My castle in the clouds.

It took hours to pack up in the morning. Another herdsman had joined us in the night, returning from Parayang to our camp. When our yaks were loaded, we helped him saddle and load up his herd before leaving the lakeside and heading up the second pass. At midday, I glimpsed the southern valley, the Great Southern Highway . . . the

Great Southern, almost invisible, two-wheel cart track. There wasn't a car to be seen, much less a car dealer. But I was happy anyway. It was still the most momentous occasion of my journey to date. It marked the end of my thousand-mile detour. I went to take a photograph of the valley, with the imposing Himalayan chain stretching across the horizon hundreds of miles away. I pulled out my telephoto lens, and out tumbled my Swiss army knife. Oh no. I had checked my camera bag a dozen times. How on earth did it get there? The vision of Lobsang standing with his arms folded, facing the mountains and seething with hatred, returned to haunt me. I felt completely devastated. Had I carried the knife all along? Had I accused Lobsang without reason? The poor child would carry the label of thief forever. I had well and truly seen to that. He would remember and hate me forever. He would probably hate all foreigners forever. But how had I missed seeing the knife in my bag? I had turned it inside-out—or had I? I ambled behind the yak herd, my eyes fixed on their swinging tails. Oh God, let me be wrong. No, right. No, wrong. Oh, just let me forget about it. I felt so guilty. Lobsang's image burned into my memory, his hatred would be with me forever.

Beyond the dry spinifex and sand underfoot, I could now see Parayang. The distant Himalayan peaks glistened in the bright sunlight. The snow caps turned a golden hue and transformed the mountains into majestic Egyptian pyramids and sphinx-like sculptures. Thousands of animals roamed the plain before Parayang. Hundreds of tents were scattered around the small mud-brick and new-concrete village. Yaks and horses, sheep and goats. No performing bears but the trading nomads resembled the fat ladies and acrobats of my circus dream. The caravans had come from every corner of the country to trade their autumn produce before winter took hold. Finally we reached the town itself. Garma and Perma wandered off to pitch their tent by the river, and I took off for the compound, in search of my hot coffee and croissants. All the traders and townsfolk gathered around and ushered me toward the goti's residence. He wasn't home.

I sat down on the worn steps of the compound and gazed over the sea of merry, curious faces surrounding me. The questions started and soon my animated tale of misadventures was known to all. Various nomads took me to their camps for tea, yogurt, and zumpa. When the afternoon sun began to descend, I returned in search of the goti. I sat by his door and waited. I brushed my hair and tried to rub a bit of the dirt from my face and hands, using a lump of rancid butter. I wrote. I fidgeted. And then the great goti appeared. I jumped to my feet, smiled, and reached out to shake his hand. The goti's face registered a look of utter disgust and loathing. He pushed me aside. I felt like a party balloon, all too quickly losing air, blown-up and bouncy, then suddenly deflated. I scrounged around in my bag and produced the three letters of introduction I had to show him. One from the sports service office in Ali, one from the goti in Yagra, and my official documentation from Jigme in Lhasa. The goti wasn't interested. He claimed he couldn't read. I was furious. He went inside his small room and shut the door. I shoved it open again and yelled at him in Tibetan. He sniggered and spat, then went about his business as if I did not exist. I stood in his doorway for a full hour, staring at him, my mouth agape. I couldn't move. Anger held me bolted to the ground. I was frightened, tired, and confused.

A few nomads came to call on the goti. They made the town mayor tea, swept his floor, and tidied his cupboards. I was horrified—proud nomads, obviously humiliated. Yet still I stood, staring. My horror turned to courage, and finally I exploded. Tears of frustration. "Look—why are you treating me like this? I've just walked halfway across Tibet. All I want is permission to rest in your town. Nothing more. I've walked through blizzards, through mountains, rivers, and deserts. I'm tired. I've got full permission to be here. And (this in English), you could at least smile or shake my hand or something." The goti's face contorted into a leering smirk. He spat at me again. Welcome to Parayang, Sorrel. Welcome to paradise.

The goti's wife came home and gave me an odd, questioning look. She turned from the doorway and asked her husband what I was doing in Parayang, in their compound. Her husband answered in as few words as possible. The woman smiled at me nervously and took my hand in hers. She led me inside and gestured for me to sit down. The goti turned a deep shade of green and walked away. I was having great difficulty working out his nationality. His skin was Tibetan, but his military uniform, heart, and mind were sickeningly Chinese. The converted kind. They say the most fanatical nonsmokers are the reformed ones, the most bigoted Christians, the middle-aged, born-again variety. The goti was a convert to Communism. The Dalai Lama wasn't worth knowing. He pointed at the Tibetan turquoise in my hair and spat again. He hissed at me when I quietly started chanting "Om Mani Padme Hum." He asked me if I spoke Chinese, and rolled his beady eyes in disgust when I replied in the dialect of western Tibet, "No, I only speak the language of the nomads." To him, I was the lowest of all life-forms. A cockroach. To me, he was even lower. We clearly repulsed each other. His wife poured me a cup of tea. He cursed and prevented her from giving it to me. He muttered something in Chinese and she turned to ask me if I had my own cup. I retrieved it from my pack. It was the ultimate insult, and she knew it. She was pathetically embarrassed, but unfortunately slave to her husband's wishes.

In between insults about my attire, journey, and country of origin, the Parayang goti asked me where I planned to stay the night. I said I had my own tent and asked him if he would mind me pitching it outside his compound. Considering the whole situation, I was being frightfully polite. I really didn't care about his opinion or permission, I would have slept on his doorstep if I had wanted to. His wife clucked her tongue and broke into the conversation in Chinese. One of the visiting nomad women left the room.

The goti pointed, and ordered me to follow her. It was already dark and cold outside. I felt pretty dark and cold inside too. All I wanted was a day or two off. A rest. I didn't really need a piña colada or a *Time* magazine. And I really didn't need the hostility I received in their house.

I was led across the compound to an infrequently used school room. A spring bed frame had been wedged between piles of squat desks and bench chairs. The nomad woman held my hands and smiled. "Goti ya bo ming-du." Goti no good. She told me not to worry, for his sentiments were not those of the townsfolk and passing traders. Word had spread about my journey, and good wishes had been voiced all round. Well, nearly all round. The nomad woman advised me to leave the town at first light—to carry on and rest for a while in Zhongba, a town some fifty miles "down the road." She said the goti's wife would try and talk her husband into loading half my belongings onto a military jeep bound for Zhongba, to save me carrying all the weight I had on my back. She told me to have all my unnecessary belongings ready, just in case the goti agreed to help. She squeezed hard on my left hand and left. I looked around, surveyed the cavernous, dank room with my torch. A large map of Tibet covered the wall nearest my bed. It was labeled in Chinese. I studied it for a few minutes. I still had an awfully long way to go. My heart felt heavy, my body exhausted. Just three more days, and I could rest.

In the morning I wandered over to the goti's quarters to thank him for his "hospitality" and say goodbye. Another guest sat by his stove, eating zumpa with a silver spoon. It was fascinating. I had never seen anyone eating zumpa with anything but their fingers before. I was stunned by the spectacle and the guest's apparently refined etiquette. What breeding! He introduced himself. "Basen (grunt) Tsering." (Another Tsering!) The poor man had one of the worst speech impediments I had ever come across. A low grunt rumbled in his throat in the middle of every second word he uttered and spilt from his lips in a hiccough-like sound at the end of every third. He told me he was the goti of Zhongba and he would happily transport any spare luggage I had to his town. He wiped a few specks of flour from the corner of his mouth with a white handkerchief, then motioned to the jeep outside and instructed me to put my extra gear on the back seat. He said something about Australia (grunt) enjoying good (grunt) relations with China (grunt) and claimed he was very pleased (grunt, grunt) to be able to assist me. Parayang's goti grunted too. In disgust.

I had a cup of tea, then set off for Zhongba. It was the first day in ages I had had all to myself. The landscape changed dramatically, and it was almost impossible to believe only a few days had passed since I had stumbled through knee-deep snow. The southern valleys were lined with sand dunes; huge desert domes, corrugated by wind, sculptured by time. I climbed them, photographed them, loved them, and cursed them. I took on their every challenge, ignoring the comparatively easy wheel-track route.

By late afternoon, a savage thirst had taken hold of me. I felt ridiculously masochistic. The roadway followed the river; but then the roadway was for wise men. Sensible men. Something strange had happened to my brain cells. I talked to myself and got upset when I refused to answer. I pushed myself over massive dunes that I could easily have avoided. I was making my life impossible, my journey unbearable, and reveling in it. I couldn't work out why. I reassured myself that it was completely sane to talk to spinifex roots, to hear conversations between the sand and loose pebbles. At the top of one sandhill, I gazed toward a lake, nestled in a valley below—convinced I could walk across its surface. It wasn't until near nightfall, thigh-deep in the water with my pack still hitched to my back, that I admitted defeat. If I couldn't walk on it, I would drink it. Drink the lake dry. I plunged my head into the icy water and started sucking.

They shoot mad dogs, don't they? I fumbled in my pocket for a gun and pulled hard on its imaginary trigger.

Zzzt. Zzzzt. He's dead, you're mad. He's dead, you're mad. I shivered all night long. I didn't want to sleep, to dream.

At dawn, I put my wet clothes on and sat for a while rocking to and fro. My tent was covered in ice again and a strong wind tried to tear me to shreds. I drank some more water, packed, and pressed on.

I passed a few nomad camps and watched like a crazed ghoul as four sheep were slaughtered in the sunlight. I waded through rivers and creeks and climbed more sand dunes. I stripped right down and dressed again, just for the sake of it. I rounded yet another bend in the valley and approached a house. A house! What was a house doing here? I tried to collect my thoughts. It wasn't Zhongba—Zhongba was supposed to be a whole town. Two men stood outside the mud-brick home, throwing teapots full of whitewash at the walls. They must have been as mad as I, they waved and said hello. "Want a cup of tea?" I panicked. I felt too out of control to carry on a conversation. A mangy dog sat in the doorway, snarling in my general direction. Oh please, someone help me. I'm coming apart! My legs are ears, my ears have eyes. I'm burning up. I'm freezing. What day is it? Who cares? Tea? Do you have any Twinnings Orange Pekoe? My insides were crying, tears of blood and fear. I must have been dying from the inside out. The men were real. The whitewash was real. Was I real too?

I drank the tea that was offered and tried desperately to sound sane. I felt like a zombie, a psychopath. Help me, help me.

Somehow I managed to continue on for another two days, crashing through ice-covered rivers and streams, wading through mud, spinifex, and over more sand dunes. I avoided nomads, I avoided the roadway. I avoided anything potentially capable of putting me in contact with the human race. Emotionally and physically I was teetering on a razor's edge—at any moment I thought I could fall. Sadness formed like a rock in my throat and tears tumbled endlessly down my cheeks. I cried about nothing.

I wept about everything. I wasn't too far off reaching Zhongba—but what comfort was that? I still had so far to go beyond it.

Still far from the town, I stumbled across a group of old mud-shelters. Although the compound was almost in ruins, it was inhabited. An assortment of ancient Tibetans sat beneath the warming sun in the courtyard, spinning and carding wool. Two of the women and the only man were blind. They were like outcasts, their days numbered. They offered me some cold, butterless tea and zumpa. I sat with them for half an hour, collecting the courage I needed to face Zhongba, and real people. The old people were little more than dry autumn leaves, waiting to be swept away by time. Like so many geriatrics everywhere. Waiting for death to free them from a society which had already labeled them useless and forgotten their past worth, their present needs.

People. All right. I think I'm ready. I marched on over the hills at the edge of the plain, and entered Zhongba. Basen (grunt) Tsering wasn't home. His effeminate house-boy led me through the littered back streets of the village to the police station.

The main office was strewn with dry sheep carcasses, sacks of barley and ground flour, piles of paperwork, tubs full of stale bread, torn cardboard boxes stuffed with packets of instant noodles, cases of beer, and great mounds of clothing and blankets. Somewhere, beneath everything, sat the sergeant's desk—a huge mahogany structure with three antique phones on it. I later found out they were the only three phones in the town and were connected to a sometimes-operational switchboard. That was as far as the line went. All messages were carried from there by foot. Such is the modernization of west Tibetan villages. The office—indeed the whole town—looked like an air raid shelter that had failed to pass the bombing test.

The round-faced sergeant led me through the piles of debris to an adjoining, less cluttered room. A row of guns in holsters lined one wall. A tinpot stove held glowing embers and I sat as close as I could to it, trying to take in its warmth. I was freezing. My nose was running like a tap and the rock of sadness in my throat had turned to a pineapple of fatigue. The policeman poured himself a beer and offered me some sweet jasmine tea and noodles. He asked to see my passes and travel permits, then gave me a small mirror and smiled. Oh my goodness! Is that really me? My eyeballs looked like two burst tomatoes and my dirt-smeared face appeared to be coming off in hunks, like well-cooked chicken flesh falling away from its bones. How awful. The policeman poured me a beer. I needed it.

Various suspicious-looking characters wandered in and out of the room during the ensuing hours. I had never seen so much money changing hands and wondered, in my usual cynical way, if the police office was not a front for a large gambling syndicate. A woman came in, half-crying, half-laughing, and stayed. She was the policeman's "bit-on-the-side." She was after love—and money. The policeman drew the curtains and poured her a Chinese vodka. He downed his fourth glass of anemic amber beer and giggled quietly to himself. He held his index finger to his lips and whispered to me, "My wife is out of town." I was amazed. Stunned. The woman could have bought a mink coat with all the money the sergeant now gave her. Money, money, money. It was bulging out of his desk drawers and pockets. My eyes were bulging out of their sockets.

The world closed in around me. The woman led me to another room on the other side of the main office, and made a bed on the floor for me out of a half a dozen chubas and blankets. I slithered inside my sleeping bag and closed my eyes and my mind. I slept. And slept and slept and slept.

Sometime after eleven the next morning, Basen Tsering knocked on the door and asked me to his home for breakfast. The policeman had disappeared. Duty must have called—two guns were missing from the wall. Outside, a low fog hung over Zhongba and absolutely nothing was visible beyond three feet.

Basen had been boiling water all morning, and it sat in a row of dented thermos flasks, ready for me to use. Hot water! Whoa boy, steady, steady. The excitement of cleaning myself up was almost too much to bear. I stripped off, donned a shirt of Basen's and my overalls again, then sat in the courtyard washing everything, scrubbing every square inch—piece by piece.

The fog lifted and the sun came out. I was happier than a pig in mud. The warm water was so soothing on my nearly mended, but oddly bent fingers. I washed my hair. I washed my feet. I felt fabulous. When my clothes were dry I felt even better. I sat and wrote a letter to Jigme, relating my tales at length, reveling in the fact that I was still alive. Alive. Yes, and sane again. Along with all the dirt and dust, I washed away the blues. Away they trickled into the street gutter. Goodbye and good riddance. I wish I could have said the same for the fleas. They were impervious to my ardent scrubbing and clung to the seams of my clothing for all they were worth. Spiteful creatures, they bit now with a vengeance. I itched and scratched till sundown.

Basen's houseboy led me down to the town's truck-stop hotel and arranged a room for me. A whole room—all to myself. Usually in this sort of accommodation, all you can be sure of is a bed. When he left, Jing Hwa, the young hotel manageress, came to ask me if I would like some sweet, milk tea. I wandered up to the dank, earthen reception room and plonked myself down among the truckies. Two Tibetan lads were perched in one corner of the room, being sick after consuming an assortment of alcoholic drinks. Their complexions were not at all appealing— gray is a most unbecoming shade—and they emitted an even more unappealing stench. I tried to smile and drink my lukewarm tea without retching. A long-haired pimply driver sauntered up and sat down next to me. "One, two, three" he said in English, "What is your name?" and beamed with pride. I nearly died with shock. English! I answered, "Sorrel. Do you really speak English?" to which the young man replied, "One, two, three. What is your name?" I was just about to say, "Sorrel. Do you really speak English?" again, but I cut myself short. This conversation could go on forever, like a warped record. The man said something else, to which I replied "Pardon?" and knitted my brow in a gesture of misunderstanding, just in case he didn't understand this. He repeated himself three times before I got it. "One, two, three. The English alphabet is merely a series of phonetic symbols." What a mouthful! Anyone who could come out with such a statement had to be capable of more. I began with, "Do you live here in Zhongba?" He answered, "One, two, three. What is your name?" I ended with, "Would you like a cup of tea?" and then came, predictably, "One, two, three . . ." Stop! I ran back to my own room before I started cracking up again.

Jing Hwa came and asked me if I would like to have dinner at her parents' home. I accepted with delight, and waited while she tossed the last few drunk truckies out of the tea room, and locked the door. I followed her up the main street, slipped behind the mud-walled "supermarket" into a narrow alleyway, ducked low to avoid braining myself on the wooden gate-beam, tripped on the front step, and tumbled into her parents' doll-size house. Quite an entry.

A big, gaudily painted cupboard opposite the doorway was cluttered with a million and one curious items. There were some great photos of Jing Hwa and her brother dressed in vinyl jackets and mirror sunglasses, leaning on an old army motorcycle, in front of the Potala Palace. There was a tape deck, several wooden window boxes planted with plastic flowers, a painted plaster Buddha, and a plastic replica of the "wise man"—the one with the gross, swollen cerebellum. There were vases and small mirrors, china cups and magazines—Chinese magazines.

Jing Hwa's family came down from the roof, which they were apparently mending, and joined us. After feasting on mutton stew with actual onions in it (the first vegetables I had eaten in ages) Jing Hwa and I ventured out into the cold, night air to watch a movie, screened on the exterior supermarket wall. A generator thumped away in the background. The town even had four street lights, three of which now emitted a low glow across sections of the main street, illuminating the dust. The movie was a *Gone with the Wind* affair—Chinese-style—and I drifted off to sleep halfway through it. I awoke to see the final dramatic (and terribly risqué) peck on the cheek, and wandered back to my hotel room. The generator went off right on cue and plunged me into darkness.

I spent the following day photographing the village school and the ruins of an ancient hilltop fort. The school was the first I had seen in operation on my journey—the first of China's acclaimed 6,500 recently established schools in Tibet. The rest must have been in Lhasa.

At midday the children all filed out of their classrooms and marched along the schoolyard several times. They marched, then jogged—shouting like regimented soliders, "Eee, Err, San, Su, Eee, Err, San, Su"—Chinese for "One, two, three, four, one, two, three, four." One little radical five-year-old was clipped across the ear for daring to keep time in Tibetan. "Jig, nee, sūm, shi, Jig, nee, sūm, shi." I thought he deserved a pat on the head, and promptly gave him one. The sixty-odd children formed themselves into rows and began performing a calisthenic routine. A seven-year-old yelled unintelligible commands at the students, and the exercises changed accordingly. He would make a good army general one day. Perhaps tomorrow. After the "recreation" period ended, all the children marched back into their dark schoolrooms. I followed one teacher inside and received a formal introduction to his class. The children were instructed to take out their paper and pencils. Judging by the wide-eyed looks of surprise on every face, it wasn't something they were frequently asked to do. A couple of kids stared at me, as if to say, "Boy, you must be pretty important." Then they tried to hold their pencils and scrawl letters on their blank notepads. The teacher articulated an order to the children. "Don't write. Just make it look as if you're writing. Don't smile; you will look ridiculous. Look serious. School is serious."

When the children were ready, the teacher permitted me to take a few flash photographs of his students. He neatly wrote some Tibetan characters on the large blackboard and produced a long bamboo stick, pointing the thin end at the first letter in the chalked series. He straightened his blue Mao cap and, thus posed, instructed me to take his own photograph. Very good. I looked around at the children; at their school dungeon. A single strand of light filtered in through a filth-smeared window. Posters of happy little Chinese children and their smiling instructors lined the walls. There were newspaper cutouts and copies of the Chinese Educational Constitution, pictures of Mao and Deng Ziaoping—a thoughtfully decorated room for five-year-olds.

I left the room, and walked up to the ruined fort. Zhongba Dzong, once a mighty power, was now used as a storage shed for grain and flour. Ugly Chinese slogans had been painted in yellow across the faded wall murals and deity-decorated doors. It wasn't hard to imagine the anti-Tibetan sentiments the graffiti expressed.

Outside, hundreds of small clay icons lay half-buried in the earth and sand. One big wind, and they would be gone forever. I looked at the medallion-like Buddhist offerings. Each had the palm print of its maker on the back and a relief sculpture of Buddha on the front. Each had once been offered to the fort as a sign of great respect. Each had long been forgotten. Bits of broken slate, bearing the carved words, "Om Mani Padme Hum," were strewn all around the ruins together with bits of broken bone and skulls of long-dead sheep. The breeze altered the patterns in the sand slightly, and caused my footprints to vanish almost as soon as they were made. Nothing up here was meant to suggest life or the living. The ruins were a symbol of a dying culture. Perhaps a dead culture.

I reached the summit of the hill and looked down over

the new Zhongba. The old mud-brick walls were deteriorating as fast as the concrete ones were going up. Corrugated iron roofs reflected the sun with blinding brilliance. The dzong had been built in harmony with the landscape; the new town appeared to strike a discordant note among the singing mountains. Music wafted by me on the breeze from the street loudspeakers below. The notes were distorted and left me feeling empty and frightened. Dead. Like the ruins around me. I ran back down the hill and into the ugly streets of progress.

Where craftsmen once molded the clay icons I had fondled on the hill, and artisans used to make cupboards and doors for the dzong by hand, hawkers now plied their trade in the street-market stalls, selling hot-pink, glow-in-the-dark long johns, mass-produced lime-green plastic cups and tin mouth organs. Behind the market, in a military compound, dozens of sheep were being slaughtered. Spilt blood flowed out onto the main road. A river of death. A river of death flowing between a dozen streams of life. I saw a greenhouse in the compound, full of rotting cabbages. A single weed, iridescent green, shot up from the decaying matter. Inside, amid the death, there was life. Outside, amid the life, there was death. Everything meant something. Could I yield to this desert again? Accept it without feeling the urge to beat it, to challenge it? Could I accept this new face of Tibet and find beauty in it? Such towns as Zhongba would be appearing with increasing frequency from here on. Would it make things easier, or emotionally tougher?

As I left town the next morning, a group of school children raced down the main road to escort me to the village limits. All of them had little red handkerchiefs knotted around their necks. School uniform. Several had red protection cords and talismans from Buddhist monks beneath their scarves. Hope. One small child tugged on my overalls, then pressed a clammy handful of sweets into my open palm. She smiled, and whispered into my ear, "Say hello to the Dalai Lama for me." I smiled too. She had made my day a perfect one. Hope, hope. Amid the dying, there is new life.

Basen Tsering had offered to place all my unnecessary belongings on a Shigatse-bound truck. All things being equal, I would reach the second largest city in Tibet in sixteen to twenty days—depending on the number of times I needed to rest. I estimated it was about four or five hundred miles away. I had left him with my climbing boots, half my camera equipment and exposed films, all my written diaries, and the address of the sports service company office in Shigatse. I trusted my Tibetan now, so I did not think it a risk. So the sixteen or twenty-day task would not seem too daunting, I broke the remainder of my journey into sections. Five days to Saga, seven or so from Saga to Lhazê, and four or five from Lhazê to Shigatse. I put Lhasa out of my mind for the moment. As long as I didn't add all the figures together, I felt capable of making it—in control of myself and the situation. My pack wasn't too cumbersome, and if rumor was correct, I could post my comparatively weighty tent from Saga to Lhasa and rely on the hospitality of farmers and road workers for nighttime lodgings.

And so the days slipped by, and the last night I was to spend alone in my tent materialized. It was a really cold night too, and I was forced—for want of a better place—to pitch it on an ice-covered bed of hedgehog-sized lumps of turf by the river. The landscape had become a boring, continuous stretch of low, brown mountains and dry, yellow valleys. I lived in a world of dreams and thoughts, drifting in and out of reality. I worried and feared for my family and friends in their city jungle across the world. I imagined myself to be a dozen different people in a thousand different places. I wrote songs and sang them. I composed poems and recited them.

I sometimes dropped in on nomad camps for a little light relief and tea. One evening, I strayed into a road worker's cabin, listened to a Radio Australia broadcast on the antiquated radio, took a photograph of their dog, bid them a hearty Merry Christmas and adieu, then wandered casually away to camp on the other side of the river. Now I was facing my last night alone. Did it matter? I was of two minds. I liked crawling into my tent at the day's end—writing in my diary in the half-light. But I liked spending time with the nomads and townsfolk too. They made the long night hours pass so much quicker. They brought sanity to my lonely mind. I used the last of my packet soups and muesli. I was tired as usual, and cold. Very cold. I shivered all night.

In the morning, I waited for the sun to rise and melt the frost from my tent fly. I felt miserable, homesick. I hadn't had more than an hour's sleep. I wanted cereal and fresh fruit for breakfast. I wanted to see Sydney Harbour full of yachts, and listen to the pop groups blaring on my sister's stereo. I didn't want to go to Lhasa. I wanted to go home. To Australia—or to any equally civilized place in fact. I remembered a small card German well-wishers had given me months before in Kathmandu. It said, "If you get lost, turn left. You have our address in Bonn." I turned left and found reality. More of Tibet unfolded. It was heartbreaking to realize I couldn't go home or anywhere without reaching journey's end first. Traversing Tibet on foot was nothing like climbing a mountain. If you want to quit Everest, you just come down. If you want to quit walking across Tibet—well, you just can't. There seemed no way out, except, of course, by truck. And if a truck had come along that morning, I would have taken it to Lhasa. I would have taken the first available plane back to China and the next, to Australia. But there were no trucks. No buses, no carts, no donkeys, or Land Cruisers. Just me and my own two feet. So off we marched again.

My journey had become a nine-to-five job. I should have stayed at home and become a secretary. It was so dreary.

Then, ahead, a house appeared. Just like that. A house in the middle of nowhere. It was nestled at the base of yet another mountain pass. The dogs sniffed me out; their eager barking alerted the road-worker owners. A woman, her face covered in smallpox scars, came to greet me and ask me in for tea. Her head looked like a black currant-encrusted Christmas pudding, swathed in a calico cloth. I sighed to myself. Yet another homesickness-induced analogy. When would this agony of images end? I wiped my feet on the worn metal doormat and entered the dark mud-brick home.

It took a few minutes to adjust to the lack of light, but when I did, I was silent in shock. Then I doubled over with laughter. There on the wall opposite me was a souvenir tea towel from Australia! A mother koala and her quarter-sized baby bear were surrounded by a circle of parakeets, kookaburras, and galahs. I couldn't believe it. Lhamo, my pudding-faced hostess, looked at me as if I was slightly crazed. I pointed at the tea towel, screaming, "Australia! Australia! That's where I come from!" I asked Lhamo how on earth she had come to have such a piece of kitsch gracing her wall. She didn't know. She didn't know what or where "Australia" was. She had never seen a foreigner before, either. The tea towel was just "there." Had been for as long as she could remember. I touched the tea towel. It was real, all right. I took a photograph of Lhamo and her husband standing next to it. As much as I hate taking posed photographs, I knew no one would believe me if I didn't have irrefutable proof. I was there, looking at it, touching it, smelling it—and I could scarcely believe it myself.

Lhamo's youngest son asked me if the koala bear was the same as an "abra." An abra is a small, half-rat, half-squirrel-like creature found throughout Tibet in tunneled burrows like those of rabbits. I squealed like an abra, then pretended to suck on a gum leaf to denote the differences between the species. For the next half-hour, I amused myself and delighted Lhamo's steadily-growing family with impersonations of the various birds on the tea towel. My sixth-grade nature teacher couldn't have done it better.

I finished my tea, hugged the children and banged foreheads with everyone, then skipped off into the sunshine. What a glorious day! Who would want to be anywhere else? This place was fantastic—every bit of it. My high spirits carried me up and over the pass. My homesickness had subsided and I felt just great! Hail Australia! Bless you Buddha and the tea towels in your lotus.

I reached the town of Saga some time in the early afternoon—at least three hours ahead of schedule. I wasn't cracking up, far from it. I didn't even need an extended rest. I checked into a hotel. (Am I foolishly starting to sound as if Tibet is littered with Hiltons? In fact my room was the usual hard-bed, very basic earth-walled accommodation.) Then I went for a wander through the village streets. There were more donkeys in town than people—donkeys carrying wool and sacks of zumpa, donkeys hee-hawing like a philharmonic orchestra tuning up for a royal command performance. Budget would truly have been in his element here. It was a shame he hadn't made it. A shame for him, that is, not me.

Back at the hotel I met a rich Chinese tradesman, a local version of the repairmen found in shopping arcades in the West. He had an amazing hand-turned sewing device which, he claimed, could repair anything. Even shoes that had marched halfway across Tibet. He told me, through his bilingual Tibetan accomplice, that he had enjoyed a profitable day, and would repair my shoes for nothing! I pulled them off with such enthusiasm, they literally fell apart in my hands.

The Chinese lad went to work, and within three-quarters of an hour, I was prancing around the room in ventilation-free footwear. The dead had been resurrected. He had done a remarkable job with his sewing machine. The ripple sole of one shoe had melted during the course of an evening spent too close to a nomad's fire, and my friend had even managed to fix it back onto the body of the shoe with nails. Surprisingly, I could not feel their large, bent heads against my heels at all. I was so impressed, I bought the young man a bottle of beer.

I left the hotel at the crack of dawn, with more fleas than ever and a smile that seemed impossible to wipe from my face. I had posted my tent to Lhasa (a process which took a good two hours to complete) on the previous evening, and my load was now as light as the proverbial feather.

At the end of each day from Saga to Lhazê, I joined the roadway and took refuge in the well-positioned camps and compounds of Tibet's wonderful army of road workers. The dirt highway was meticulously maintained by these rural (as opposed to nomadic) Tibetans. A road grader in these parts was a bar of metal pulled by a mule. Bulldozers were unheard of, and the road gangs used spades. They were collectively a curious mob of people, but all hospitable and extremely friendly. There were young ones, old ones, fat ones, thin ones, gregarious, and garrulous ones. Days were made for marching, evenings for entertainment—and if I was very lucky—sleep. I was always warm, physically and emotionally. No pass was too high, no valley too long. Everything was just right. Especially my shoes.

The colors of the landscape changed again and again. The mountains were always there, admittedly, but always they were different—sometimes dull brown or jagged and fortress-shaped, sometimes soft-pink or striped, sometimes even polka-dotted. The river was nearly always close—cool and translucent.

On the morning before my late-evening arrival in Lhazê, I passed one of the most beautiful and serene lakes I had ever seen. The purple-tinged mountains on the far side of the water and tufts of gentle white cloud were reflected on the mirror-smooth surface of the lake. I ran down from the high roadway to the water's edge and ambled along it, enjoying the still silence of the morning. I curved around a tight bend in the lake's embankment and surprised several hundred sunbaking water geese and ducks, bobbing up and down like floating lilies on the gentle ebb of the vast pond. As one, they took off in fright, an awesome cloud of flapping wings, swirling from the lake's surface. They circled just a few feet above the lake, then settled again. I sat back and watched. The geese quacked and squawked to each other, readjusting their feathered coats in a noisy flutter, rippling the water surface as they glided effortlessly across it. Suddenly I was in a large, opulently decorated room, at a harborside cocktail party. Snippets of conversation were echoed in the goslings' chatter. Crystal champagne glasses, touched in toasting, hummed like the song of the breeze. The fur coats of rich widows ruffled like the water birds' feathers. The silver flash of a huge diamond ring caught my eye— the sunlight fragmented into a thousand jewels across the water's skin. I was spellbound by the beauty before me and the beauty of my illusion, a contrast again between lifestyles. Yet reality was far more beautiful than anything my dreams could create. It was going to be a day where I loved Tibet more than anything, or anyone, or anyplace in the world. I sat, feeling intensely satisfied with my lot, for just a moment longer; then I pressed on.

My valley narrowed, widened, narrowed, and widened again. I saw many small communes—some far in the distance and others close enough to explore. I reached one such farming settlement and stopped dead in my tracks. Before me, there was a tree. Although without leaves, it was the first I had seen in months, the first I had ever really *seen* in my life. I wanted to prostrate myself before it, hug it, dance around it as if it were a maypole and decorate it with streamers. Beneath it, a wind-wrinkled couple were sorting grain from the chaff of a late spring harvest. They smiled and chatted to me as if I were some long-lost friend they had been expecting to see for weeks. Three small, runny-nosed boys played in the hay—wriggling and laughing with the innocent freedom we lose with our youth. I handed out my last Dalai Lama pictures and moved on, down to the river.

The river was suddenly deep, wide, and turquoise, snaking like a perfect glistening necklace across the bare, brown shoulders of the earth. The only way across was via a large, rusting barge. I shared the ride with a couple of vehicles, two local cyclists, and three disgruntled donkeys. It took only a few minutes to reach the other side. It sure beat wading—risking one's life and precious camera equipment.

From the other side, it was just two miles to Lhazê. The Kathmandu roadway met the dirt track at this point, and the traffic consequently thickened. In the short space of twenty minutes, a truck, a jeep, and a bus had rattled past me. The sun was beginning to descend, but I wasn't in any particular hurry to get anywhere. I stopped to talk to farmers and commune workers, to take photographs and wish them well.

Two hundred yards from the center of town, a new white Land Cruiser pulled up alongside me. The driver jumped out, beaming with joy. He had been hearing stories about me from the roadworkers for days. He had passed me several times—spied me from the roadway, floundering over the rivers and plains. He shook my hand and introduced himself—"Nima." He turned to introduce me to the three official-looking Chinese men he was apparently chauffeuring around. They were really friendly and anxious to hear my tales, and they asked Nima to translate them from Tibetan into Chinese.

Nima asked me if I would consider changing my plans and venture with his officials down to Sakya—a very special monastic town about fifteen miles from Lhazê, off the main Lhasa-bound road. It was the center of the powerful Sakyapa Buddhist sect that once ruled Tibet. "The Red Hats" allowed their abbots to marry, and established a hereditary system among their ranks. I had been to the village before—with Hyo and Shubu and their party—on my way out to Burang. It felt like a decade ago. I was tempted, but what would my sponsors think? What if foreign tourists saw me accepting a lift in a car? They

would tell the world I had cheated. They would call me a
liar if I dared to claim I had crossed Tibet on foot. But
Sakya, I loved the place, and I could be there that night.

I tried to justify my yearning to accept the tempting
offer. It was only a detour. An aside. I wouldn't have to tell
anyone I did it. If no one saw me, I could even lie and say I
walked there.

Out of the blue, Nima asked me when I had last had a
bath. "A bath? What's that?" I replied. It had indeed been
a while. I think it was in Australia, actually. I had had the
odd shower in India and Nepal, but never a real bath. I
didn't think Tibetans knew what they were. I had soaked
my feet and washed my hair in ahhh, Zhongba. Yes.
Zhongba was the last time water had ventured further
than my face and hands. Nima told me there was a natural
hot spring just four miles away, right near the Sakya road
turnoff. He was planning on stopping there on route to
Sakya. I threw my backpack into the rear of the car and
dived into the back seat with the officials. I had my justifi-
cation. I had more than that, I had Nima's warm smile
and his clammy pink bar of soap wedged in the palm of
my hand. Wow. A lake, a tree, and now a bath. All my
Christmases had come at once.

A bathhouse complex had been built around the hot
spring source, and boiling water flowed continuously into
large concrete tanks inside an assortment of spartan
rooms. They were communal baths, but being of still just-
recognizably female build, I had to wait a while for a room
to be free. It was not the done thing to place a woman in a
room full of naked truckies and traveling army sergeants.
I played a game of kickball with the two little daughters of
the bathhouse managers while I waited. The ball was an
old handkerchief tied around a small handful of pebbles.
The object was to kick the thing with the inside of your
foot as many times as possible without it touching terra
firma. The only thing that bit the dust, of course, was me.
My balance left a lot to be desired. Perhaps it was the
decreasing altitude. I got steadily dirtier during the

course of the game and was more than relieved to stop when the bathroom was free.

I stripped off. I looked down at my naked body in absolute horror. Half of it was missing. All my ribs were visible and my bosom had shrunk to half size. The fleas had eaten me down to skin and bone! I eased my way into the scalding tub. The water was so hot, it hurt. But, oh, how I loved that sort of pain! I wallowed in the water for half an hour, in a steamy, boiling heaven. My kickball mates came in to watch me dress. One sat me down and dragged a comb through my matted but squeaky-clean hair. The other sniffed at my putrid clothing and said "Go naked. This smells. You smell good." She pointed at my hand. "What is that?" My little gold ring. I touched it and laughed. It was my lucky ring. My mother had found it on the footpath near her home, on the very day I had launched my preposterous plan to cycle across Asia. On Christmas day 1983 . . . a few days before I flew out of Sydney, she had slipped it into my slice of Christmas pudding. I had very nearly choked on it. It was lucky, all right. I was the luckiest person on earth and never would I remove that ring from my finger. And then there was another ring to claim. Jigme's. The one that was my prize. The turquoise. How I longed to see him again! Imagine the look on his face when I spoke to him in Tibetan!

I climbed into my overalls, then into the back of the Land Cruiser, and sped off to Sakya. The sun was setting the evening sky on fire as it slipped toward the horizon. Fifteen miles were there and gone in well under an hour. Nima dropped the officials off at their military-compound hotel, then whisked me away to visit some of his farmer friends.

It was pitch-dark outside. Hundreds of tiny candle flames and gas lamps illuminated the windows of the small houses clinging to the mountainside on the left-hand bank of a narrow river. Torches lit the way for farmers coming home, for their wives and children returning from the day's harvesting. They looked like fireflies, swarming across a honeycombed cave wall. Night had rendered the mountains invisible, the sky was a vast, black void. There was no moon and as yet, no stars.

Nima and I tripped up the mountainside pathways and though a dozen alleys and dark stairwells before reaching his friend's home. An old gray mare was asleep in the first room. In the second, a baby was gurgling—not crying—to be fed. An old woman was squatting by the fireplace in the main parlor, using fox-skin bellows to rekindle the still-smoldering embers of the morning's fire. She stopped to greet Nima and me, and ushered us to sit on a bench, covered in an assortment of worn Tibetan rugs and sheepskins. Heavy wooden beams and pillars supported the mud-brick walls and ceiling of the house. It had that familiar, cozy feeling of the nomad tents. I felt at home. Utterly accepted.

Nima interrupted his fast-paced conversation with his friends to ask me if I had a man, if I was married. I thought of Hyo, and lied. Yes. But in reality Hyo was many thousands of miles away—emotionally and mentally. There was a time when I needed to believe there was something lasting between us, but now, I knew in my heart there would never be. I had stopped clinging to the romantic illusion, stopped pretending to myself that I meant something special to him. I never would. I was no proper match for anybody, but I lied because I thought it would make the conversation simpler. For no logical reason, Nima's question had suddenly made me feel like a jilted lover, drinking away the blues in a smoke-filled bar. I felt vulnerable, and so I lied—yes—to protect myself.

One of the old farmer's daughters looked at me questioningly and said, "Oh—only one husband? Why is that?" I was confused. What did she expect me to have? A bearded harem? Then I remembered reading somewhere that polygamy was often practiced by Tibetan women. They marry brothers and in theory all children born are sons and daughters of the oldest man. I tried to explain that Western women, almost without exception, have only one

husband at a time. Wasn't one more than enough? The
farmer's daughter laughed and agreed, with a knowing
nod and smile. Her three husbands came in from the fields
and she stopped feeding her smallest child in order to help
her old mother prepare their meal.

The evening zumpa was freshly ground and lashings of
rancid sheep's butter was offered as a side dish. It tasted
like sulphur. Nima raved on and on, detailing my journey
to his attentive friends. I was weary. Clean, dry, warm
and above all, emotionally content. We visited a few more
families and finally, just after midnight, Nima dropped
me off at a civilian hotel compound and returned to the
officers' rooms. I made polite conversation with the plump
proprietor of the place for an hour. Eventually she noticed
my eyelids sagging, and led me down the wooden veran-
dah to an unlocked and very basic room. I collapsed in an
exhausted heap on the closest bed. So much for the early
night I had planned. So much for sleep.

After a huge breakfast of barley-flour flat bread and tea
with the hotel manageress, I wandered down to Sakya
Monastery to meet Nima. This is one of the most impres-
sive in all Tibet, and seems free of the ravages of time and
the Chinese invaders. A small sign in English blemished
the entrance gate to the internal courtyard. No photographs inside. Three-yuan entrance fee for foreigners.
Foreigners. What an ugly word. I was on the outside
again. I was "one of those," as opposed to "one of us." That
was the first shock. The second was the less obvious implication. Sakya—a town in the middle of nowhere—was
gearing up for foreign guests. Tibet's tourist industry was
booming. It was 1986 and no place in the world was considered sacred ground anymore. I felt saddened by the
inevitability of progress. No doubt highways would one
day sever the great Gangdisê Ranges, and nomads would
be exposed to bus loads of insensitive tourists, anxious to
goggle at the "natives" in their natural habitat. Tibet
would become a vast zoo with Tibetans, the caged mon-
keys. Tourists and terrorists. One and the same in the end.

I wasn't one of those. I was one of *us*. Tibetan. After all my long days there I did not take kindly to being called a foreigner.

I resented it. I got up on my high horse and protested vehemently to the ticket seller. I did not win the argument. I paid my three yuan, relinquished my camera, and moaned audibly when two, huge, bodyguards led me inside the temple. They wouldn't leave me alone. Even when I started chanting "Om Mani Padme Hum." They had their orders from faraway Beijing.

The throng of dust-covered pilgrims and monks inside were far more trusting. They held my hands and talked to me and asked me innocently if I had any pictures of the Dalai Lama or the exiled Sakya sect leader, now living in India. All I knew about the latter was that his cousin's son—the next in succession for this title—was a great consumer of pizza and romantic fiction. Magazine trivia—I could hardly share the knowledge with anyone there, they wouldn't understand.

I looked around the temple. I had been there before, but still it fascinated me. Gold oozed from every inch of the room. Massive gold-plated statues stood behind wire, tourist-proof cages, dripping with turquoise and silver-studded jewelery. Butter candles, sitting in neat rows on the tops of massive altars, cast a warm glow onto the shadowed, gold gods, onto the offerings of old coins and barley grain piled before each image. Photographs of past Dalai Lamas and Sakya sect overlords were all but obscured by a mountain of silk and cotton scarves, tossed there in respect by the faithful.

A withered monk sat in one corner of the massive room, printing new scriptures from ancient stone tablets. The black printer's ink he used made the area in which he worked smell like a newspaper pressroom. Traces of the thick paint striped his wrinkled old face and hands. On the far side of the temple were the fruits of his labors, together with that of other past monks. The entire western wall of the room was hidden behind a daunting array of

shelves, piled high with cloth-covered scriptures, fifteen
or twenty feet high, right up to the dim ceiling. A young
monk, balancing precariously on a long ladder, was trying
to adjust a wad of scriptures halfway up the wall. The
whole lot looked as if it would topple at any moment. I
moved away from the huge library in case I was trapped
beneath the avalanche. I pushed the fact that I had paid a
three-yuan entrance fee to the back of my mind, and fanta-
sized that I was Indiana Jones discovering the Temple of
Doom, that I was opening the door to Tutankhamen's
tomb, or stubbing my toe on the hidden ruins of Boro-
budur. At least I was getting my three-yuan's worth.

Nima looked at his watch and excused himself, arranging first to meet me in two hours outside the monastery
complex. With my mind flooded with Sakya temple pag-
eantry—real or otherwise—I soon went outside into the
strong sunlight and wandered across town to the mountainside farmers' village. Like the external walls of the
monastery itself, every mud-brick house was painted
charcoal-gray, with ochre and white vertical stripes. The
village just seemed to grow out of the pastel-hued mountain. It was beautiful. An environmental gem.

I sat high above the village amid the ruins of an old fort
for an hour, watching the beehive of activity in the streets
below; listening to the people singing as they worked sift-
ing grain. Their voices were as harmonious as the setting,
their song wafted to me on the gentle midmorning breeze.
There was such a strong feeling of love woven through
every fiber of the place—every fiber of the people. I belonged on the outside, looking in. I loved Tibet, but I knew
it really wasn't my home. I was merely passing through. A
silent observer—a one-time participant. It was beautiful
to look, to see and admire everything the gods tried to
show me. I felt privileged enough for that alone. My hillside aerie was a haven of delight and the village below, a
wonderland. In fact it would have been perfect, were it not
for the donkeys. They were everywhere. (Perhaps they
were following me!) But donkeys were better than human

asses, and soon there would be busloads of them too, littering the streets of Sakya. Progress, change. Perhaps I was too selfish and idealistic.

I met Nima at the appointed time and he drove me back to the turnoff, four miles east of Lhazê. His Chinese officials, still in tow, burdened me with exotic gifts—bottled pineapple pieces, sardines in black-bean sauce, two packets of sickly sweet biscuits, and a bar of my very own pink soap. They were heading back to Shigatse, then Lhasa, and flying from there to Beijing. They wished me well. I couldn't remember such a thing happening before; their thoughts gave me some faith in things Chinese. They were okay. Two out of a billion wasn't a bad ratio.

So, there remained four days to go before I would reach Shigatse. Just a hundred miles. I could phone Jigme and tell him I was alive. He could phone my parents in Australia, and break the happy news. Shigatse would be full of foreign tourists and travelers. (Note the distinction.) The prospect of actually talking English to the latter group had me on the tip of my toes, flying over the long, winding pass which now confronted me. I was singing. Imagine speaking English to someone other than myself! It had been a long time, indeed!

For four days, I consciously prepared myself for lucid English conversation. I practiced a dozen different opening gambits. "Good afternoon. How nice to meet you." "Would you be so kind as to tell me what month this is?" "November? Good heavens! And what year, pray tell?" No, that wasn't quite right. No one in their right Western mind would converse with some emaciated, filthy waif who didn't know what day it was—let alone the year. I altered my focus. The weather. Ah yes, the weather. A perfectly acceptable topic for openers. "Frightfully cold, eh what?" Yes, that would do nicely. I could make references to the weather for hours.

As I walked, I talked and thought. I sorted out my attitudes to the country and its people. I sorted out my feelings toward change and progress. I was ready to answer anything about Tibet and to ask everything about life beyond it. What had been going on in the outside world during my absence? I hadn't been away very long—even if it felt like it. It had only been a few months. I reassured myself nothing much would have happened.

The miles ticked off like the dollars on the meter of a taxi stuck in heavy traffic. I mostly stayed close to the road—on it, or near it, always with the telegraph line somewhere in view. I didn't want to get lost, or stray from my course. I had attempted shortcuts before and invariably I wound up falling through ice-covered rivers and into muddy swamps. I backtracked, doubled-up, got stuck, and walked in circles. Shortcuts were not my forte. They made the days longer, my hair grayer.

I climbed over more mountains and met with more hospitable, road-working settlements at each day's end. Long hours were spent instructing the more modern-minded Tibetan road gangs in the gentle art of Western disco dancing. Longer hours were spent drinking chang (Tibetan beer) and eating soup-inflated sheep lungs, a delicacy in the central-southern regions through which I now wandered. Few hours were spent admiring the landscape, and fewer still crying about it. I pushed myself to the very limit, every day. But the limit was growing wider and my journey comparatively easier. My fingers had healed. My face had ceased to exfoliate like a leper's and my eyes only occasionally burned as if branded by a devil's trident.

By late afternoon on the fourth day, I was all but worn out. I was just four miles short of Shigatse. There were two options open to me. One: I could stay the night in the farming commune at hand and enter the big city on the following morning, happily refreshed and ready for anything. Two: I could struggle on. I could be there at dusk, albeit in a state of collapse. Now, if I chose the first option, I would undoubtedly regret it. I would toss and turn all

night in anticipation and excitement. I surely wouldn't
sleep. If I chose the second alternative, I could well wind
up in the hospital, suffering from complete exhaustion.
However, if I hitched a ride on a truck, there would be no
dilemma. There was a buildup of traffic on the roadway:
buses, cars, donkeys, and mule-drawn carts. Plenty of
trucks. Everything and everybody was Shigatse-bound.
My feet kept moving ahead and finally I gave in to tempta-
tion. I flagged down a donkey driver and leaped aboard
his small, hay-filled cart. It seemed a more appropriate
way to enter civilization than on the back of a truck.

As soon as the majestic Tashilhunpo Monastery came
into view, I jumped off the cart and resumed walking.
What a euphoric feeling. It wasn't journey's end, but it
was close enough, cause enough to feel fantastic. The
streets were bursting with life. The dusty intersection
before the monastery was crammed with traffic and pilgrims, tents and piles of tradeable produce. More truck-
loads of people and paraphernalia were arriving by the
minute. Pilgrims were coming from everywhere to the
city to welcome and pay respect to the visiting Panchen
Lama, after the Dalai Lama, the most loved religious
leader of Tibet. Tashilhunpo was the seat of the particular
sect he led, and still an active center of religious life. It
was the most amazing monastic labyrinth on earth. I stood
outside the main entrance, in awe once more.

Jigme had brought me here when I was ill—so long
ago—and we had circled the outside of the complex and
quietly explored its interior together. I remembered the
sun-drenched kitchen where the monks had prepared tea
for us. I remembered the maze of rooms and external rust-
red walls, the window boxes brimming with flowers, the
sculptures, and above all else, the devoted faces of the
pilgrims who had filed through the hallways and stairwells, hypnotized by love and reverence.

Suddenly, I knew the foreign onslaught could wait—the
"Good afternoons" and inquiries about the weather. I felt a
sudden urgency to thank the musketeers, my brothers-in-

arms, my two-fold god. And what better place to do it than inside Tashilhunpo?

An old monk sat by the entrance to the monastery. New pilgrims, deep in meditative chant, filed through the gates to the temple. A big sign loomed above my head. "Foreigners permitted 9:30 A.M.–12:00 A.M." Three yuan. I looked down at the monk. I remembered him from my first visit to the temple. He remembered me too. He actually recognized me. He stood up and looked at my ragged clothes. He praised me in Tibetan, "You have walked. You have made it." It felt like Buddha himself was patting me on the back.

A single tear rolled down my face. It came from the very bottom of my heart. It was not for myself. It was for all the people who I knew were deserving of my thanks and the old monk's praise. All those nomads who had helped me, fed me, taught me, and kept me alive. Why had they done it? It wasn't because of my passes and permits. They hadn't done it for money, none of them even mentioned it. They clearly had nothing to gain in a material sense from helping me. Standing outside Tashilhunpo, holding the old monk's hands in mine, I realized Tibetans knew the beauty of giving, that they believed in a power cynically labeled "ideological"— the power of love which knows no bounds of creed or color, status or purpose. They had even forgiven the Chinese, their oppressors.

It was 7 P.M. The old monk swallowed his fear of reprimand and let me join the throng of pilgrims. I was one of them. There was no need for external metamorphosis. Being one of them was an attitude, a belief—not a costume or guise. In two weeks, I would leave Tibet, but Tibet would never leave me. The mountains and the people were in my heart forever. My tear was both for sadness and joy, for my discovery of new wisdom and in acknowledgment of the fact that I still had so far to go, so much to learn. I would soon reach Lhasa, but it would not be the end, as I had thought. It would be a new beginning. The journey would go on and on. There would be more knowledge; more understanding. Many, many more milestones. Tibet was just a chapter in the endless book of life.

The sun slipped off the edge of the earth and I left the temple courtyard. The old monk had disappeared with the late afternoon wind. I bowed my head in respect once more, turned, then crossed the still-busy road and entered the reception room of my favorite guest house frequented by pilgrims and truck drivers. Dolma, the manager's young daughter, remembered me too. How familiar the place seemed. She squealed with delight when I blurted my joy at seeing her again—in Tibetan, no less. She giggled at my country-bumpkin accent and delved in her pockets for a set of keys. I found the energy to race her up the narrow, warped stairway to the second landing. My heart pounded. I could see a couple of blond-haired travelers through the dirt-smeared window of one room. We slipped past them. Was I seeing things? Was I still real? I turned to Dolma. "Ingiss?" Foreigners? She laughed and nodded, then turned the key and opened the door to a warm, empty room. It was the same one I had stayed in three months before. Dolma tossed my pack on the bed nearest the doorway. She was so happy. I was so happy. We giggled like two schoolgirls and stepped back onto the veranda. I bumped straight into another girl. A girl with long, strawberry-blonde hair and a fine-bone-china complexion. My rehearsed, introductory speeches bubbled inside my brain. I tried to speak, instead laughter—nervous, hysterical laughter—rose to my lips. I blew it. I couldn't care less about the weather. "Do you speak English? Do you really speak English?" I prayed she wasn't French. "I'm in heaven! I can't believe it! Speak to me!" The girl smiled. "You look like you could use a beer . . ."

For the next four or five hours I blurted out everything I had experienced and seen to a more-than-stunned group of five lovely, adorable, wonderful, understanding English women. I was flooded with joy. Nothing, absolutely nothing, could bring me down from a state of euphoria. I was in heaven indeed.

CHAPTER 9
The Journey's End
and a New Beginning

At ten o'clock the next morning, I cleaned myself up a bit, ran around smiling "Good mornings" at everyone, then raced down to the sports service branch office, anxious to phone Jigme and tell him to have the champagne ready. He had ten days to import some before I arrived in Lhasa! I spent half an hour getting lost. Someone had painted the office building a revolting duck-egg blue and I had walked past without recognizing it. A lot of development had gone on in the city since my last visit. The massive supermarket and department store had been completed. The three-star hotel for wealthy tourists had officially opened. The roads had all been dug up and some were now surfaced with asphalt. There were new concrete constructions going up everywhere. I found a familiar landmark and got my bearings. It was comforting to notice amid the progress, the hands of the clock on the post office tower were stuck in the same five-to-four position as always. Finally, I found the office.

I crept in silently, and sat down in the first empty room.

The door to the second was shut; a meeting of the clan was obviously in progress. I stared at the phone, the furniture, the walls, and waited. And waited. I was amazed by my capacity for appearing patient. Finally I heard a chorus of laughter and throat-clearing, a few chairs scraping on the bare concrete floor as they were pushed back. The door creaked open. I swung around and grinned like a contented Cheshire Cat. "Hi guys! I'm back!"

There were gasps of surprise and joy; lots of hugs and handshakes, lots of comments about my loss of weight and my apparently pungent odor. (How sweet the English girls were, not to have commented on the latter!) I retold my great saga with renewed enthusiasm, drank a toast in tea to the great Tibetan Sports Service Company, then asked the branch director if I could phone Jigme. I couldn't wait any longer. He had to know I was nearly there.

The branch director's eyes grew wide. His face went gray.

"No, Miss Sorrel. You cannot phone Mr. Jigme." I didn't understand.

"Why? What's the problem?" "Ka ba ya bo ming-du gay?" Telephone no good?

"Mae. Jigme ya bo ming du." No. Jigme no good. I still didn't understand. Had he gone to America again? What did they mean, "Jigme's no good?" Surely he hadn't been sacked from the company, he was the head of it. My heart was racing, I was sweating. The room was suddenly claustrophobic.

"What on earth is the matter? Why can't I phone him?"

The Shigatse man tried to explain, but I couldn't understand his city dialect. He resorted to gesture, to body language. He made a rasping sound low in his throat and ran his hand across his neck. He made noises like a car engine, an explosive sound like a bomb, then whipped his flattened hand across his Adam's apple again. He closed his eyes and tilted his head to one side. Oh, no. Not Jigme.

Not Jigme Surkhang, my friend. Not dead. It just couldn't be.

Everyone in the room was silent. Then I pieced the story together. On September 12th, just days before his youngest daughter was to be married, Jigme had been killed in a car accident. He was driving out to the airport to welcome and escort a party of Everest climbers to Lhasa. He took a blind corner too fast and too wide, collided with a bulldozer, or something similar, and the long arm of the road-building machine burst through the windscreen of his Land Cruiser and decapitated him. He died instantly.

I couldn't speak. I couldn't cry. My heavenly happiness dissolved around me. I was falling. Echoes of my sinister dreams returned. He's dead, you're mad. He's dead, you're mad. Oh Jigme. It can't be true.

Stunned, I walked from the office. If anyone said anything to me in the way of condolences, I didn't hear them. It wasn't fair. Why was I alive when the man who had inspired my dream was dead? It was all wrong. I remembered his words at our last parting. "Sorrel, I know I'll never see you again." He was right all along. But surely he couldn't have known. It was all wrong. I was the one who was meant to perish. I was the one who wasn't supposed to survive. The odds were against me, not Jigme. Perhaps someone had made a mistake. Perhaps Jigme was just sitting in his office, waiting for me to call. I raced back inside the company building and tried again.

"Jigme. Let me phone Jigme. You must have the wrong person." But there were no two Jigme Surkhangs in the world. No two Jigme—Tibetan Sports Service Company Director—Surkhangs. There was only one. And he was indeed dead. The reality was the hardest pill I ever had to swallow. I choked on it and finally it went down. But it wouldn't stay there. I could not accept what I did not wish to believe.

I walked through the city streets in a daze. It was still five minutes to four. Time was standing still. It always did

when you wanted it to race—backwards or forwards. I
tried to visualize the accident, then I tried to imagine
Jigme's funeral in an effort to finish everything. His funeral—such an ugly vision. For the traditional Tibetan
burial rite had become even more of a tourist attraction in
Lhasa since the city had opened its doors to all and sundry;
it was, to Western sightseers, a macabre circus sideshow.
All I could see in my mind's eye was a row of ghoulish
tourists perched near the burial rock, taking photos at the
funeral of my friend. I shuddered. I had to stop thinking
about it.

I knew that Jigme was a Tibetan. Forty-nine days had
passed since his death, and according to Buddhist belief
he would be someone else now. Alive again. Reincarnated.
There was some comfort in knowing this, but never again
would I see the Jigme I knew and loved. He wouldn't be
there at my journey's end. He would never hear me speak
his language, we would never toast together the land he
had let me discover and explore. We would never laugh,
cry, hug, or dance together again. Time did move on, only
in my mind could I make it go backwards, only on the post
office clock did it appear to stand still.

Eventually, I met up with some of the other travelers at
the guest house and together we went off to have lunch at a
small Chinese cafe, rather appropriately called Restaurant of The New Wind. All the cabbage and pork fat in
Chinese food was well-renowned for the rather flatulent
side effects it had on even the most experienced eaters.
Rosemary, the English girl who had poured the beers
during my five-hour monologue on the previous evening,
asked me if I had put my call through to Lhasa. I had told
her—and everyone—about Jigme. And now I had to tell
them what had happened. I had to say it in English. Hear
the indigestible facts again.

The next morning I went to Tashilhunpo monastery
once more with my new roommate, Ian. He was also from
England and spoke Chinese fluently. He had studied and

worked in Taiwan and was traveling from Lhasa to Kathmandu, via Everest base camp. We both paid three yuan to the attendant and wandered into the complex. I tried to forget about Jigme. We listened to the monks chanting and watched the pilgrims perform their devotions for an hour or so.

The burning butter candles made the maze of temple rooms heavy with their pungent scent. We stopped in one massive hall to talk to master sculptors and their apprentices, busy restoring the huge, clay Buddhist deities. In the main courtyard of the monastery, the monks were having a white elephant sale, selling off a huge pile of second-hand clothing. Behind them, a new temple building was under construction. I bought a hat from the stall for three yuan, and Ian took a photograph of me. At midday I went back down to the sports company offices to collect my belongings, sent there by Basen Tsering from Zhongba. Takla, Jigme's young assistant, was there. His face was badly scarred, yet despite the disfigurement he managed a brilliant smile for me. He had been in the car with Jigme. But he had survived. We laughed, cried, and teased each other about our present looks. Takla was going back to Lhasa and agreed to take my extra gear with him. Lhasa. My Mecca. Jigme. I still couldn't face the truth.

Later in the day, Ian and I went to the new Summer Palace. Thousands of pilgrims were standing in queues, winding all the way around the external wall, through the thinly forested parkland before the massive palace gates. The crowds inched slowly inside. They would pass, one by one, before the great Panchen Lama, pay their respects, and receive his blessings. We talked to some, photographed others, touched, teased, tickled, and tormented the young and the old. They loved it. Everything was said and done in good fun.

Suddenly a white Land Cruiser came charging out of the palace compound. It screeched to a halt and was swallowed by the dust ball it created. Out hopped Nima. What a rascal! He came over and beamed me a winning welcome. I introduced him to Ian, and asked him how long he was in town. He lived in Shigatse itself. He was currently chauffeuring the Panchen Lama backwards and forwards across the city. Tomorrow he would drive the lead car in the lama's entourage halfway to Lhasa. A new team of drivers and vehicles would escort the religious leader and his army of bodyguards and assistants the remaining distance to the holy capital. Nima asked Ian and me if we would be at our hotel that night. He said he would call on us with a small surprise.

That was an understatement. The surprise turned out to be a wife, two daughters, tea, a huge sack of zumpa flour for the remainder of my journey (minus the mule I would have needed to carry it), and a scarf and ready-blessed protection cord from the Panchen Lama himself. I was touched to hear Nima had told him all about me. He was so proud. His wife sat smiling at us, the eyes of his two beautiful daughters were as wide as saucers. Nima, who could also speak Chinese, told Ian of meeting me in Lhazê and about the trip to Sakya. He smiled and smiled. The English girls, Rosemary, Catrina, Hilary, Victoria, and Kirsty all came in and Nima smiled some more.

In the morning, I left my sack of flour outside a pilgrim's tent, pitched in front of Tashilhunpo. Ian walked with me to the start of the Lhasa roadway. The weekend was over and I was back at work. My nine-to-five job. My boss would have to be there at the end to see me sign off. I could not believe otherwise.

In two-and-a-half days I reached Gyantse. I kept going. I reached Nagarzê. I dragged myself around the great Lake Yamzho Yumco (Yamdrok Tso) to the base of the last pass before Lhasa, and then stopped. I couldn't go on. I was emotionally and physically drained.

I had caught the flu in Shigatse and it had worked its way down into my lungs. I had been wheezing from sunrise to sunset for days. I couldn't lie flat at night, my lungs rattled, and I coughed continuously. I had lost another five pounds. My body ached with fatigue. I collapsed at the foot of the mountain and decided with detachment that I would go no farther. I looked up at the long, winding pass, then I lay back and looked at the sky, the vast Tibetan sky. It was as empty as my reservoir of energy and as barren as my soul.

A truck came along, passed me, and then stopped. The driver jogged toward me, his shadow obscured the sun. A look of disbelief swept over his face as he realized I was still breathing.

He crouched down and wiped away the sweat pouring down my face with a greasy rag. I was burning. I couldn't speak—apart from everything else, I had lost my voice. My rescuer helped me into the cab of his vehicle. I looked down at my hands and my fingers seemed to fragment and disperse across my lap. The dashboard fell apart, the sky shattered. I couldn't focus without blacking out or having the world disintegrate before me.

Just before dusk, we rattled to a standstill. I strained my eyes, ears, and mind. I was back in Gyantse again. The truck driver helped me into the hotel where I had stayed a few days before. The manager tucked his arm around me and led me upstairs to the same bed I had slept in. "I told you so, I told you you wouldn't make it." Now look at you, you've had it old girl. You'll never get there now. You'll never reach Lhasa alive. I told you so, I told you so. I just need sleep. I just need medicine. I'll try again in the morning.

He buried me beneath a huge mountain of eiderdowns and went back to his office to fetch a flask of hot butter tea. He was so kind. He came back making jokes about chopping off my nose to cure my ills; but realized decapitation would probably be more successful. Decapitation. Jigme. I had to reach Lhasa. I had to get better and keep on going.

I had a few visitors during the evening. A Beijing-based film crew had taken lodgings in the room next to mine and my continuous coughing worried them enough to call a doctor. The cameramen ushered him in and introduced themselves simultaneously. I looked up from my sickbed. Heads were separating from necks, arms and legs from bodies. The doctor took my temperature and confirmed the suspicion that I wasn't very well. 105°F. He gave me an injection, a handful of tablets which looked like wombat droppings, and a dose of sickly sweet syrup. The Chinese cameramen stayed by my bedside, forcing me to drink tea and continuously wiping the sweat which poured from my body. I still couldn't talk. I could squeak a bit and manage the odd smile of gratitude. My lungs were pounding in my chest, my heart was in my head. Things grew blurrier. My eyelids closed and I slept.

I felt better in the morning. The hotel manager came to replenish my tea and see how I was doing. I was doing fine. So fine, I thought I could manage the quarter-mile trek down to the temple where the film crew were apparently shooting footage. And eventually I made it. But it wasn't easy. With my resistance to disease at an all-time low, the little Nepali stomach bug awoke from his hibernation in my lower bowel and made a most unwelcome reentry into the limelight. I crawled toward the temple—ducking down side streets to relieve myself, then sitting down on people's doorsteps to gain the strength to continue.

Everyone in Gyantse was heading for the temple, armed with picnic baskets and thermos flasks. They would be the unpaid extras in a sequence for the film. Hollywood had come to town. The crew had imported a busload of monks from Tashilhunpo and they arrived at the great gates just seconds before I did, dressed in their ceremonial regalia and exotic headgear. Their hats were yellow felt, and crescent-shaped like cockatoo combs. Stagehands were up on the temple roof, hanging colored cloth decorations from the verandas and windows. Cast members roamed around the courtyard in an array of stunning costumes. The cameramen were positioned on high, scaffolding towers and the producer and his assistant were shouting instructions at the crowd of spectators and extras through dented tin megaphones.

Word had spread like wildfire through the village. "The girl from Kailas is back, you know—the one who speaks Tibetan. The one from Australia, the one who lost the donkey!" The elusive Budget. His escape was well and truly the high point of my tale, the story which won the most laughs among Tibetans. He was fast becoming as legendary as Pegasus, the mythological horse he had emulated.

Everyone in Gyantse wanted me to join the cast, to feature in the film. But I was foreign and didn't quite fit in. It was a film about the life and ordination of a woman lama and since it dated back to the early part of the century, an Australian girl in torn ski overalls would have been a touch out of place. One group of women were determined to have me in the movie and protested to the cameramen at length. "She is Tibetan, we tell you! Look at her nose! Our friend Dolma has a nose as big as hers and you're letting her take part in the film!" I was touched and amused but willingly retired to the sidelines to watch the action from afar.

It took hours for the initial organization of the masses to be completed. And then hours to shoot one elaborate scene from several dozen angles. I had plenty of opportunity to take photographs of the spectacular costumes of the cast and crowds and plenty of tea-break time to simply doze in the sunlight. Late afternoon came and the crowd was dismissed. See you tomorrow. Same time, same place. I scraped myself together and embarked on the long trek back to the hotel.

My fever was down, but my diarrhea had worsened. I headed straight for the toilet block. On the way back to my room, I spied a dusty group of Westerners collapsed across the beds in the room next door to that occupied by the film crew. I poked my head around the door. I could do with their company. "Hi! Where are you from?" I croaked in greeting. "Lhasa." "No, no, I mean what country?" My spirits soared. Two of them, Patricia and David, were from Australia. "Terrific! Mind if I join you?"

The worn-out souls had just arrived by jeep from the holy capital. They were heading to Kathmandu, but Patricia was going via Mount Everest. A woman after my own heart, she was trekking to base camp from the turnoff near Xêgar. We talked on and on about everything and eventually provoked an interested groan from David. He had curled himself up in a ball on arrival—all aching and miserable from the rough ride into town. Later, he confided in me: he had thought I was a derelict sixties hippie trying to cadge a ride to the border. He had rolled over and pretended to be asleep in order to avoid confrontation with what he considered to be a very low life form. It just goes to show you should never judge a book by its cover!

Patricia gave me some tablets for my headache and cough. David gave me six whole squares of his "No Frills" toilet paper for the other end. Toilet paper! I hadn't seen the stuff in months. It's amazing how irrelevant such a thing seems in a land like Tibet. Months ago I had realized that if Tibetans didn't need to use the stuff, then neither did I. I mimicked the way they squatted and had quickly developed a no-frills-necessary method.

But I held on to my six squares for all they were worth. I've still got them. They symbolized the civilized world, the world to which I was returning. The world with a perplexing obsession for socially acceptable behaviors. It seemed fitting to place the toilet paper alongside the five-yuan note the inebriated pilgrim had given me in Yagra— souvenirs with a difference.

The sun went down and I was still talking, or rather croaking. We moved to the dumpling shop next door to the hotel for dinner. The evening chill failed to kill our conversation.

In the morning, David and I crawled down to the temple to watch more of the filming. The main monastery buildings were open and inviting. We slipped past the camera crew and entered the main temple room. A single shaft of light fell from the high ceiling onto the center of the floor. Its translucent brilliance caught a cloud of dust and smoke and pierced a conical mound of deep burgundy robing. Rows of similar mounds were visible when my eyes adjusted to the darkness, row after row, echoing the slumped forms of monks in prayer. Still. Silent. They seemed to sit on the thick shaggy carpets of indigo blue and red, positioned in lines between the heavy supporting columns of the massive room. The floor was hard, cold earth, the ceiling detail sculptured wood, with tapestries and colored, kite-like cloths suspended from the edges— red and gold, green and pink. Mahogany and burgundy. Bare earth. Buddhist scriptures lay before the empty robes, their owners outside in the courtyard for the filming. Clay pots and brass drinking-vessels were strewn between them. Suddenly the wooden supports became trees—the abandoned robing, a group of gnomes, meeting in secret deep in the heart of an enchanted forest. It was beautiful to behold the richness of colors and subtle qualities of light; beautiful to know, to understand something so different, so fascinating.

We moved clockwise around the open room and entered the main altar room of the temple. Gold on gold. Butter candles flickered soft light on the gentle, gnarled hands of an ancient lama. He was chanting, polishing the knee of a massive, seated Buddha. At three years old, I saw for the first time a Christmas tree ablaze with twinkling lights and shining glass baubles. I experienced here that same feeling of delight and wonderment. We lose so much with the years, we lose our innocence, we lose our dreams. May I be lucky and never lose my fascination for the unfamiliar, the mysterious.

Outside, we shared in the picnic-style parties of the people, shared in their laughter and simple joy. It took all afternoon to get back to the hotel; every stallholder in the street marketplace begged us to sit with them for tea and sweet biscuits, cheese, or dried apricots. When we finally returned, it was to say goodbye, for the time had come for Patricia and David to move on. Everest called. Kathmandu called. And for me, more sleep.

But—well, I didn't get any. Another two Western travelers arrived, and I couldn't resist the urge to talk some more, especially since one of them, Andrew, was a good-looking Australian.

My English friends from the Shigatse hotel had reached Lhasa and were frantically telling anyone heading toward Kathmandu or Everest to watch out for me. To stop and talk. To keep me going, to give support. Andrew stood up. "I don't have anything to give you. I don't have any medicine or books for you to read. All I have is this." He wrapped his arms around me and hugged. "From one koala bear to another." This was the greatest gift of all. It meant everything to me. It was just what I needed. It said more than a thousand words, calmed more than an ocean full of feelings and thoughts. Andrew understood. I didn't need his congratulations. I didn't need to be put on a pedestal, or slapped on the back like an Olympic medalist. I needed acceptance, understanding. I needed people to acknowledge my human frailty, to see the truth beyond the image newspapers and magazines might create for me.

At the temple the next morning, all my Tibetan picnic friends were humming and bubbling over with joy. By sheer chance, Andrew's big Nepalese sweater was identical to mine, even down to the layers of dust and dirt half obscuring the natural colors. The match delighted the crowds to a point of ecstasy. "Oh look! The girl from Kailas has found her husband!" I couldn't believe their simple perception. All stories, all fairy tales, had to have a happy ending. Word spread that I had been reunited with my man. Smiles spread, and laughter too. It was such a glorious day, but the story wasn't over yet. The happy ending had come too soon.

The next day the film crew took me back to Shigatse with them. My health wasn't getting any better and they had taken it upon themselves to get me to a real doctor. Several hours later, one of their backup vehicles whisked me away to the gentle shores of Lake Yamzho Yumco and settled me down for the night in a small farmer's cottage. I was drugged to the eyeballs, but by morning, I was fighting-fit and seemingly ready for the final onslaught.

The farmer's old father took me across the lake in an antiquated boat powered by a small outboard motor. I reached the point where I had collapsed. The point of return. I looked up at the pass, full of courage. Those Shigatse pills must have been laced with Valium. I climbed upwards.

The view over the lake from the top of the pass was as beautiful as I had often remembered.

I caught my breath then began to descend via a steep foot track into the valley below—the valley which wound its way to Lhasa. Lhasa . . . my circus dream returned to haunt me. "He's dead, you're mad. He's dead, you're mad." I knew I still couldn't face the empty chair in Jigme's home or his family and friends. Surely my mentor, my partner, the real hero of the story would be there after all to share the happy ending, the laughter and dancing?

Just twenty-five miles short of the holy city, I turned back again. Journey's end was supposed to be for us, not me alone. I hitched a ride in a truck back to Shigatse. My thoughts consumed me. Hour after hour, experience after experience, I relived my Tibetan adventure, my dreams, my life. There would be no end until I faced and confronted reality—the final challenge.

Fear stops all of us from moving on, from growing, from gazing beyond the mere reflection in the mirror. We all dare to dream, but few of us dare to act. We spend our lives hesitating in the wings, not dancing on the stage of life. And part of life is death. It's the final act, but not the end, just a new beginning.

Jigme had shared not only my dreams but my philosophy as well. We both knew that mountains were there to be climbed, that languages and cultures were there to be learned and shared. We both knew how to reach for the sky and soar toward freedom in weightless planes of thought.

We both knew, too, how easy it was to run away and avoid coming face to face with reality, with our own selves. Jigme would be crushed if I ran now, if I let the final curtain fall without saying goodbye.

In three and a half months I had walked 1,900 miles. I returned to Lhasa by jeep in a day. I returned for Jigme. And for myself.

His office lay in ruins, surrounded by the rubble and paraphernalia of new construction work. Jigme's dream to build a bigger and better administrative and accommodation center for foreign expeditioners was slowly becoming a reality. I could hear his laughter whistling down the steel scaffolding: "I'm going to have the only elevator on the roof of the world!" Soaring toward freedom. . .

I walked the few blocks to Jigme's home. I sat in his old green chair and listened to his wife's practiced English. She laughed at my nomadic dialect and together we looked at old photographs of Jigme and their family and talked in both languages about old times. And reaching out, across oceans of time and mountains of misunderstanding, we held hands and smiled. Jigme had brought our cultures together. Through sport and mountaineering he had brought people from all over the world together, forever seeking to unite our fragmented societies. As I looked across the years and beyond all my fears toward his wife, I realized that Jigme had taught me this final lesson.

I looked around at all that remained of his life and at all he had accomplished in it. I said goodbye to his profile and came face to face with the end of that life. Then I turned to face the beginning of the rest of mine.

Adventura is a popular line of books from Seal Press that celebrates the achievements and experiences of women adventurers, athletes, travelers and naturalists. Browse the list of books below—and discover the spirit of adventure through the female gaze.

Dream of a Thousand Lives by Karen Connelly. $14.95, ISBN 1-58005-062-X.

A Woman Alone: Travel Tales from Around the Globe edited by Faith Conlon, Ingrid Emerick and Christina Henry de Tessan. $15.95, ISBN 1-58005-059-X.

The Unsavvy Traveler: Women's Comic Tales of Catastrophe edited by Rosemary Caperton, Anne Mathews and Lucie Ocenas, introduction by Pam Houston. $15.95, ISBN 1-58005-058-1.

Hot Flashes from Abroad: Women's Travel Tales and Adventures edited by Jean Gould. $16.95, ISBN 1-58005-055-7.

No Hurry to Get Home: The Memoir of the New Yorker *Writer Whose Unconventional Life and Adventures Spanned the Twentieth Century* by Emily Hahn. $14.95, ISBN 1-58005-045-X.

Girl in the Curl: A Century of Women in Surfing by Andrea Gabbard. $29.95, ISBN 1-58005-048-4.

Pilgrimage to India: A Woman Revisits Her Homeland by Pramila Jayapal. $14.95, ISBN 1-58005-052-2.

Solo: On Her Own Adventure edited by Susan Fox Rogers. $12.95, ISBN 1-878067-74-5.

Seal Press publishes many books of fiction and nonfiction by women writers. If you are unable to obtain a Seal Press title from a bookstore, please order from us directly by calling 800-754-0271. Visit our website at www.sealpress.com.